YOUNEEK STUDIOS

Malika™: Warrior Queen
Part One

www.youneekstudios.com
ISBN 978-0-9966070-5-6

For All Inquiries Contact: info@youneekstudios.com

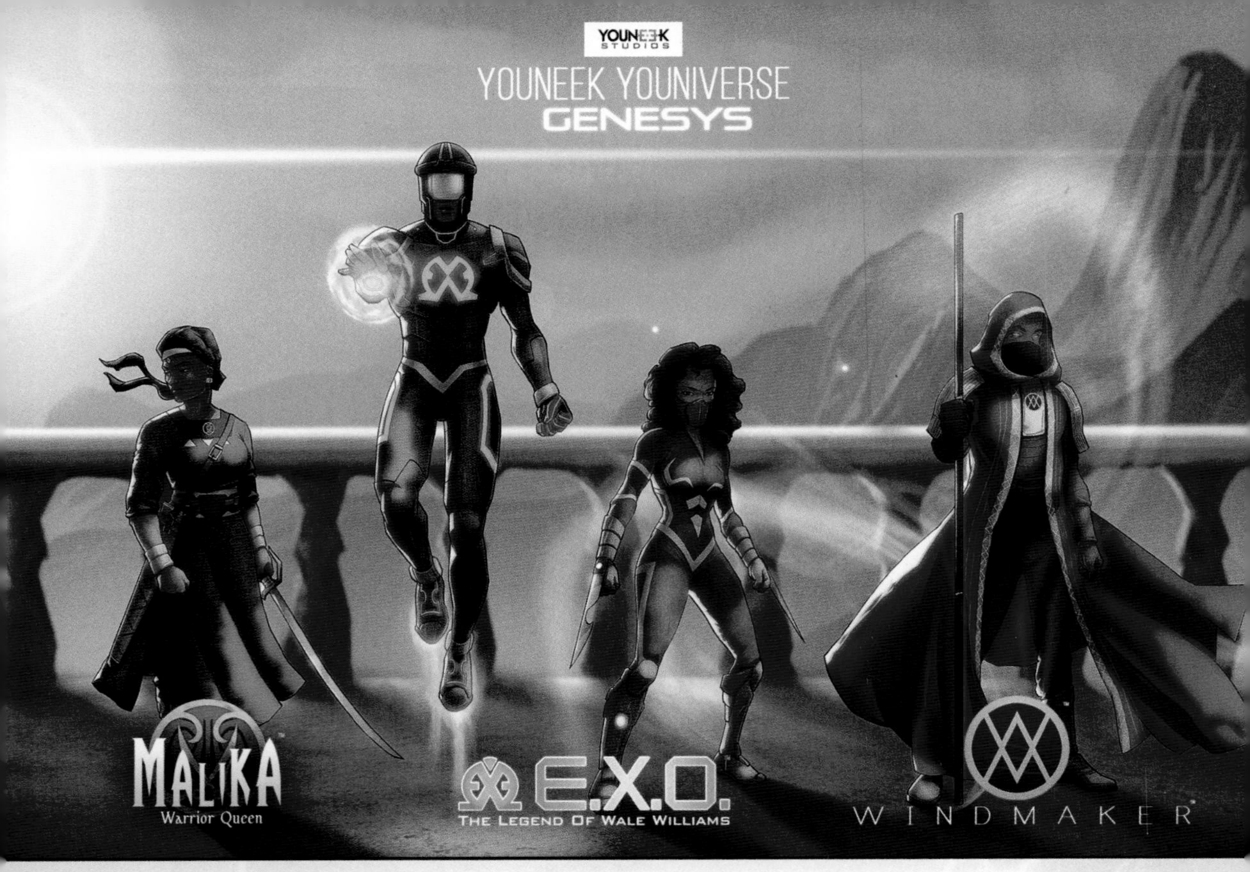
YOUNEEK STUDIOS
YOUNEEK YOUNIVERSE
GENESYS
MALIKA
Warrior Queen
E.X.O.
THE LEGEND OF WALE WILLIAMS
WINDMAKER

Dubbed "The MCU of graphic novels," the YouNeek YouNiverse is a combination of individual graphic novel series tied together with one continuous, overall plot that weaves through each individual story.

Recommended reading before Malika: Warrior Queen Part One

NONE

Optional reading before or after Malika: Warrior Queen Part One

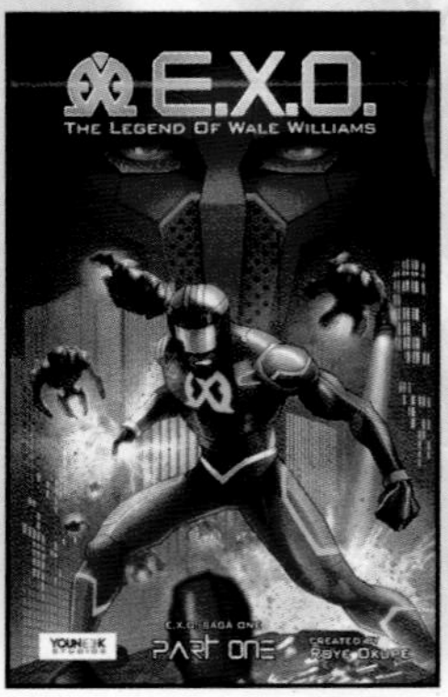
E.X.O.
THE LEGEND OF WALE WILLIAMS
PART ONE

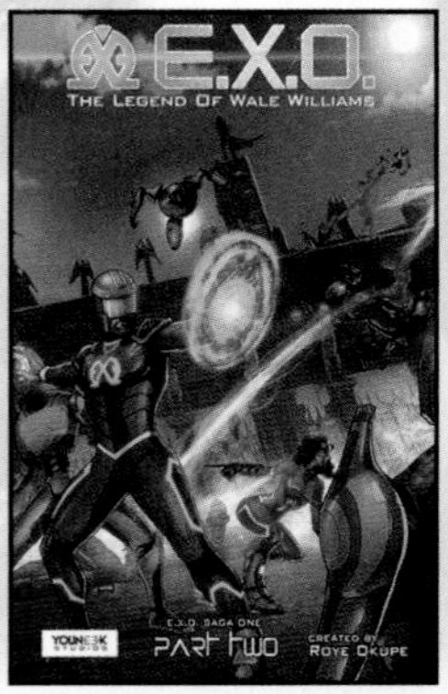
E.X.O.
THE LEGEND OF WALE WILLIAMS
PART TWO
CREATED BY ROYE OKUPE

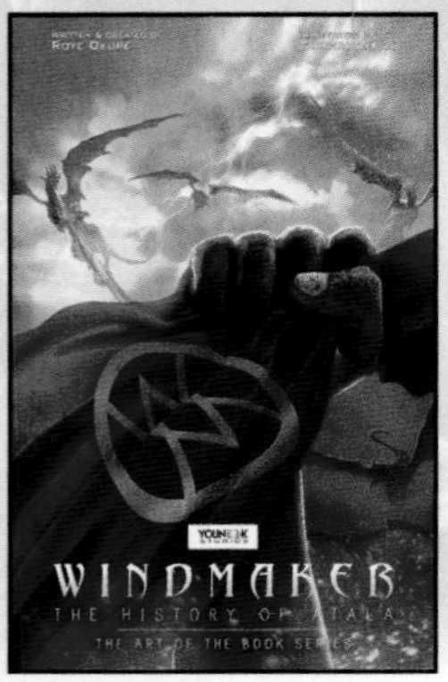
WINDMAKER

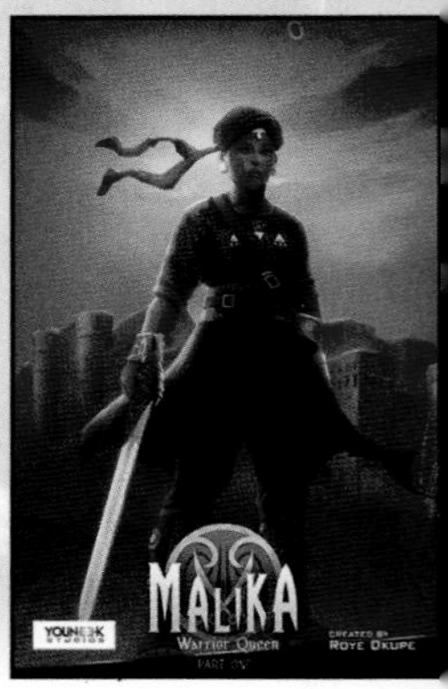
MALIKA
Warrior Queen
CREATED BY ROYE OKUPE

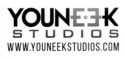

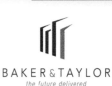

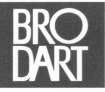

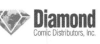

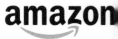

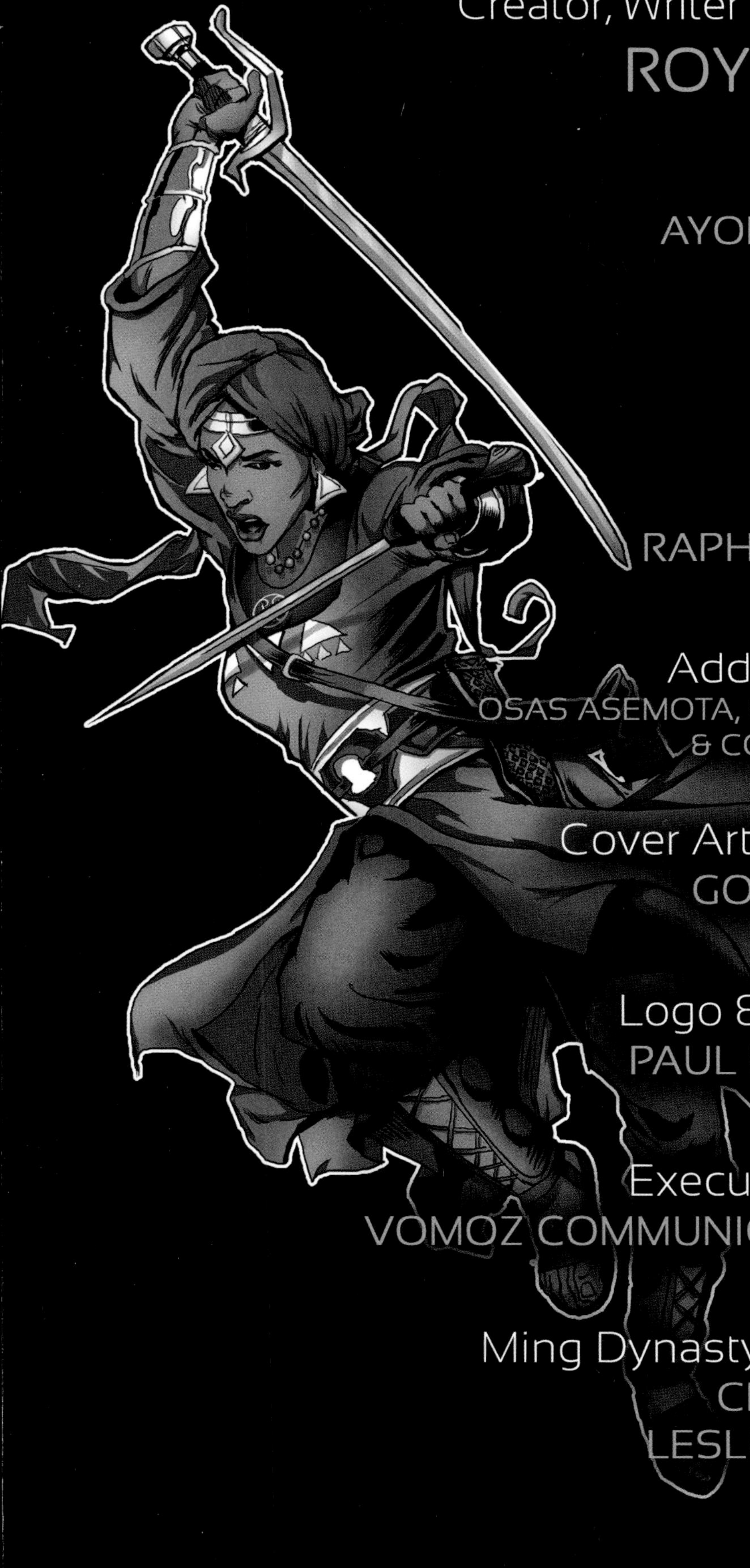

Creator, Writer & Art Director
ROYE OKUPE

Editor
AYODELE ELEGBA

Pencils/Inks
CHIMA KALU

Colors
RAPHAEL KAZEEM

Additional Colors
OSAS ASEMOTA, OMOTUYI EBOTA
& COLLINS MOMODU

Cover Art/Concept Art
GODWIN AKPAN

Logo & Map Design
PAUL LOUISE-JULIE

Executive Producer
VOMOZ COMMUNICATIONS INC.

Ming Dynasty Concept Art
CHYI MING LEE
LESLIE NG KAZUKI
AARON LIN
WILLY WONG
KAIJU DEN LLP, SINGAPORE

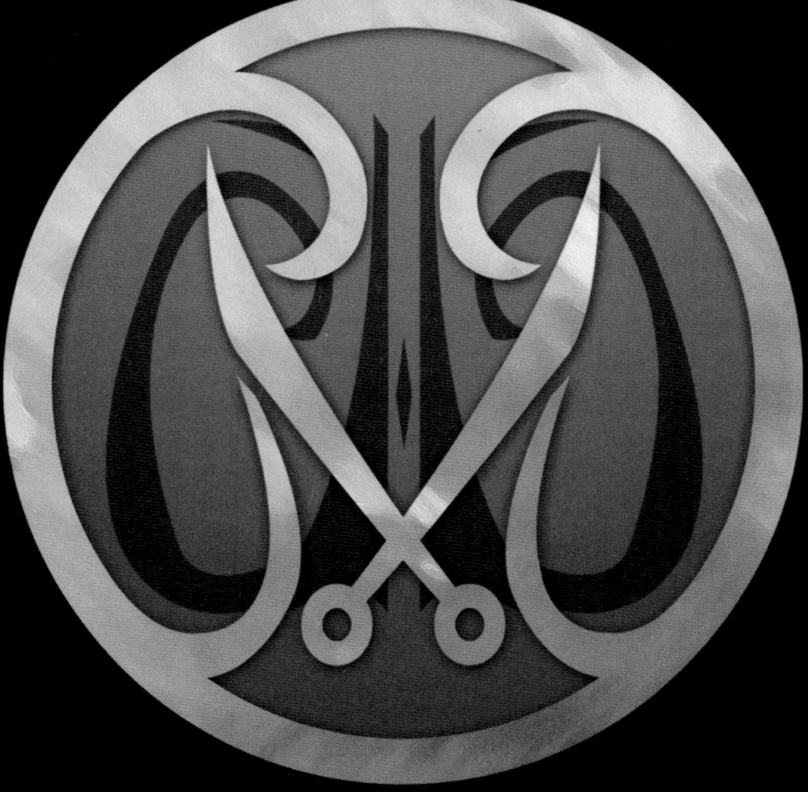

HOUSE OF BAKWA FAMILY CREST

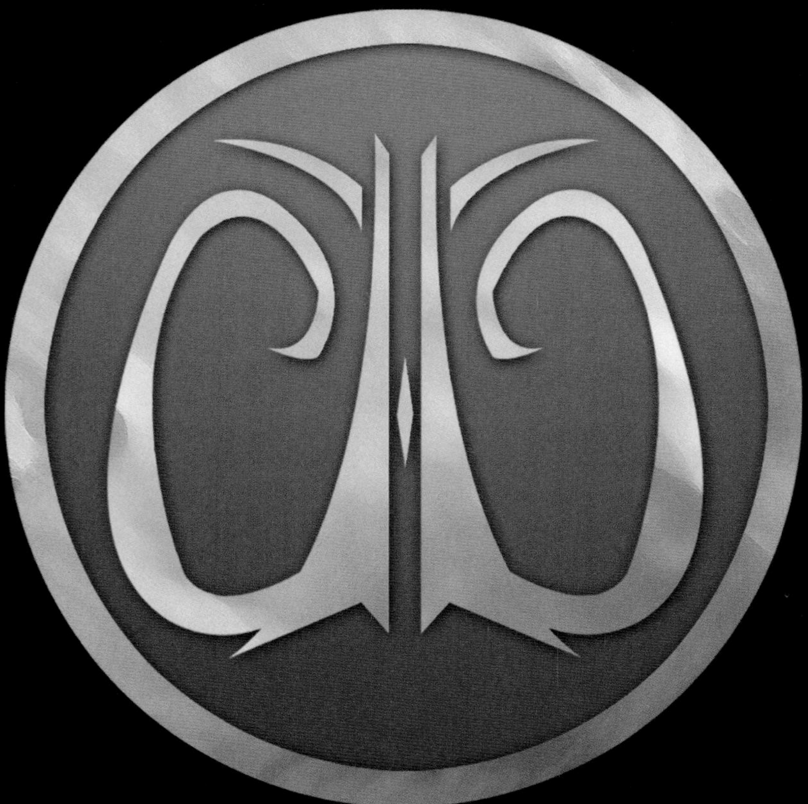

AZZAZIAN IMPERIAL CREST

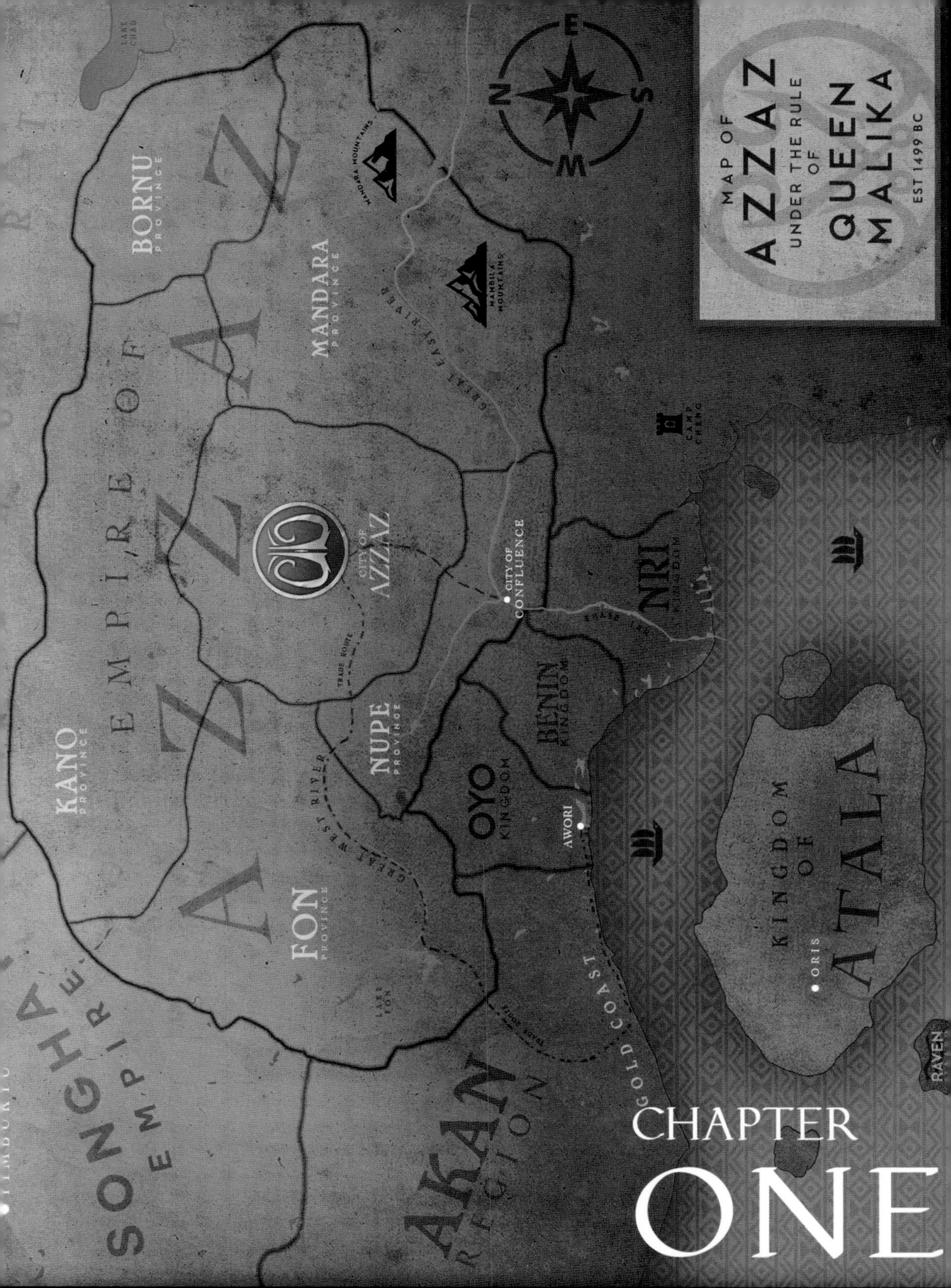
MAP OF
AZZAZ
UNDER THE RULE
OF
QUEEN
MALIKA
EST 1499 BC
N
E
S
W
EMPIRE OF
AZZAZ
BORNU
PROVINCE
MANDARA
PROVINCE
MANDARA MOUNTAINS
MAMBILA MOUNTAINS
GREAT EAST RIVER
CAMP CHENG
CITY OF
AZZAZ
CITY OF
CONFLUENCE
TRADE ROUTE
KANO
PROVINCE
NUPE
PROVINCE
GREAT WEST RIVER
NRI
KINGDOM
BENIN
KINGDOM
OYO
KINGDOM
AWORI
FON
PROVINCE
LAKE FON
TRADE ROUTE
GOLD COAST
KINGDOM OF
ATALA
ORIS
RAVEN
SONGHAI
EMPIRE
AKAN
REGION
LAKE CHAD

CHAPTER ONE

The empire of Azzaz is made up of five provinces, all of which surround the capital city at the center. Each province pays a tribute and as a result gets to elect a chief who both governs its people as well as represent them on the Council (commonly called "The Council of Five"). The council, in turn, advises the ruler of Azzaz. Although not law, no Azzazian ruler can have absolute power over the Council

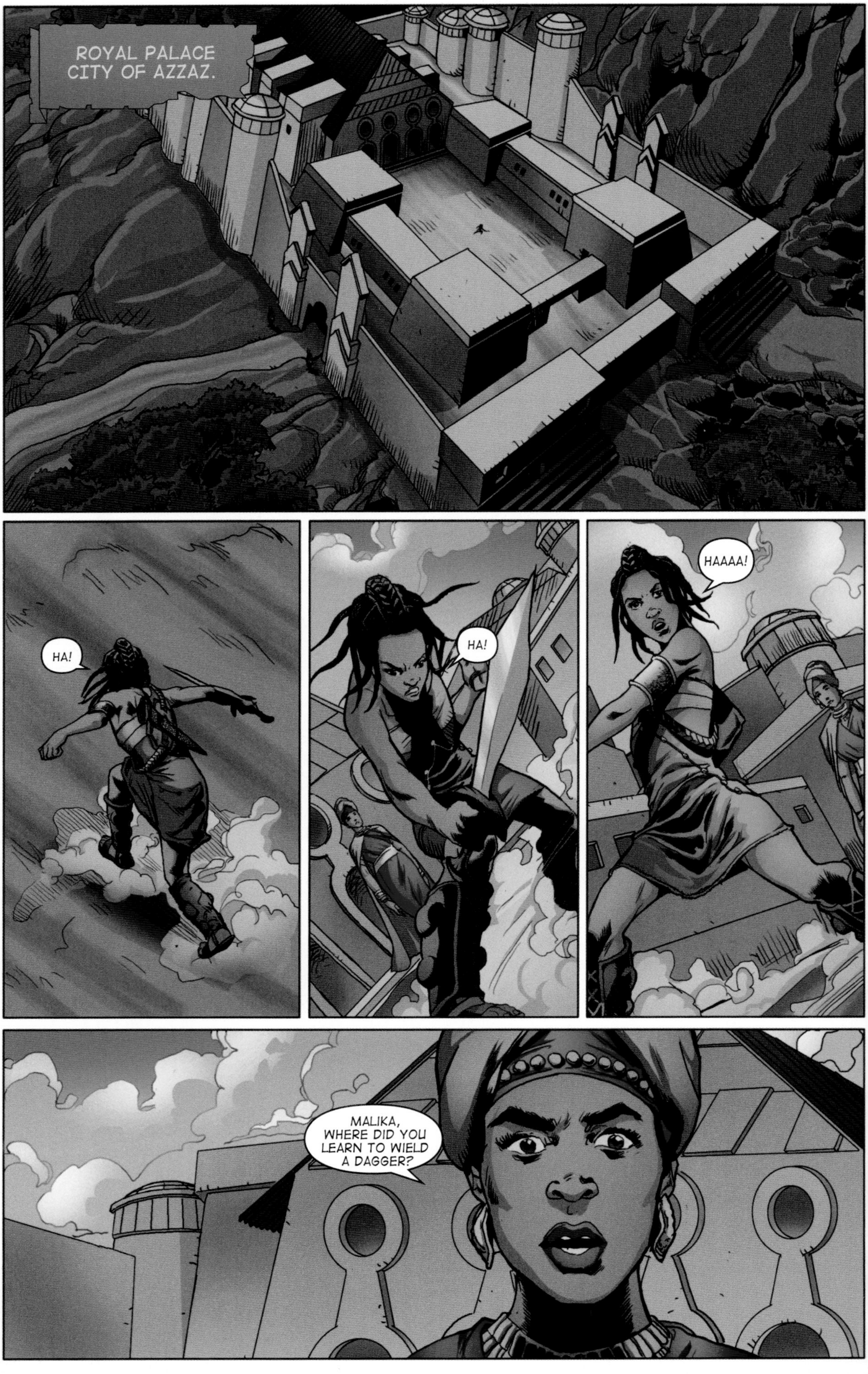
ROYAL PALACE
CITY OF AZZAZ.
HA!
HA!
HAAAA!
MALIKA, WHERE DID YOU LEARN TO WIELD A DAGGER?

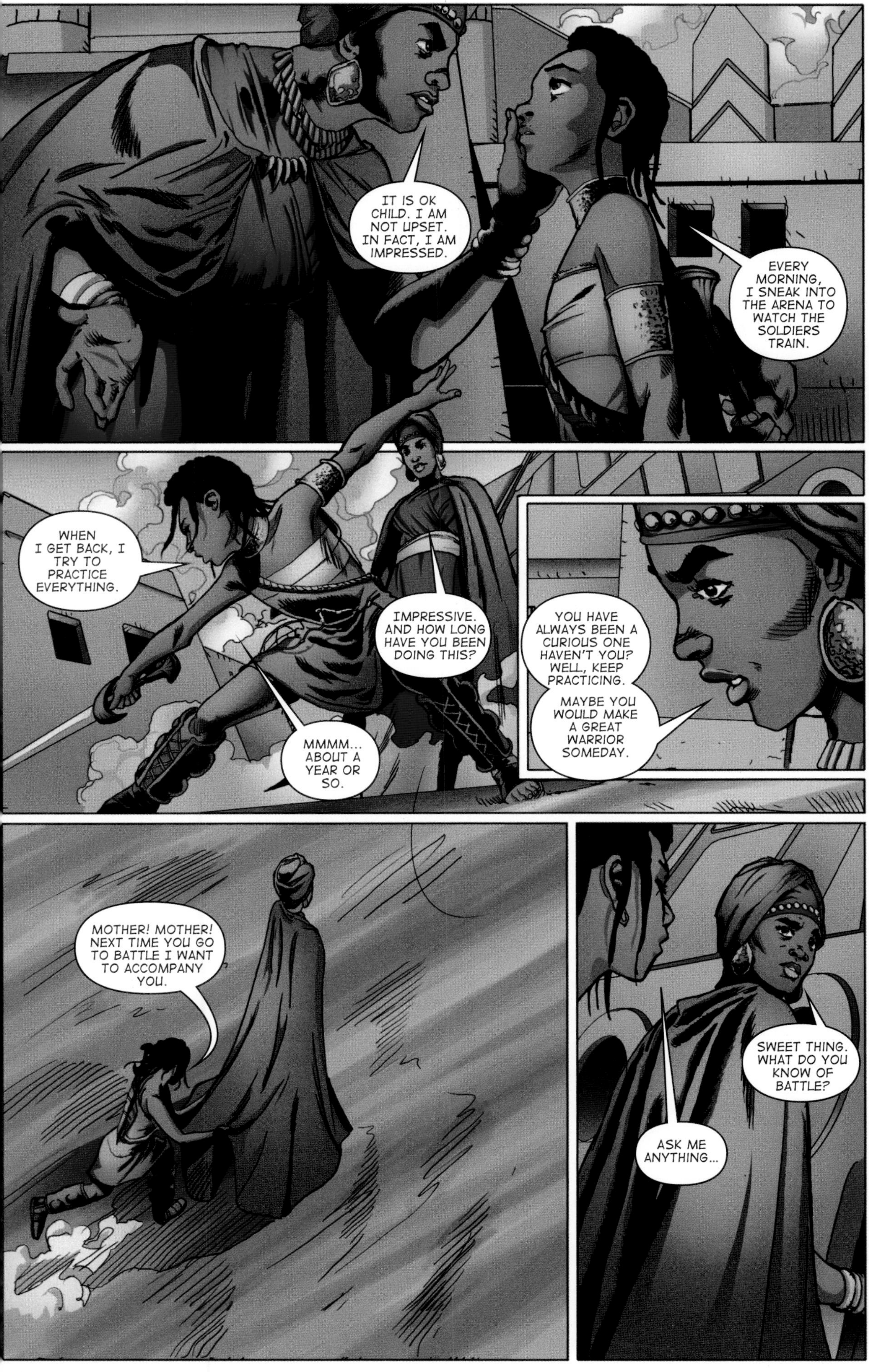
IT IS OK CHILD. I AM NOT UPSET. IN FACT, I AM IMPRESSED.
EVERY MORNING, I SNEAK INTO THE ARENA TO WATCH THE SOLDIERS TRAIN.
WHEN I GET BACK, I TRY TO PRACTICE EVERYTHING.
IMPRESSIVE. AND HOW LONG HAVE YOU BEEN DOING THIS?
MMMM... ABOUT A YEAR OR SO.
YOU HAVE ALWAYS BEEN A CURIOUS ONE HAVEN'T YOU? WELL, KEEP PRACTICING.
MAYBE YOU WOULD MAKE A GREAT WARRIOR SOMEDAY.
MOTHER! MOTHER! NEXT TIME YOU GO TO BATTLE I WANT TO ACCOMPANY YOU.
SWEET THING. WHAT DO YOU KNOW OF BATTLE?
ASK ME ANYTHING...

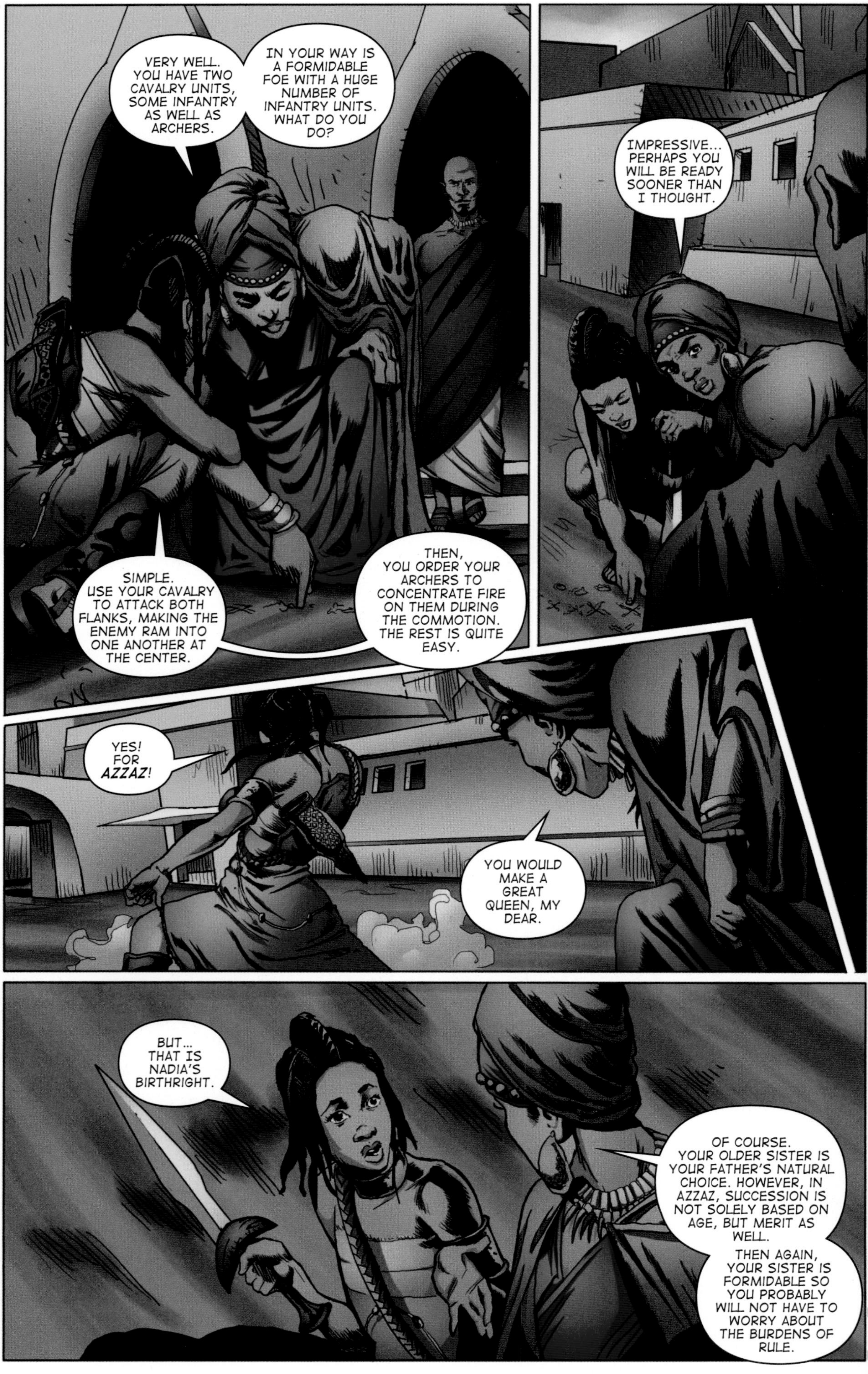
VERY WELL. YOU HAVE TWO CAVALRY UNITS, SOME INFANTRY AS WELL AS ARCHERS.
IN YOUR WAY IS A FORMIDABLE FOE WITH A HUGE NUMBER OF INFANTRY UNITS. WHAT DO YOU DO?
SIMPLE. USE YOUR CAVALRY TO ATTACK BOTH FLANKS, MAKING THE ENEMY RAM INTO ONE ANOTHER AT THE CENTER.
THEN, YOU ORDER YOUR ARCHERS TO CONCENTRATE FIRE ON THEM DURING THE COMMOTION. THE REST IS QUITE EASY.
IMPRESSIVE... PERHAPS YOU WILL BE READY SOONER THAN I THOUGHT.
YES! FOR *AZZAZ*!
YOU WOULD MAKE A GREAT QUEEN, MY DEAR.
BUT... THAT IS NADIA'S BIRTHRIGHT.
OF COURSE. YOUR OLDER SISTER IS YOUR FATHER'S NATURAL CHOICE. HOWEVER, IN AZZAZ, SUCCESSION IS NOT SOLELY BASED ON AGE, BUT MERIT AS WELL.
THEN AGAIN, YOUR SISTER IS FORMIDABLE SO YOU PROBABLY WILL NOT HAVE TO WORRY ABOUT THE BURDENS OF RULE.

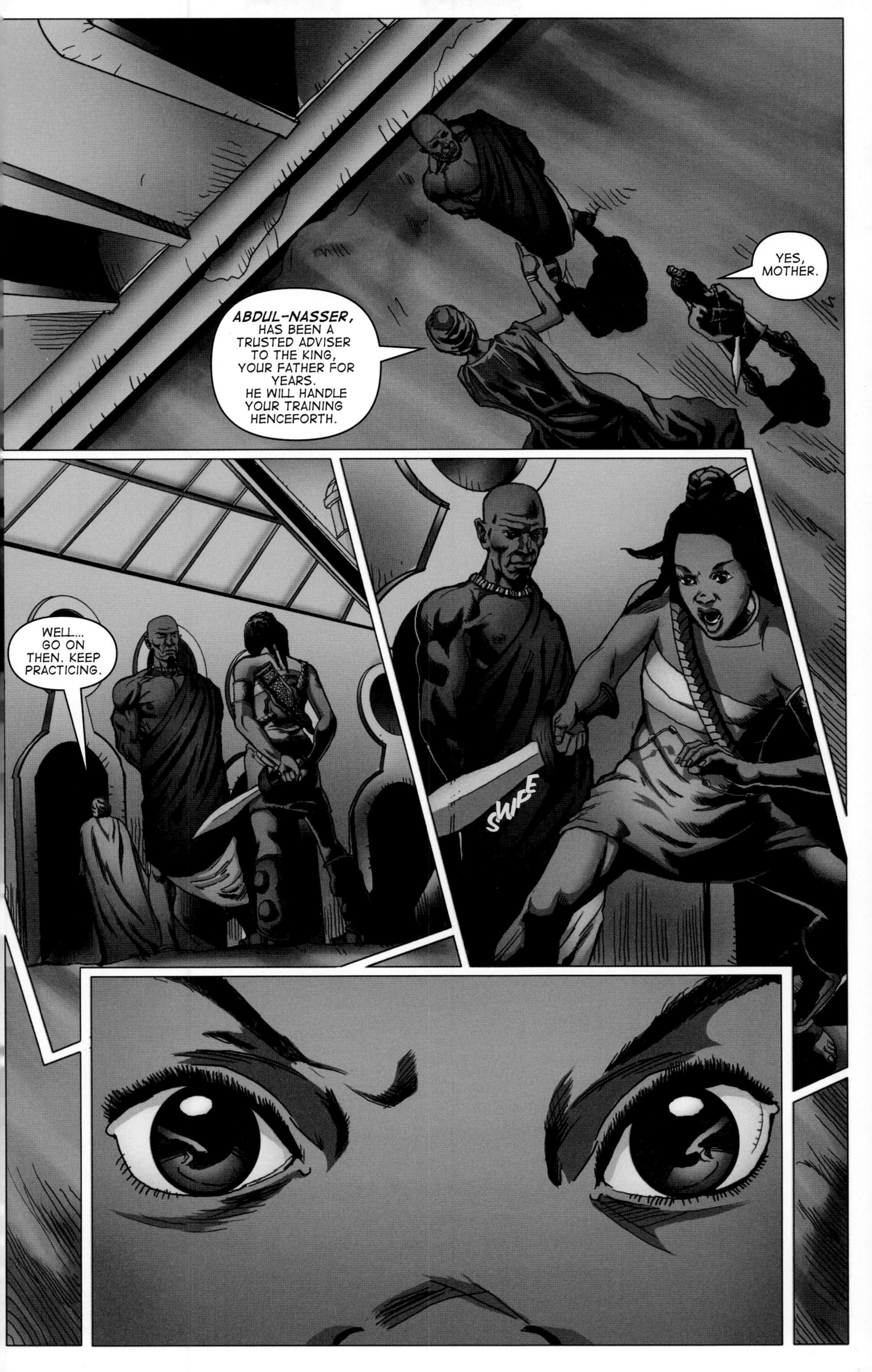
ABDUL-NASSER, HAS BEEN A TRUSTED ADVISER TO THE KING, YOUR FATHER FOR YEARS. HE WILL HANDLE YOUR TRAINING HENCEFORTH.
YES, MOTHER.
WELL... GO ON THEN. KEEP PRACTICING.
SWIRE

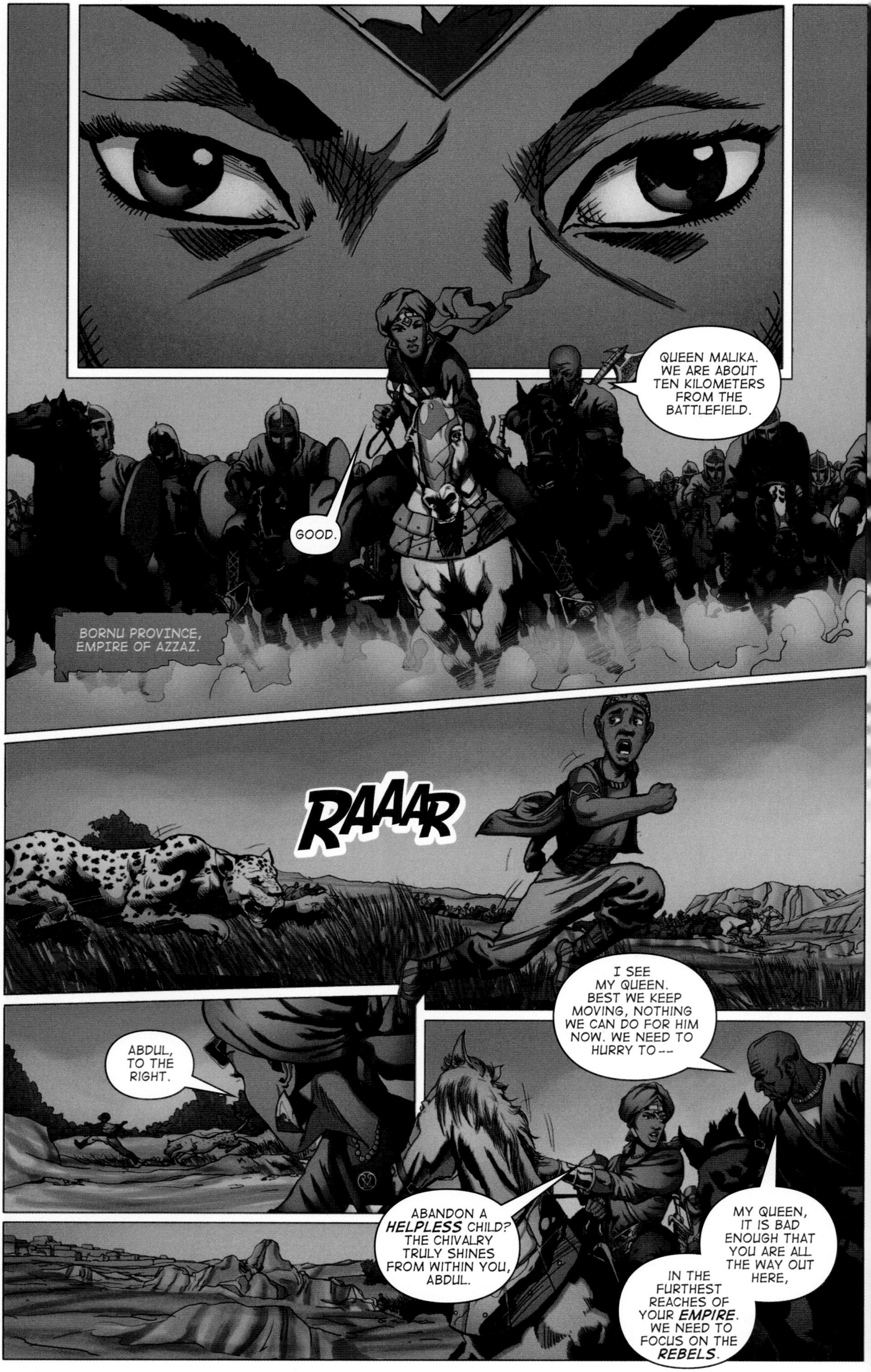
QUEEN MALIKA. WE ARE ABOUT TEN KILOMETERS FROM THE BATTLEFIELD.
GOOD.
BORNU PROVINCE, EMPIRE OF AZZAZ.
RAAAR
ABDUL, TO THE RIGHT.
I SEE MY QUEEN. BEST WE KEEP MOVING, NOTHING WE CAN DO FOR HIM NOW. WE NEED TO HURRY TO--
ABANDON A HELPLESS CHILD? THE CHIVALRY TRULY SHINES FROM WITHIN YOU, ABDUL.
MY QUEEN, IT IS BAD ENOUGH THAT YOU ARE ALL THE WAY OUT HERE,
IN THE FURTHEST REACHES OF YOUR EMPIRE. WE NEED TO FOCUS ON THE REBELS.

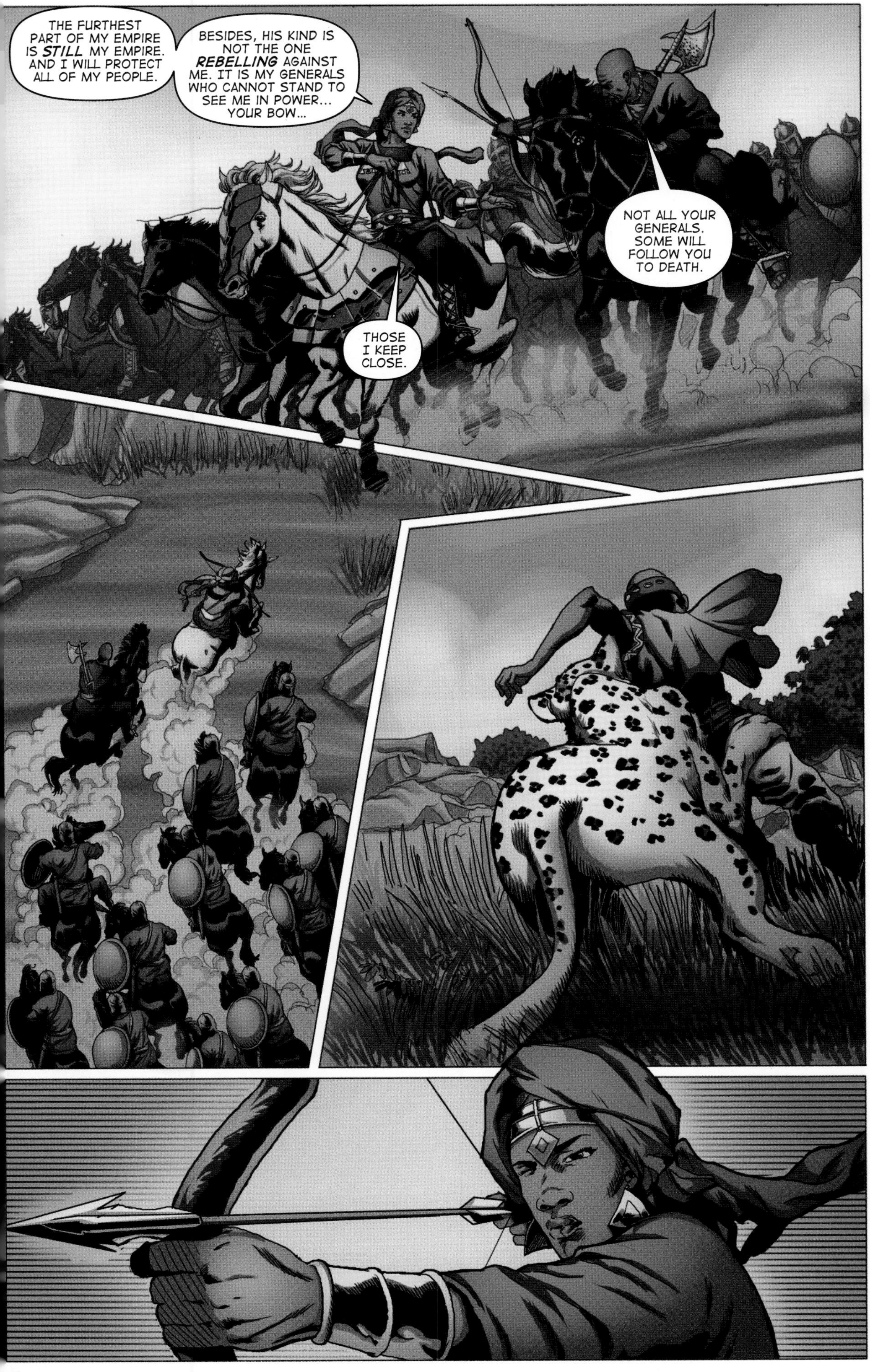
THE FURTHEST PART OF MY EMPIRE IS *STILL* MY EMPIRE. AND I WILL PROTECT ALL OF MY PEOPLE.
BESIDES, HIS KIND IS NOT THE ONE *REBELLING* AGAINST ME. IT IS MY GENERALS WHO CANNOT STAND TO SEE ME IN POWER... YOUR BOW...
NOT ALL YOUR GENERALS. SOME WILL FOLLOW YOU TO DEATH.
THOSE I KEEP CLOSE.

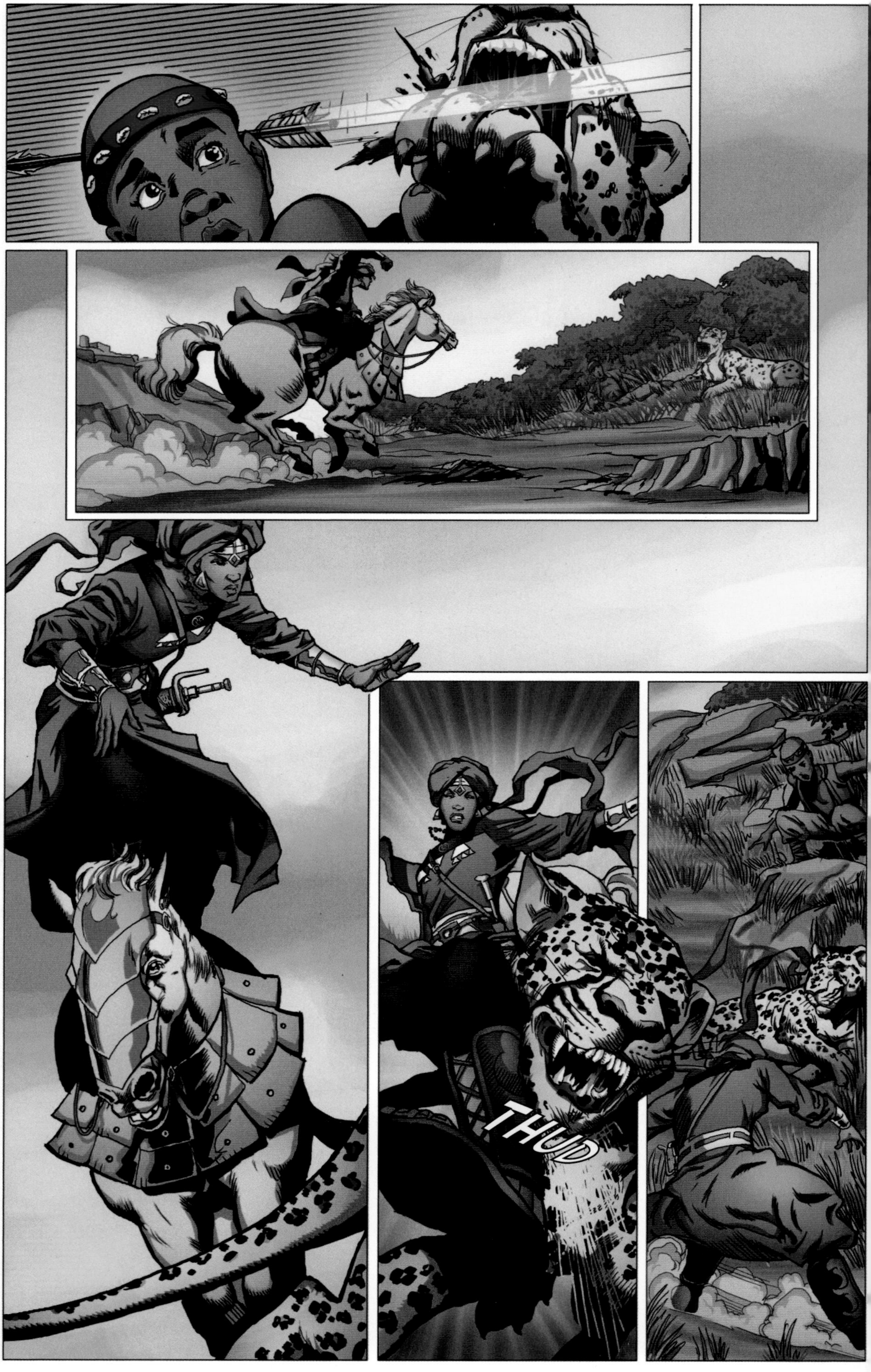
THUD

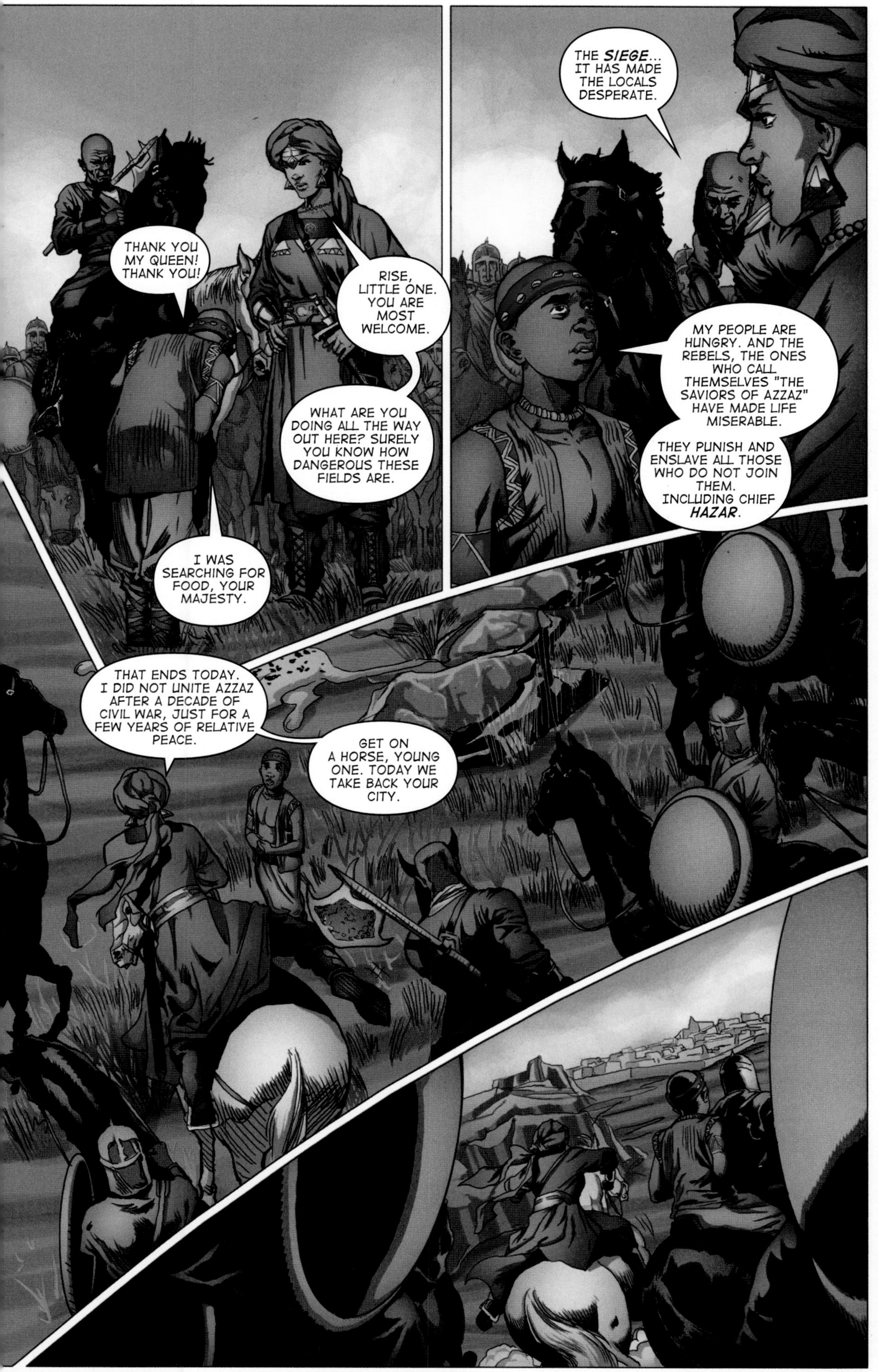
THANK YOU MY QUEEN! THANK YOU!
RISE, LITTLE ONE. YOU ARE MOST WELCOME.
WHAT ARE YOU DOING ALL THE WAY OUT HERE? SURELY YOU KNOW HOW DANGEROUS THESE FIELDS ARE.
I WAS SEARCHING FOR FOOD, YOUR MAJESTY.
THE SIEGE... IT HAS MADE THE LOCALS DESPERATE.
MY PEOPLE ARE HUNGRY. AND THE REBELS, THE ONES WHO CALL THEMSELVES "THE SAVIORS OF AZZAZ" HAVE MADE LIFE MISERABLE.
THEY PUNISH AND ENSLAVE ALL THOSE WHO DO NOT JOIN THEM. INCLUDING CHIEF HAZAR.
THAT ENDS TODAY. I DID NOT UNITE AZZAZ AFTER A DECADE OF CIVIL WAR, JUST FOR A FEW YEARS OF RELATIVE PEACE.
GET ON A HORSE, YOUNG ONE. TODAY WE TAKE BACK YOUR CITY.

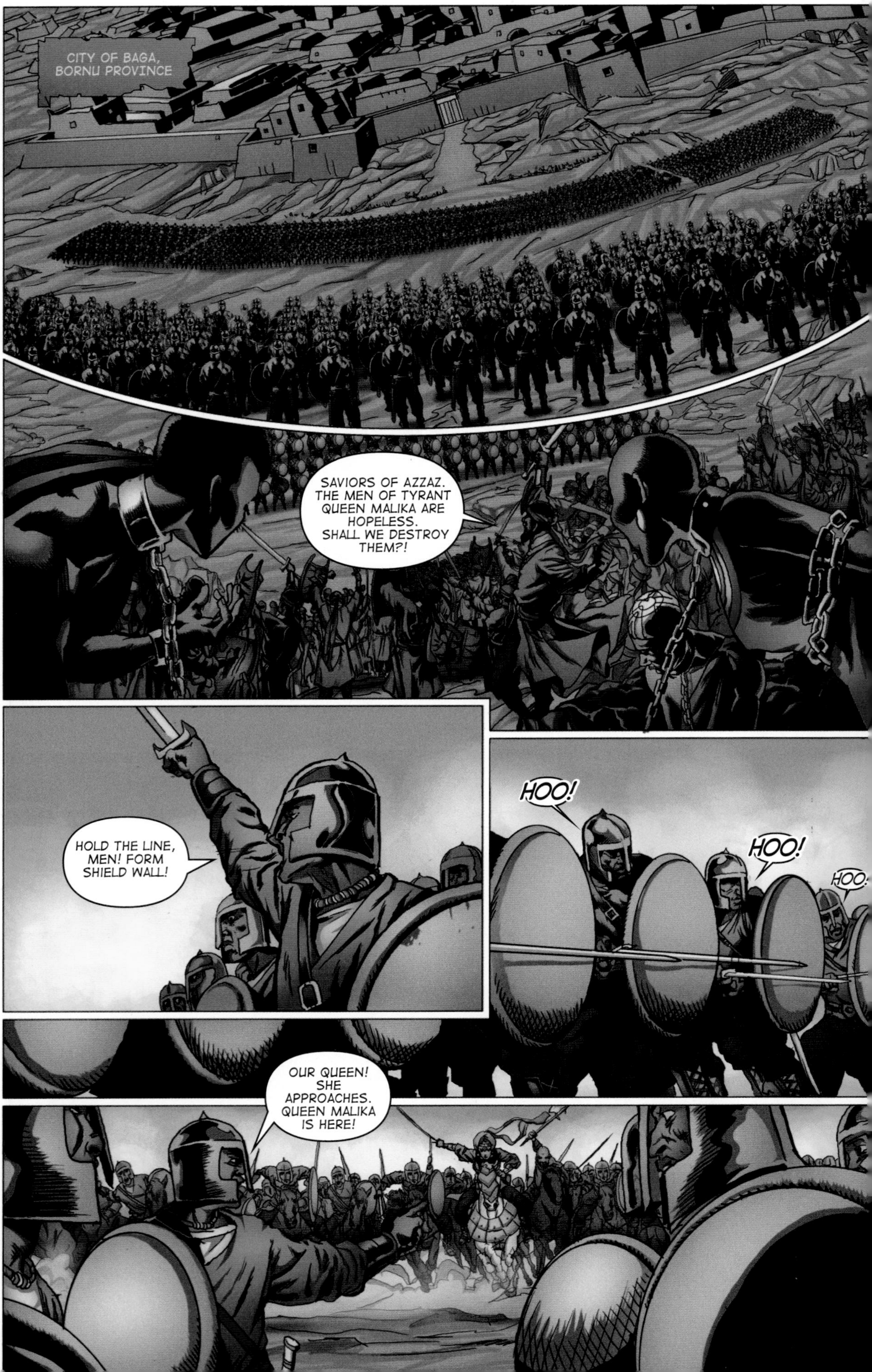
CITY OF BAGA,
BORNU PROVINCE
SAVIORS OF AZZAZ. THE MEN OF TYRANT QUEEN MALIKA ARE HOPELESS. SHALL WE DESTROY THEM?!
HOLD THE LINE, MEN! FORM SHIELD WALL!
HOO!
HOO!
HOO!
OUR QUEEN! SHE APPROACHES. QUEEN MALIKA IS HERE!

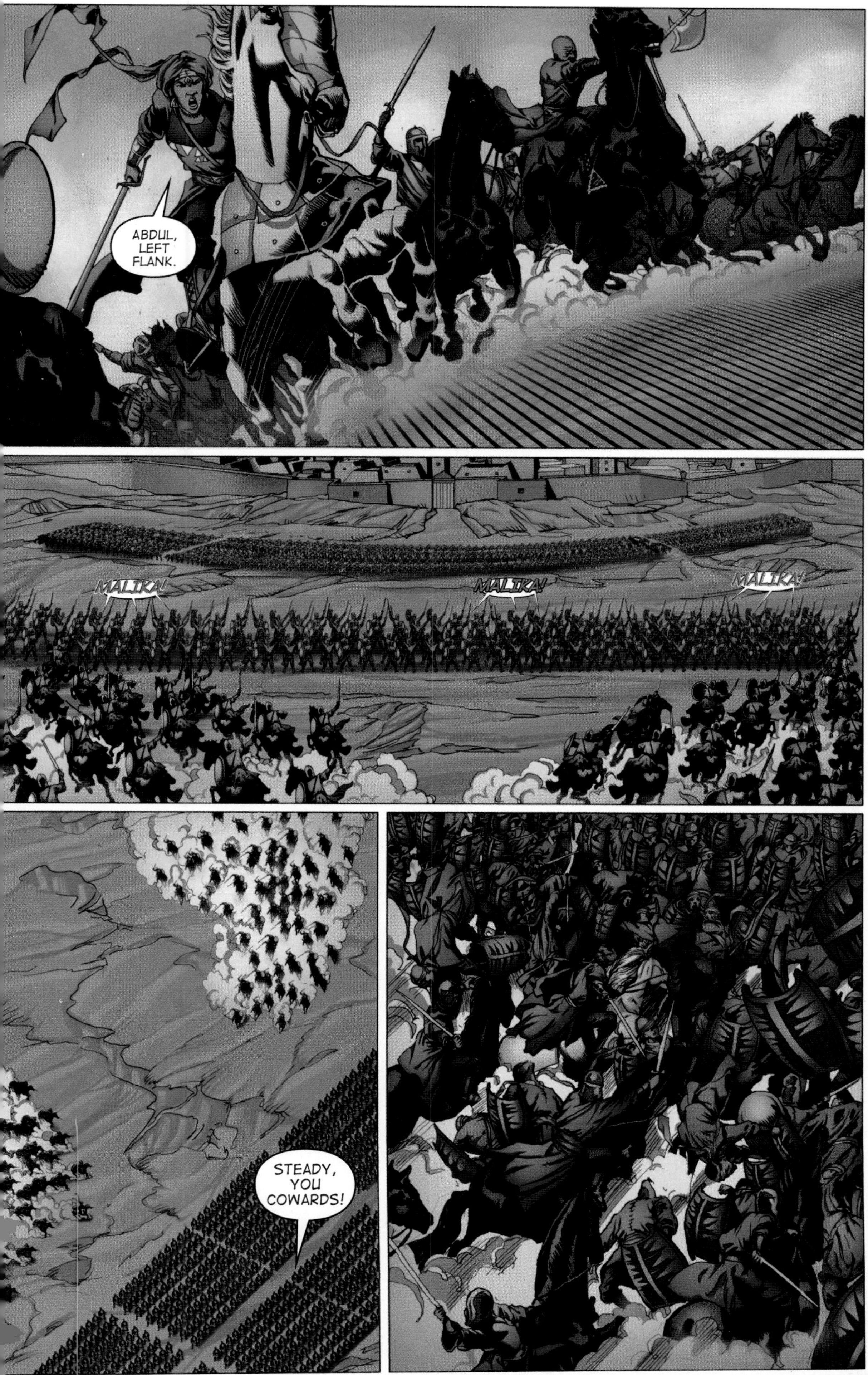
ABDUL, LEFT FLANK.
MALIKA!
MALIKA!
MALIKA!
STEADY, YOU COWARDS!

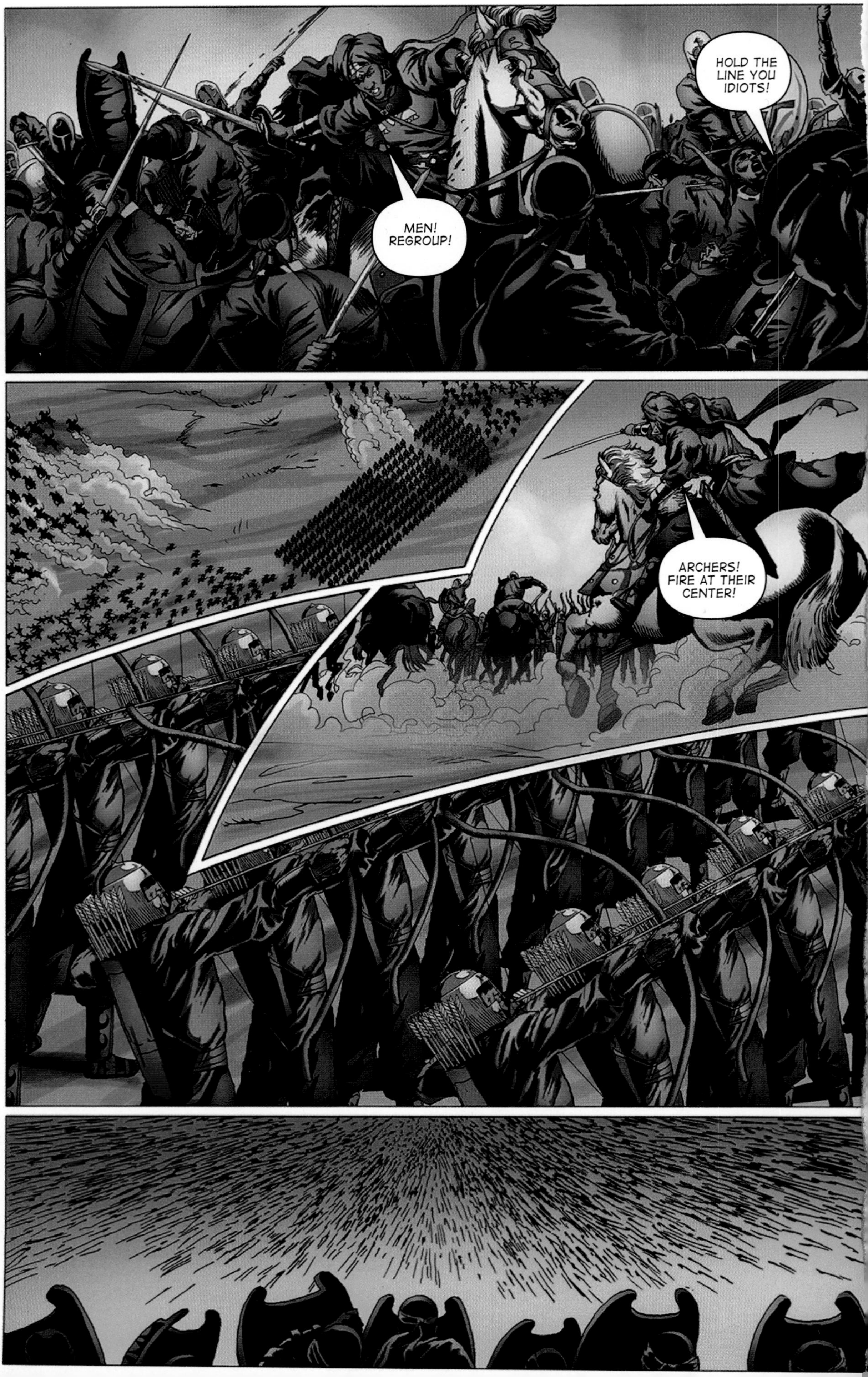

HOLD THE LINE YOU IDIOTS!
MEN! REGROUP!
ARCHERS! FIRE AT THEIR CENTER!

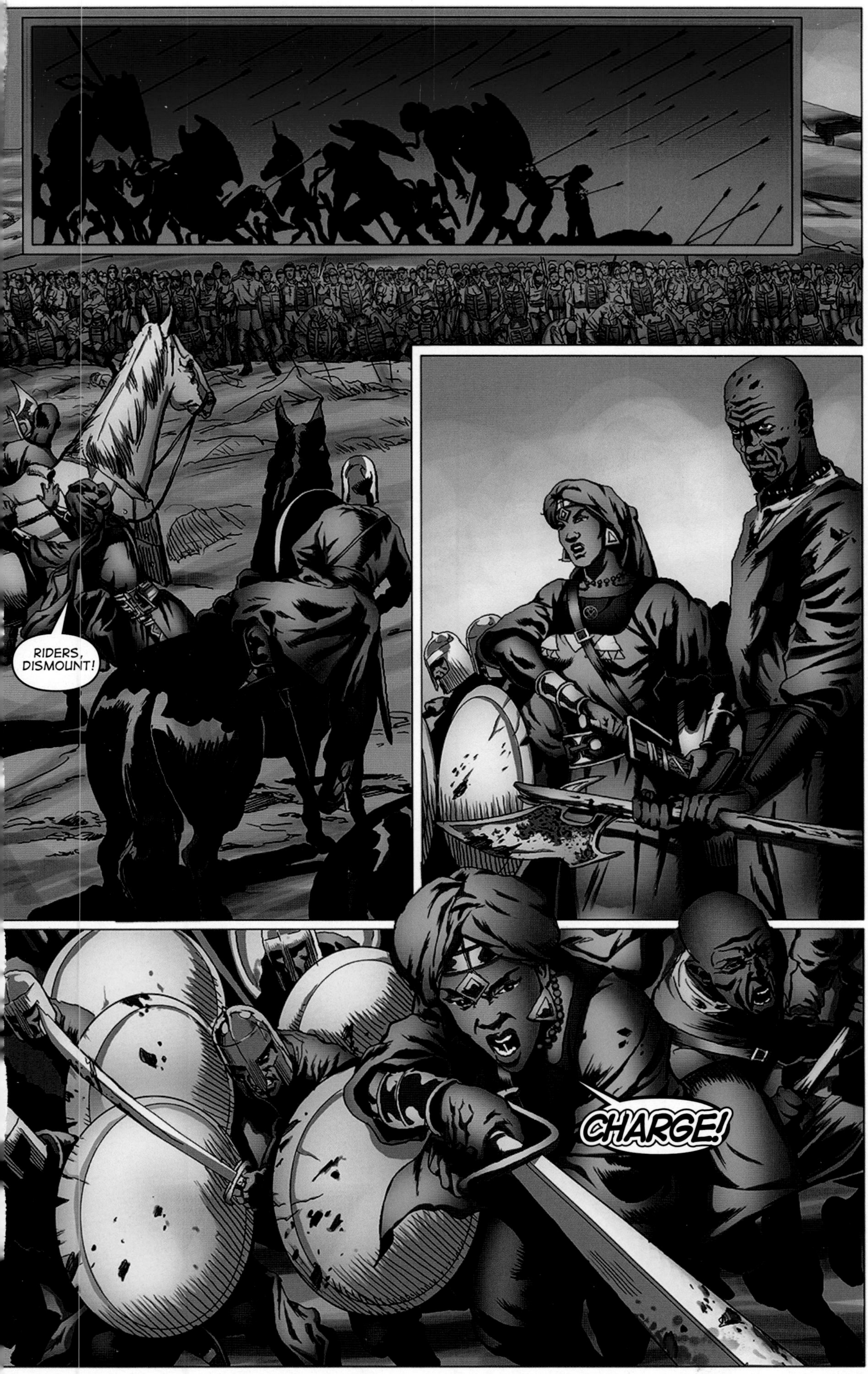
RIDERS, DISMOUNT!
CHARGE!

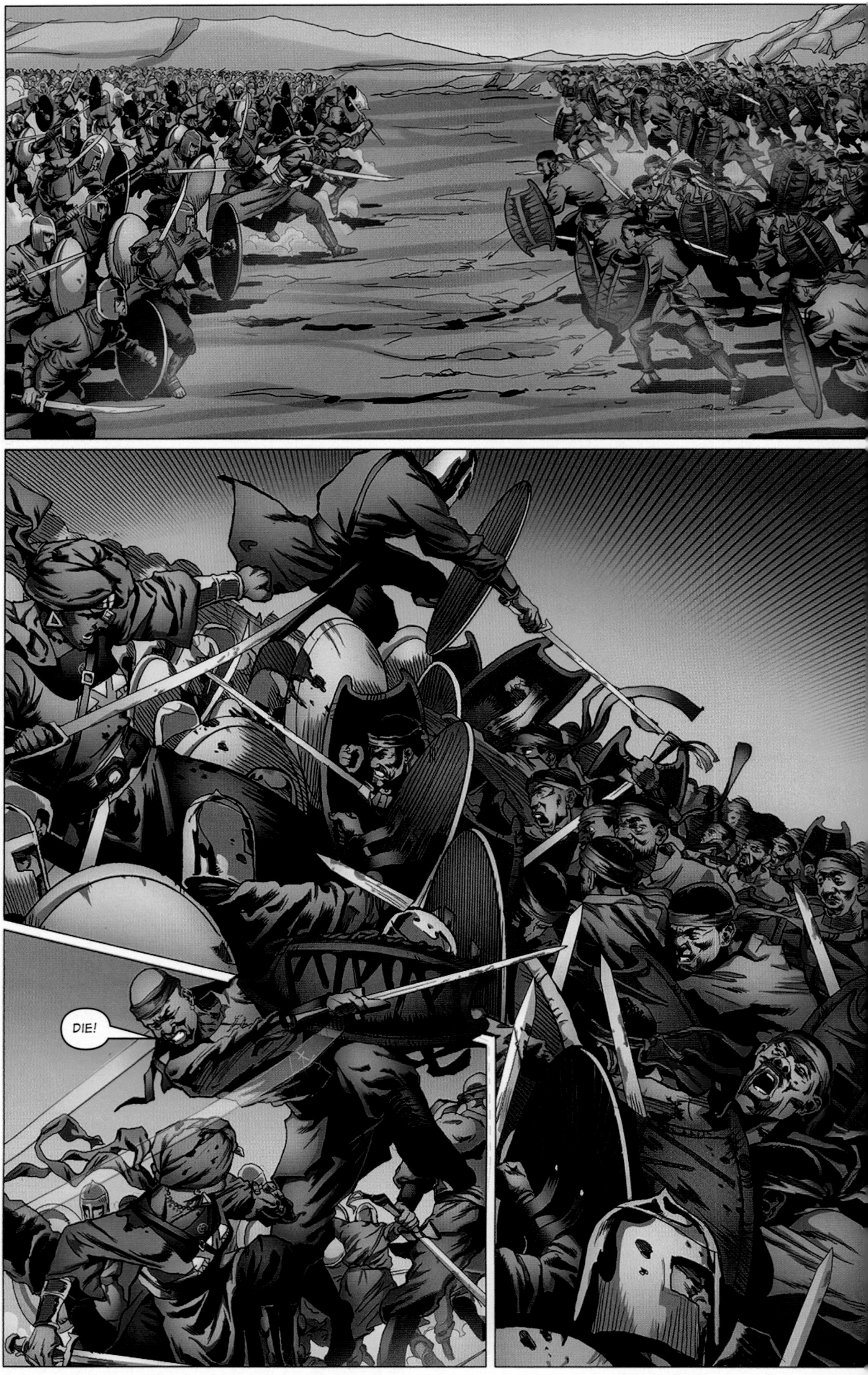
DIE!

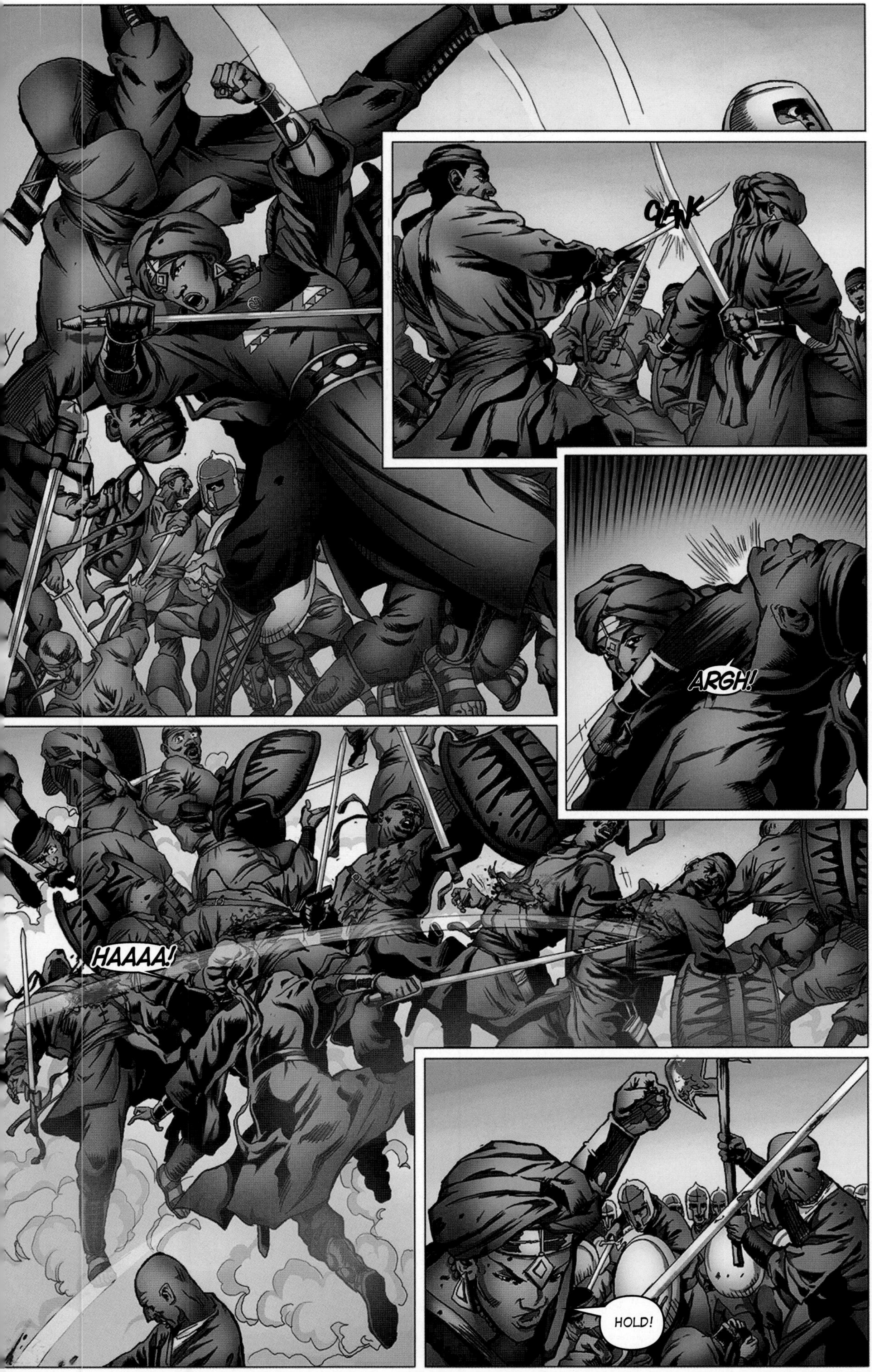

CLANK
ARGH!
HAAAA!
HOLD!

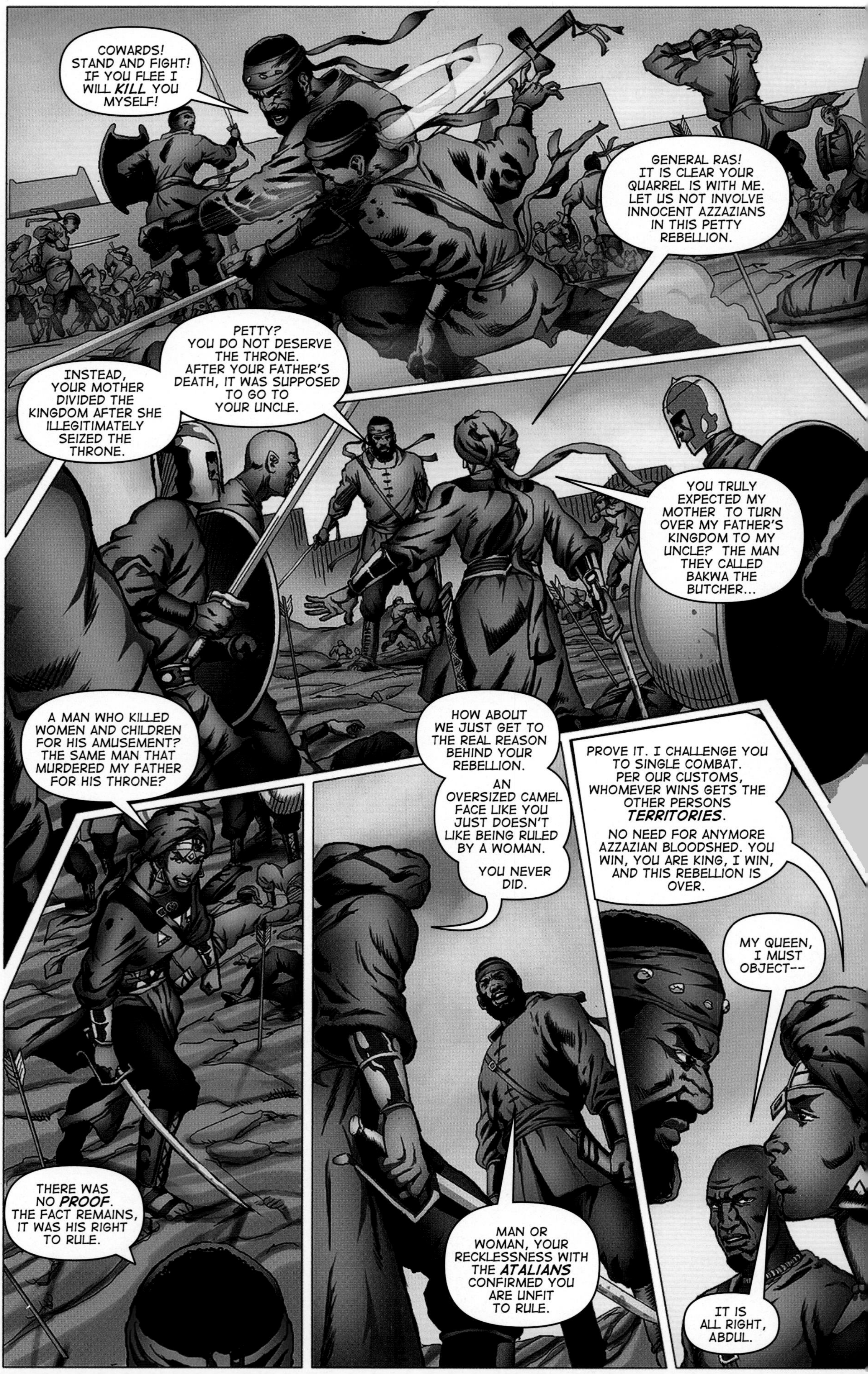
COWARDS! STAND AND FIGHT! IF YOU FLEE I WILL KILL YOU MYSELF!
GENERAL RAS! IT IS CLEAR YOUR QUARREL IS WITH ME. LET US NOT INVOLVE INNOCENT AZZAZIANS IN THIS PETTY REBELLION.
PETTY? YOU DO NOT DESERVE THE THRONE. AFTER YOUR FATHER'S DEATH, IT WAS SUPPOSED TO GO TO YOUR UNCLE.
INSTEAD, YOUR MOTHER DIVIDED THE KINGDOM AFTER SHE ILLEGITIMATELY SEIZED THE THRONE.
YOU TRULY EXPECTED MY MOTHER TO TURN OVER MY FATHER'S KINGDOM TO MY UNCLE? THE MAN THEY CALLED BAKWA THE BUTCHER...
A MAN WHO KILLED WOMEN AND CHILDREN FOR HIS AMUSEMENT? THE SAME MAN THAT MURDERED MY FATHER FOR HIS THRONE?
THERE WAS NO PROOF. THE FACT REMAINS, IT WAS HIS RIGHT TO RULE.
HOW ABOUT WE JUST GET TO THE REAL REASON BEHIND YOUR REBELLION.
AN OVERSIZED CAMEL FACE LIKE YOU JUST DOESN'T LIKE BEING RULED BY A WOMAN.
YOU NEVER DID.
MAN OR WOMAN, YOUR RECKLESSNESS WITH THE ATALIANS CONFIRMED YOU ARE UNFIT TO RULE.
PROVE IT. I CHALLENGE YOU TO SINGLE COMBAT. PER OUR CUSTOMS, WHOMEVER WINS GETS THE OTHER PERSONS TERRITORIES.
NO NEED FOR ANYMORE AZZAZIAN BLOODSHED. YOU WIN, YOU ARE KING, I WIN, AND THIS REBELLION IS OVER.
MY QUEEN, I MUST OBJECT--
IT IS ALL RIGHT, ABDUL.

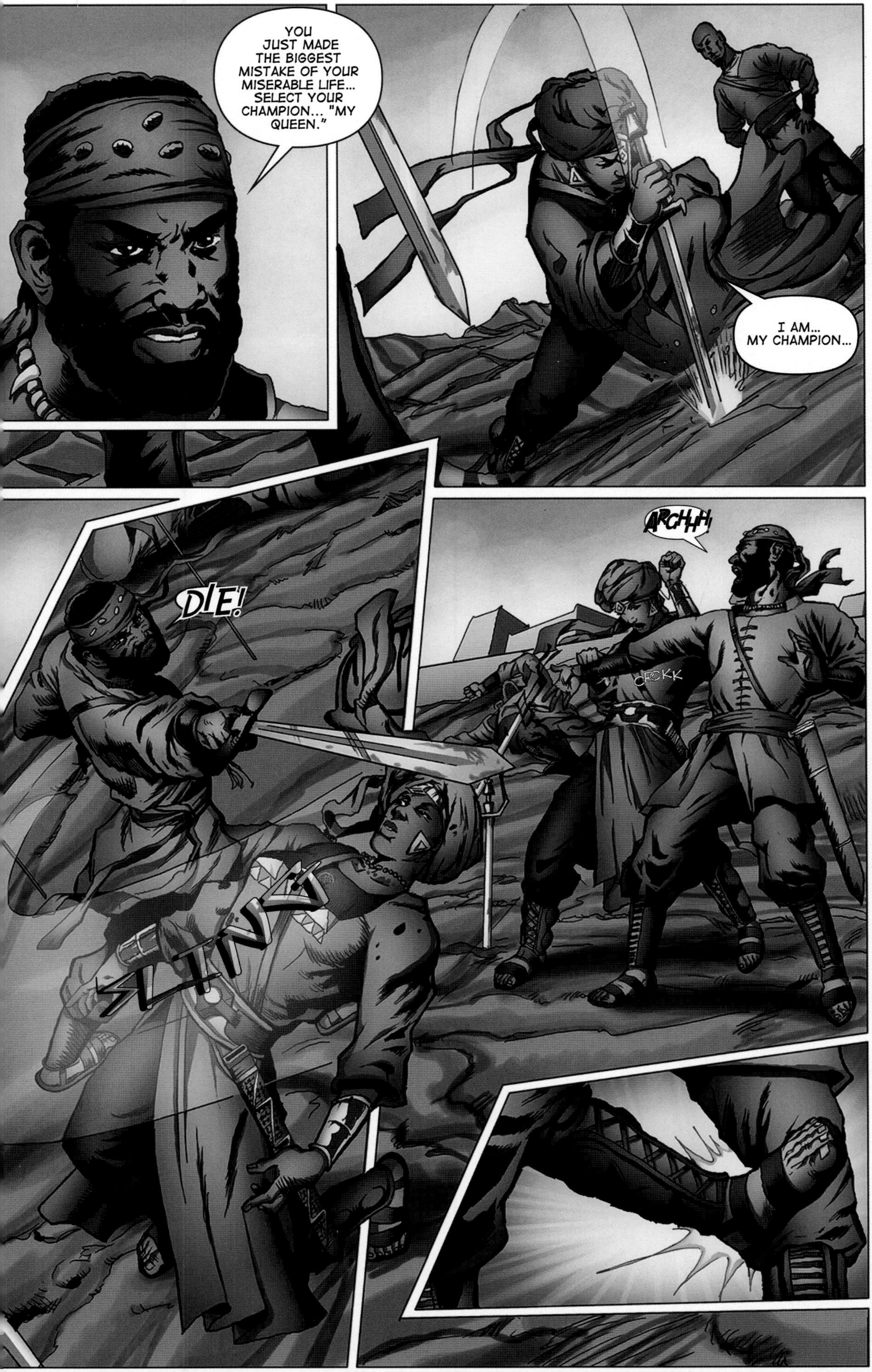
YOU JUST MADE THE BIGGEST MISTAKE OF YOUR MISERABLE LIFE... SELECT YOUR CHAMPION... "MY QUEEN."
I AM... MY CHAMPION...
DIE!
ARGHHH!
CRCKK

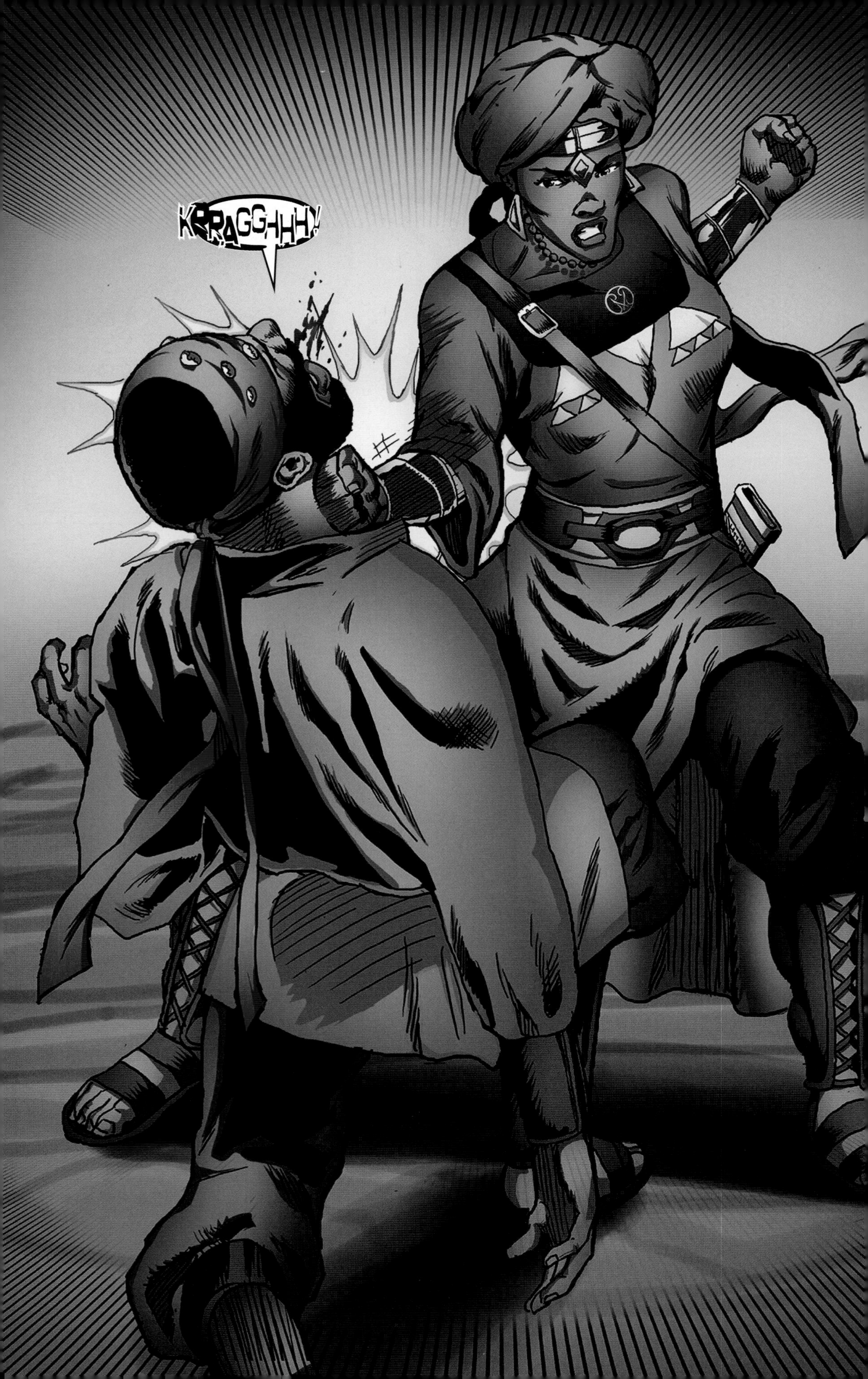
KRRAGGHHH!

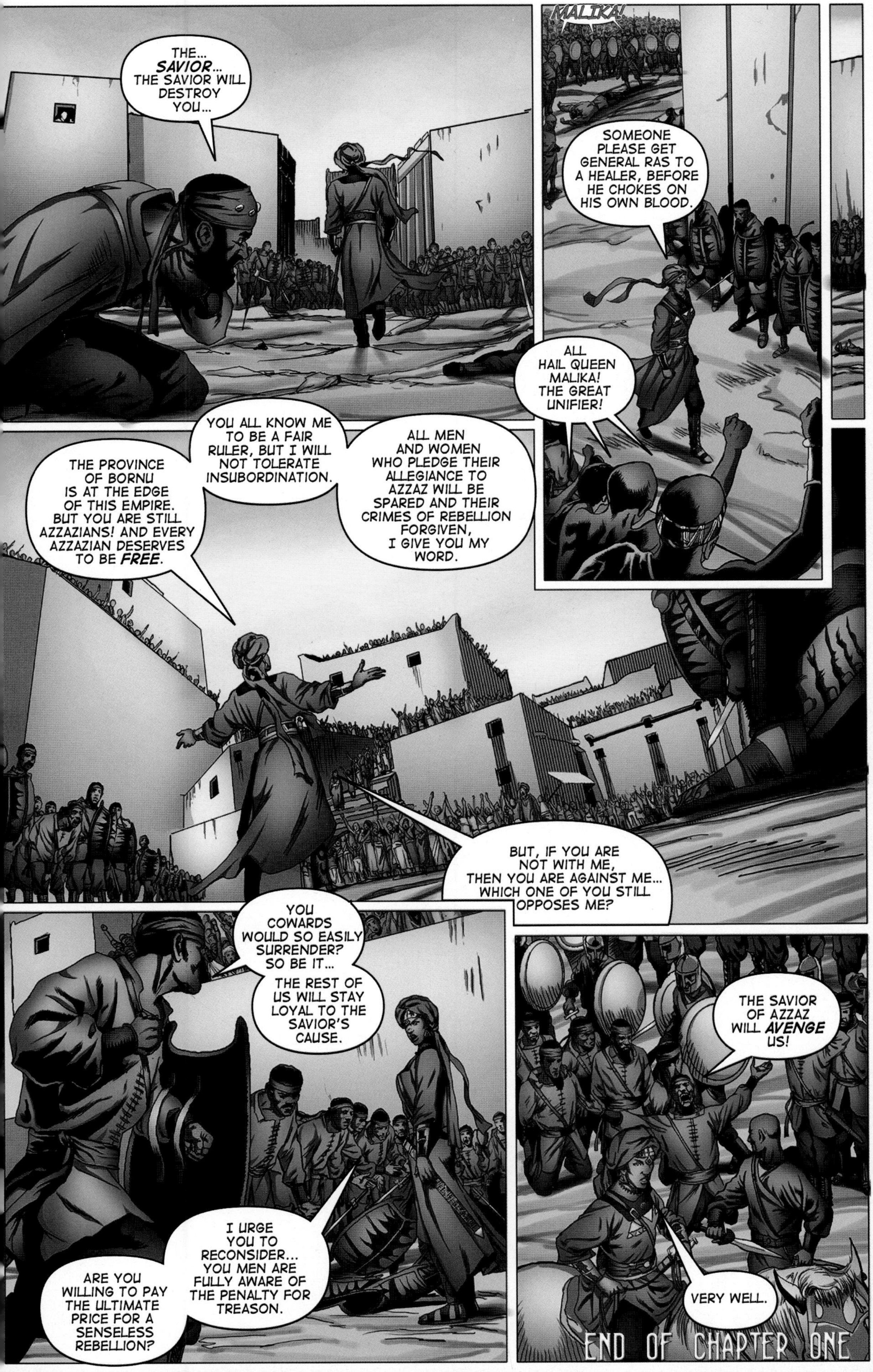
THE... SAVIOR... THE SAVIOR WILL DESTROY YOU...
MALIKA!
SOMEONE PLEASE GET GENERAL RAS TO A HEALER, BEFORE HE CHOKES ON HIS OWN BLOOD.
ALL HAIL QUEEN MALIKA! THE GREAT UNIFIER!
THE PROVINCE OF BORNU IS AT THE EDGE OF THIS EMPIRE. BUT YOU ARE STILL AZZAZIANS! AND EVERY AZZAZIAN DESERVES TO BE FREE.
YOU ALL KNOW ME TO BE A FAIR RULER, BUT I WILL NOT TOLERATE INSUBORDINATION.
ALL MEN AND WOMEN WHO PLEDGE THEIR ALLEGIANCE TO AZZAZ WILL BE SPARED AND THEIR CRIMES OF REBELLION FORGIVEN, I GIVE YOU MY WORD.
BUT, IF YOU ARE NOT WITH ME, THEN YOU ARE AGAINST ME... WHICH ONE OF YOU STILL OPPOSES ME?
YOU COWARDS WOULD SO EASILY SURRENDER? SO BE IT...
THE REST OF US WILL STAY LOYAL TO THE SAVIOR'S CAUSE.
I URGE YOU TO RECONSIDER... YOU MEN ARE FULLY AWARE OF THE PENALTY FOR TREASON.
ARE YOU WILLING TO PAY THE ULTIMATE PRICE FOR A SENSELESS REBELLION?
THE SAVIOR OF AZZAZ WILL AVENGE US!
VERY WELL.
END OF CHAPTER ONE

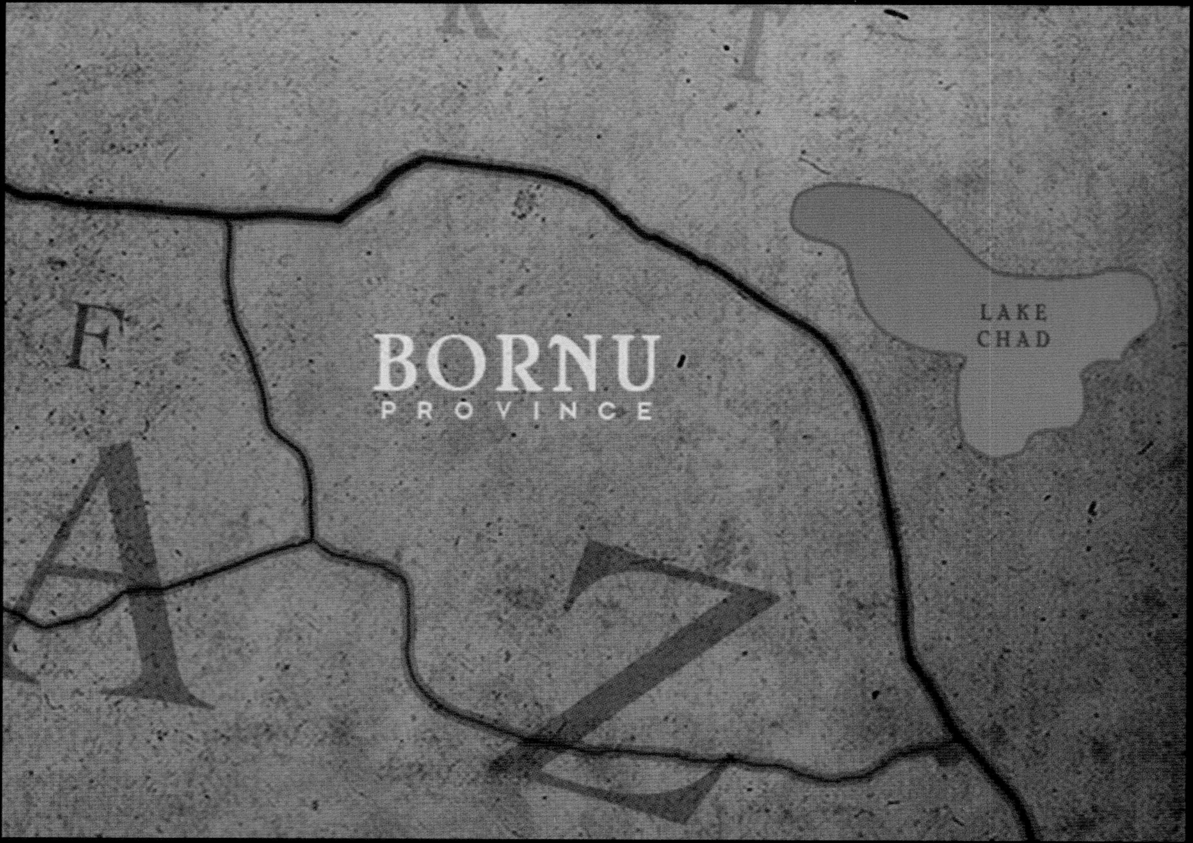
LAKE
CHAD
BORNU
PROVINCE
F
A
Z

THE BORNU PROVINCE

The Bornu Province, located in the northeast, just west of Lake Chad, provides the Azzazian empire valuable access to trans-Saharan trade routes. Chief Hazar currently governs the Bornu Province.

Fun fact: The creation of the Bornu Province was inspired by the real life Bornu Empire, which existed from 1380 - 1893. The Bornu Empire was located around the area of what is now northeastern Nigeria.

CHAPTER TWO

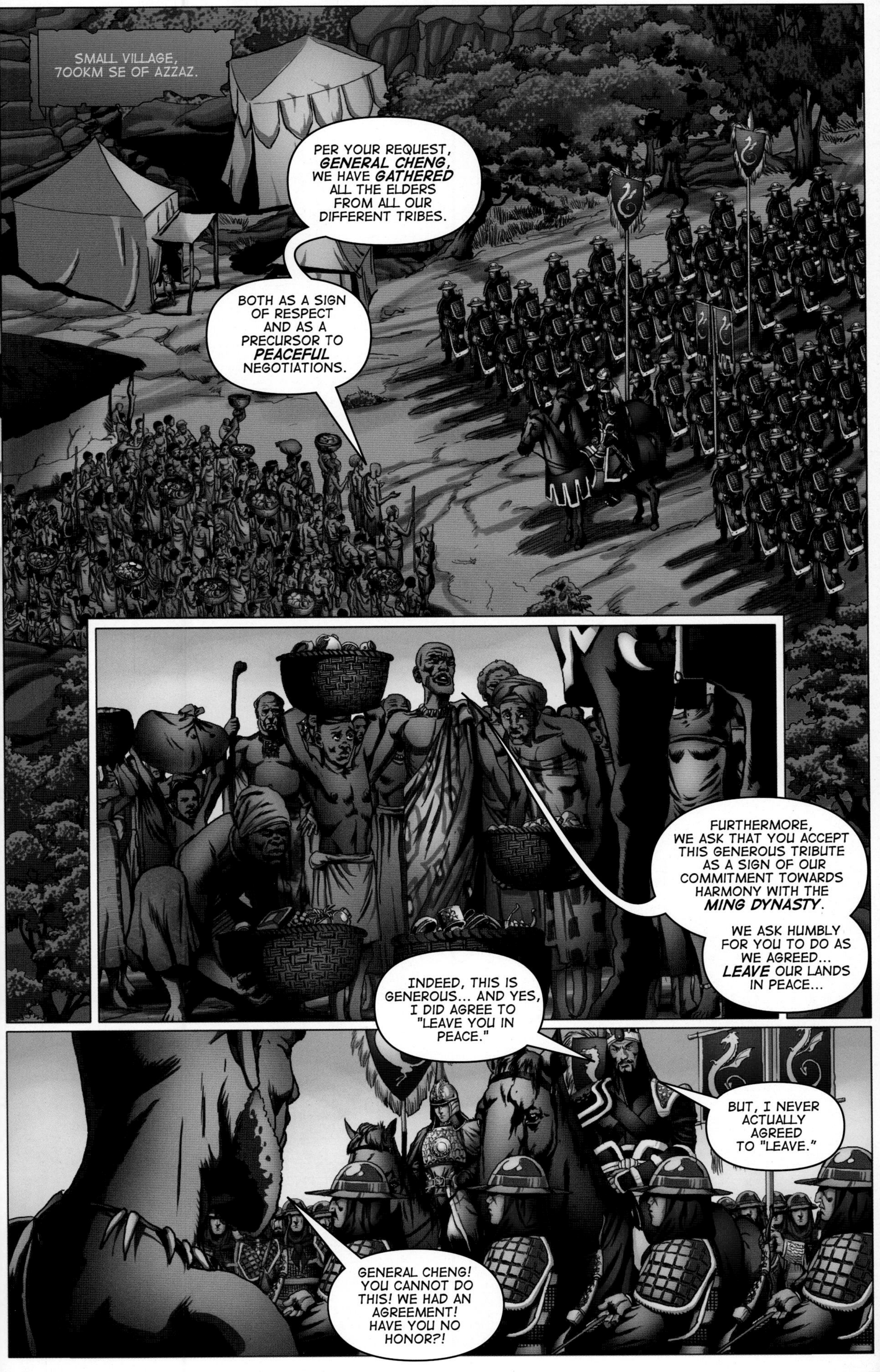
SMALL VILLAGE, 700KM SE OF AZZAZ.
PER YOUR REQUEST, GENERAL CHENG, WE HAVE GATHERED ALL THE ELDERS FROM ALL OUR DIFFERENT TRIBES.
BOTH AS A SIGN OF RESPECT AND AS A PRECURSOR TO PEACEFUL NEGOTIATIONS.
FURTHERMORE, WE ASK THAT YOU ACCEPT THIS GENEROUS TRIBUTE AS A SIGN OF OUR COMMITMENT TOWARDS HARMONY WITH THE MING DYNASTY.
WE ASK HUMBLY FOR YOU TO DO AS WE AGREED... LEAVE OUR LANDS IN PEACE...
INDEED, THIS IS GENEROUS... AND YES, I DID AGREE TO "LEAVE YOU IN PEACE."
BUT, I NEVER ACTUALLY AGREED TO "LEAVE."
GENERAL CHENG! YOU CANNOT DO THIS! WE HAD AN AGREEMENT! HAVE YOU NO HONOR?!

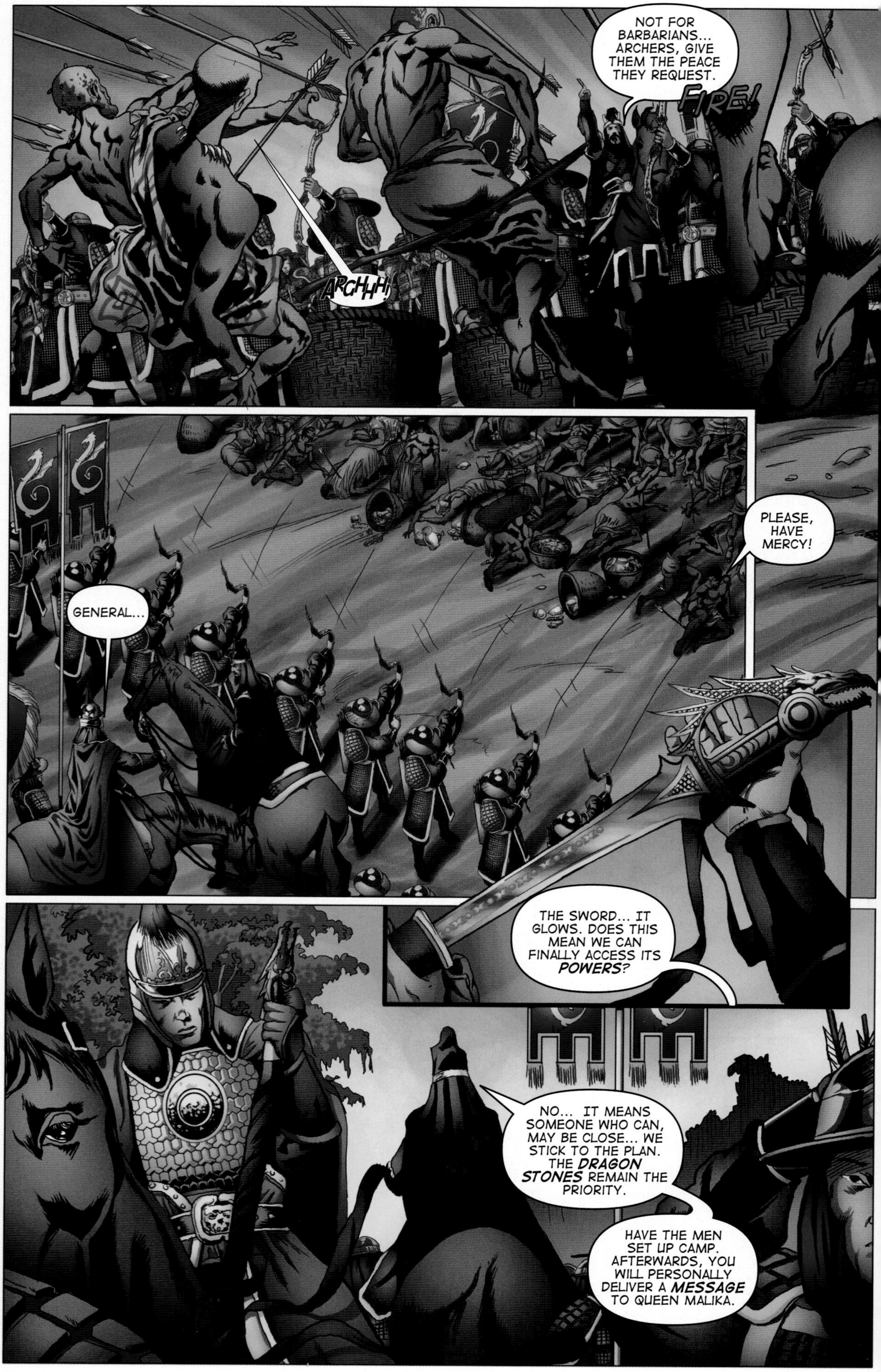
NOT FOR BARBARIANS... ARCHERS, GIVE THEM THE PEACE THEY REQUEST.
FIRE!
ARGHHH!
PLEASE, HAVE MERCY!
GENERAL...
THE SWORD... IT GLOWS. DOES THIS MEAN WE CAN FINALLY ACCESS ITS POWERS?
NO... IT MEANS SOMEONE WHO CAN, MAY BE CLOSE... WE STICK TO THE PLAN. THE DRAGON STONES REMAIN THE PRIORITY.
HAVE THE MEN SET UP CAMP. AFTERWARDS, YOU WILL PERSONALLY DELIVER A MESSAGE TO QUEEN MALIKA.

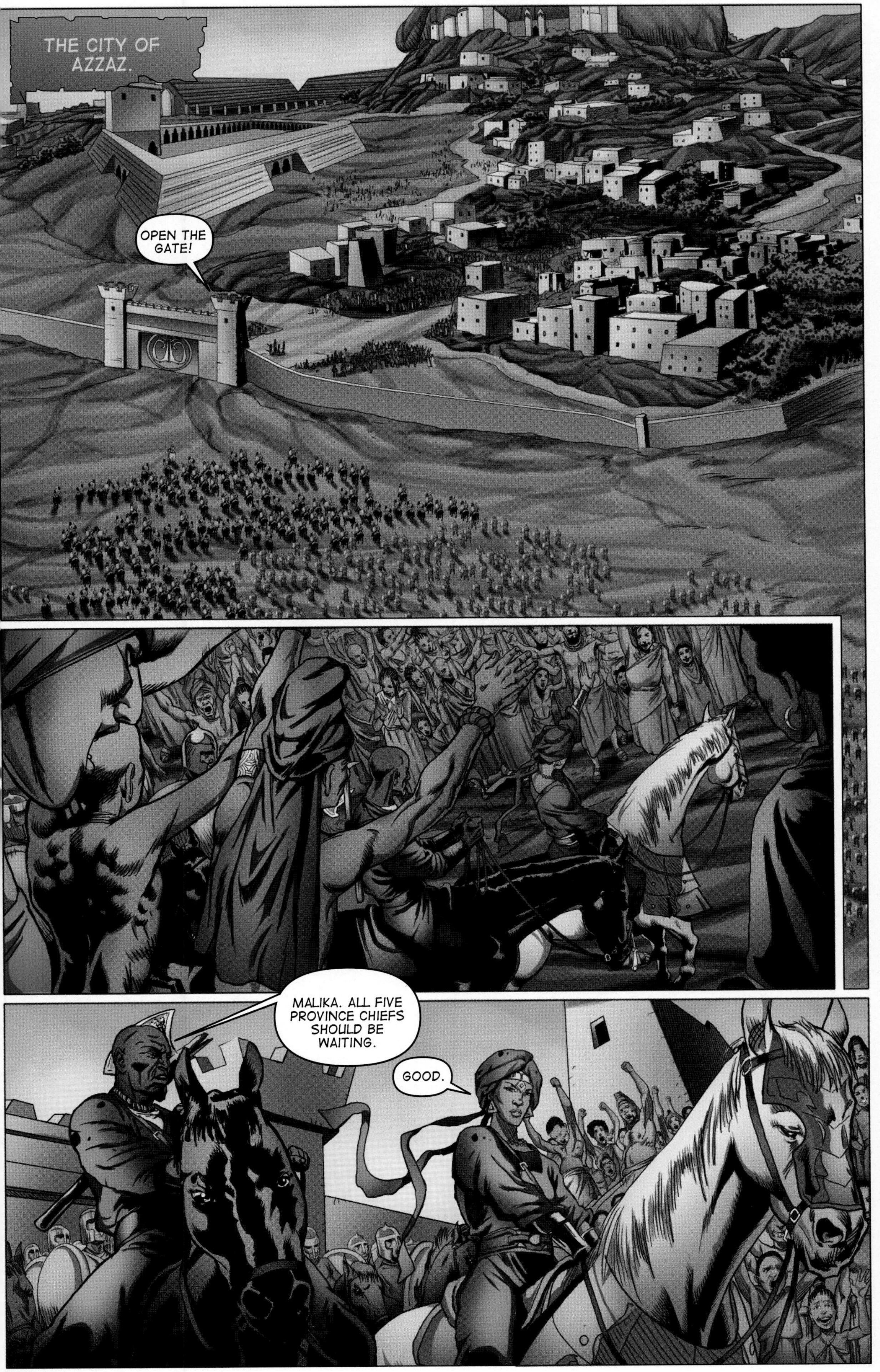
THE CITY OF AZZAZ.
OPEN THE GATE!
MALIKA. ALL FIVE PROVINCE CHIEFS SHOULD BE WAITING.
GOOD.

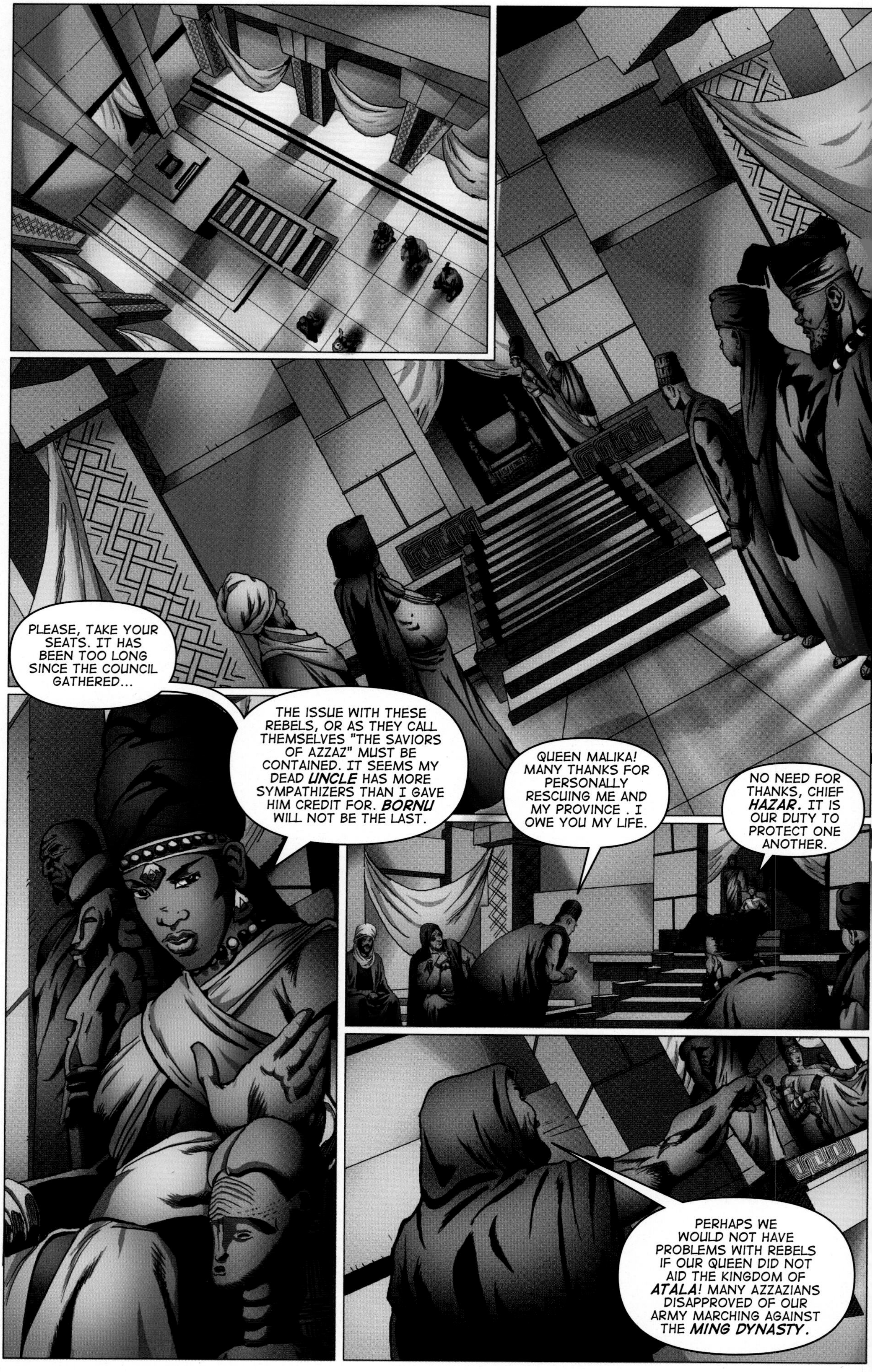
PLEASE, TAKE YOUR SEATS. IT HAS BEEN TOO LONG SINCE THE COUNCIL GATHERED...
THE ISSUE WITH THESE REBELS, OR AS THEY CALL THEMSELVES "THE SAVIORS OF AZZAZ" MUST BE CONTAINED. IT SEEMS MY DEAD UNCLE HAS MORE SYMPATHIZERS THAN I GAVE HIM CREDIT FOR. BORNU WILL NOT BE THE LAST.
QUEEN MALIKA! MANY THANKS FOR PERSONALLY RESCUING ME AND MY PROVINCE . I OWE YOU MY LIFE.
NO NEED FOR THANKS, CHIEF HAZAR. IT IS OUR DUTY TO PROTECT ONE ANOTHER.
PERHAPS WE WOULD NOT HAVE PROBLEMS WITH REBELS IF OUR QUEEN DID NOT AID THE KINGDOM OF ATALA! MANY AZZAZIANS DISAPPROVED OF OUR ARMY MARCHING AGAINST THE MING DYNASTY.

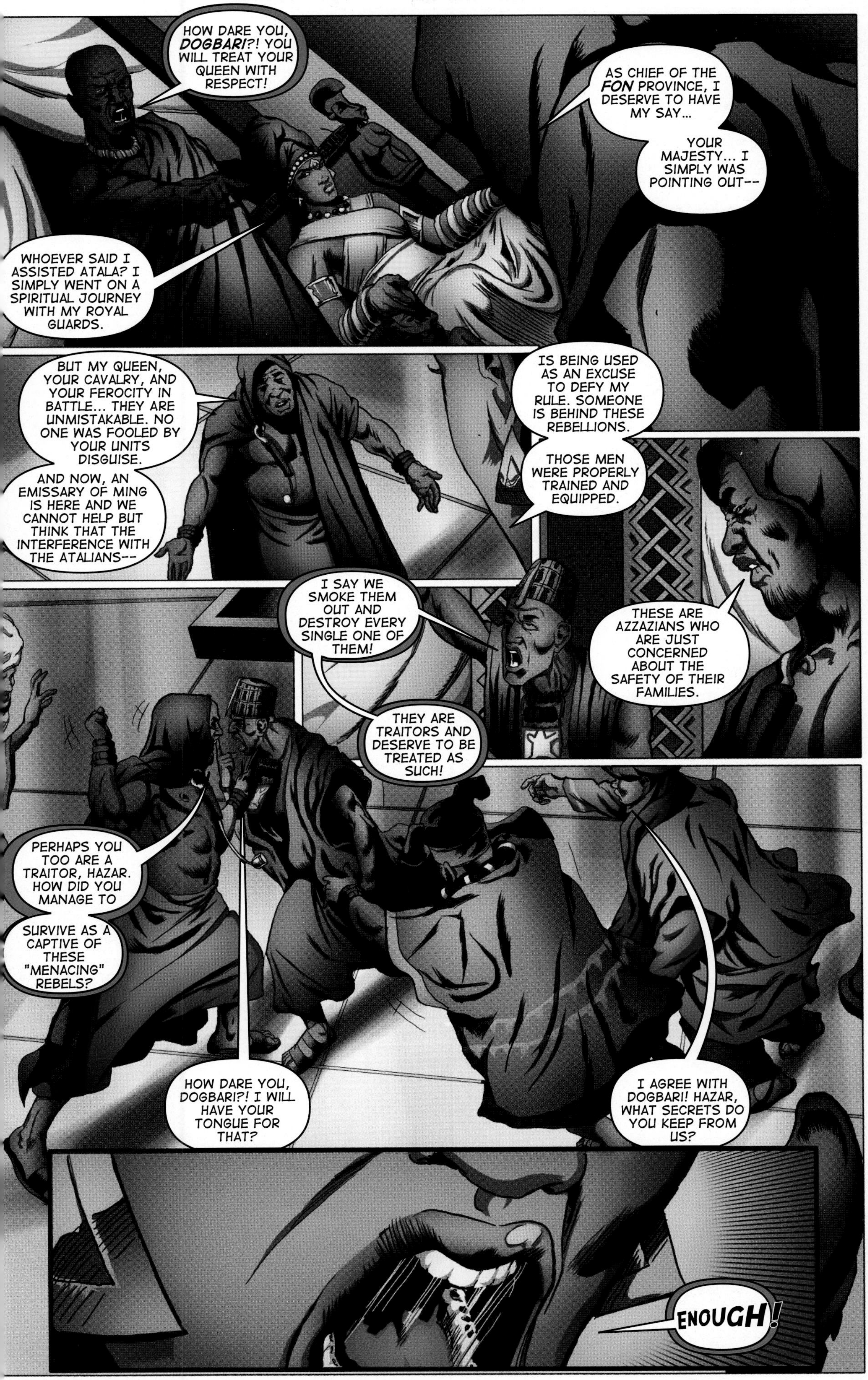
HOW DARE YOU, DOGBARI?! YOU WILL TREAT YOUR QUEEN WITH RESPECT!
AS CHIEF OF THE FON PROVINCE, I DESERVE TO HAVE MY SAY...
YOUR MAJESTY... I SIMPLY WAS POINTING OUT--
WHOEVER SAID I ASSISTED ATALA? I SIMPLY WENT ON A SPIRITUAL JOURNEY WITH MY ROYAL GUARDS.
BUT MY QUEEN, YOUR CAVALRY, AND YOUR FEROCITY IN BATTLE... THEY ARE UNMISTAKABLE. NO ONE WAS FOOLED BY YOUR UNITS DISGUISE.
AND NOW, AN EMISSARY OF MING IS HERE AND WE CANNOT HELP BUT THINK THAT THE INTERFERENCE WITH THE ATALIANS--
IS BEING USED AS AN EXCUSE TO DEFY MY RULE. SOMEONE IS BEHIND THESE REBELLIONS.
THOSE MEN WERE PROPERLY TRAINED AND EQUIPPED.
I SAY WE SMOKE THEM OUT AND DESTROY EVERY SINGLE ONE OF THEM!
THEY ARE TRAITORS AND DESERVE TO BE TREATED AS SUCH!
THESE ARE AZZAZIANS WHO ARE JUST CONCERNED ABOUT THE SAFETY OF THEIR FAMILIES.
PERHAPS YOU TOO ARE A TRAITOR, HAZAR. HOW DID YOU MANAGE TO
SURVIVE AS A CAPTIVE OF THESE "MENACING" REBELS?
HOW DARE YOU, DOGBARI?! I WILL HAVE YOUR TONGUE FOR THAT?
I AGREE WITH DOGBARI! HAZAR, WHAT SECRETS DO YOU KEEP FROM US?
ENOUGH!

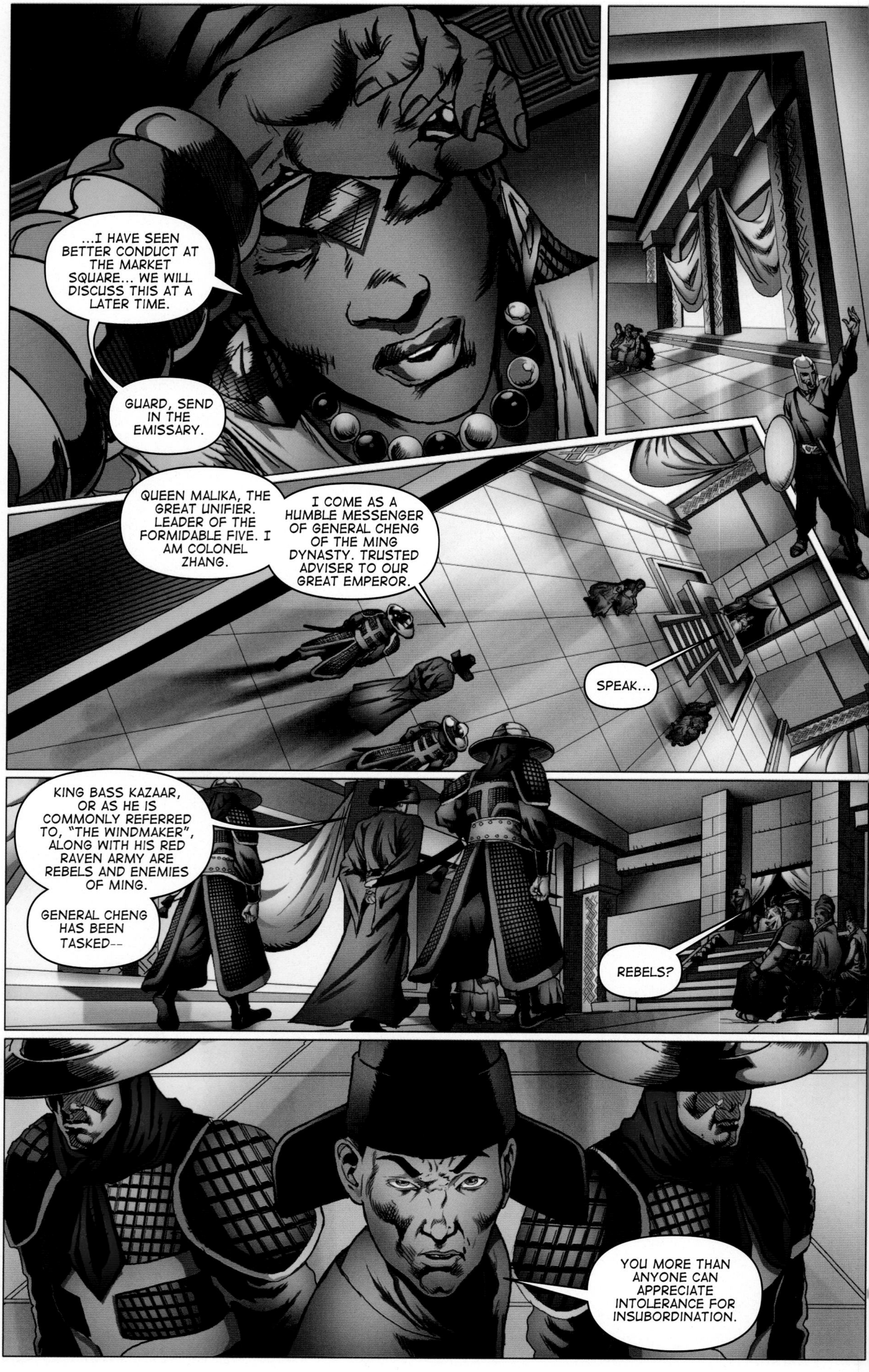
...I HAVE SEEN BETTER CONDUCT AT THE MARKET SQUARE... WE WILL DISCUSS THIS AT A LATER TIME.
GUARD, SEND IN THE EMISSARY.
QUEEN MALIKA, THE GREAT UNIFIER. LEADER OF THE FORMIDABLE FIVE. I AM COLONEL ZHANG.
I COME AS A HUMBLE MESSENGER OF GENERAL CHENG OF THE MING DYNASTY. TRUSTED ADVISER TO OUR GREAT EMPEROR.
SPEAK...
KING BASS KAZAAR, OR AS HE IS COMMONLY REFERRED TO, "THE WINDMAKER", ALONG WITH HIS RED RAVEN ARMY ARE REBELS AND ENEMIES OF MING.
GENERAL CHENG HAS BEEN TASKED--
REBELS?
YOU MORE THAN ANYONE CAN APPRECIATE INTOLERANCE FOR INSUBORDINATION.

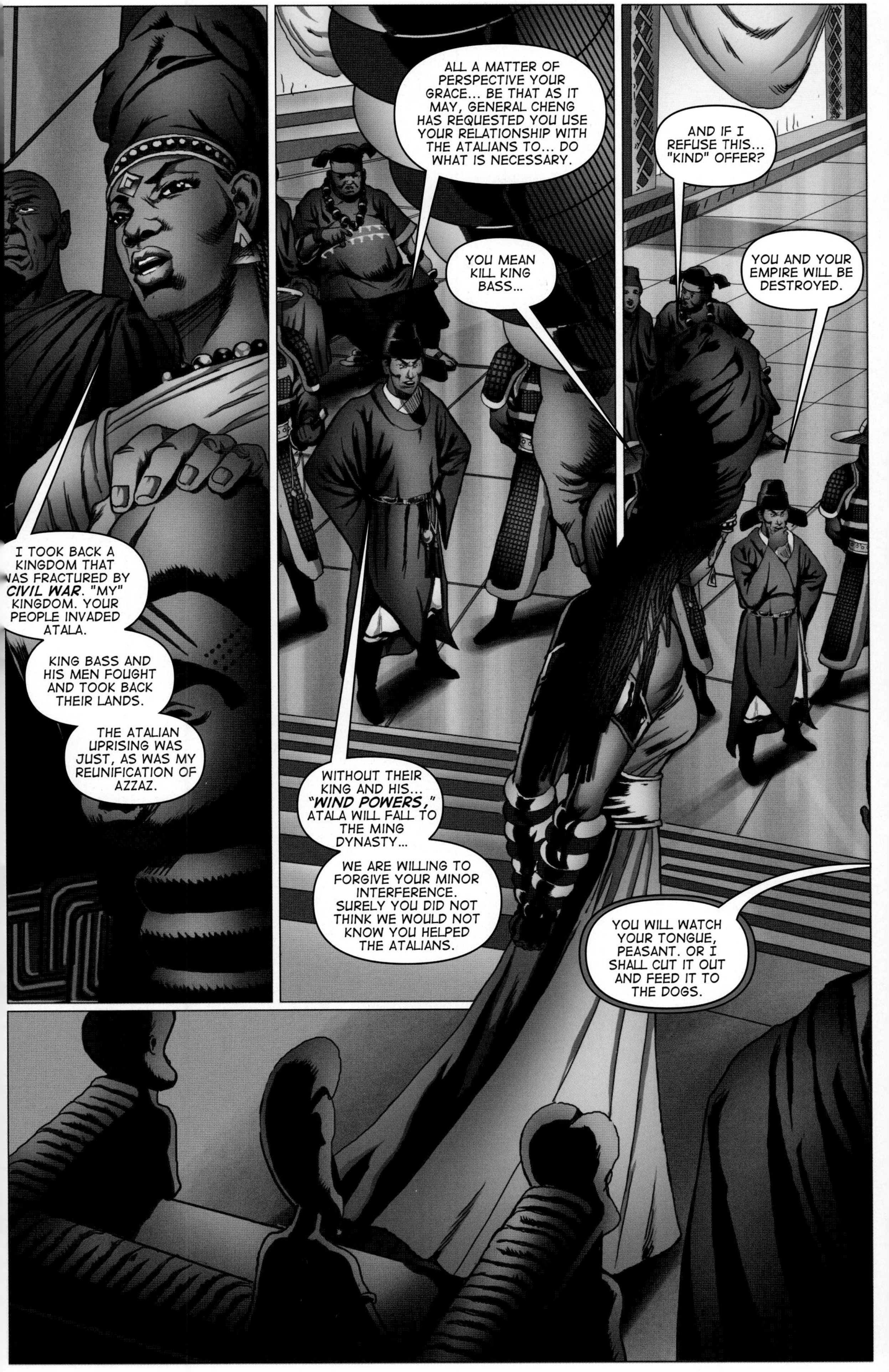
I TOOK BACK A KINGDOM THAT WAS FRACTURED BY CIVIL WAR. "MY" KINGDOM. YOUR PEOPLE INVADED ATALA.
KING BASS AND HIS MEN FOUGHT AND TOOK BACK THEIR LANDS.
THE ATALIAN UPRISING WAS JUST, AS WAS MY REUNIFICATION OF AZZAZ.
ALL A MATTER OF PERSPECTIVE YOUR GRACE... BE THAT AS IT MAY, GENERAL CHENG HAS REQUESTED YOU USE YOUR RELATIONSHIP WITH THE ATALIANS TO... DO WHAT IS NECESSARY.
YOU MEAN KILL KING BASS...
WITHOUT THEIR KING AND HIS... "WIND POWERS," ATALA WILL FALL TO THE MING DYNASTY...
WE ARE WILLING TO FORGIVE YOUR MINOR INTERFERENCE. SURELY YOU DID NOT THINK WE WOULD NOT KNOW YOU HELPED THE ATALIANS.
AND IF I REFUSE THIS... "KIND" OFFER?
YOU AND YOUR EMPIRE WILL BE DESTROYED.
YOU WILL WATCH YOUR TONGUE, PEASANT. OR I SHALL CUT IT OUT AND FEED IT TO THE DOGS.

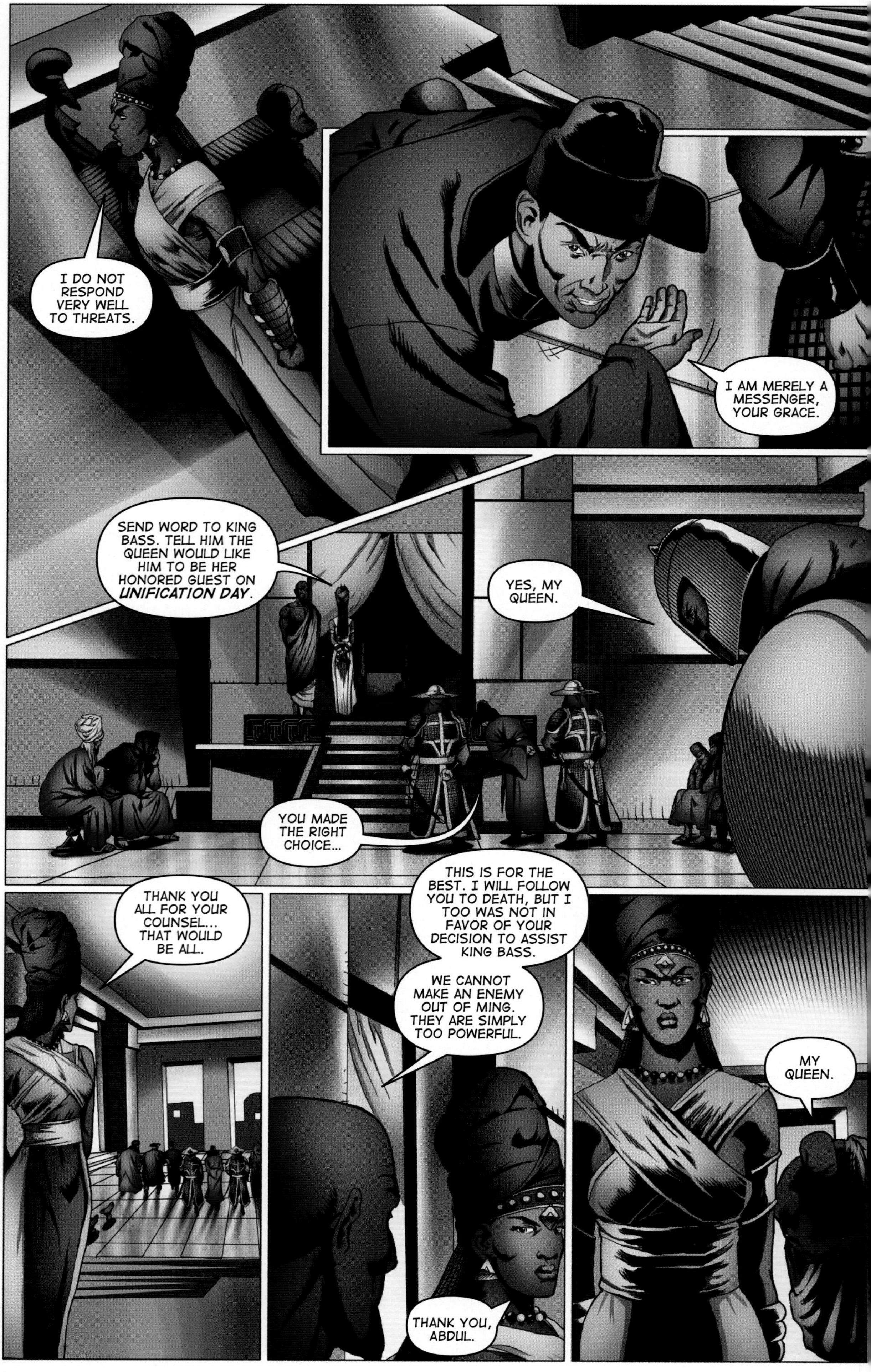
I DO NOT RESPOND VERY WELL TO THREATS.
I AM MERELY A MESSENGER, YOUR GRACE.
SEND WORD TO KING BASS. TELL HIM THE QUEEN WOULD LIKE HIM TO BE HER HONORED GUEST ON UNIFICATION DAY.
YES, MY QUEEN.
YOU MADE THE RIGHT CHOICE...
THANK YOU ALL FOR YOUR COUNSEL... THAT WOULD BE ALL.
THIS IS FOR THE BEST. I WILL FOLLOW YOU TO DEATH, BUT I TOO WAS NOT IN FAVOR OF YOUR DECISION TO ASSIST KING BASS.
WE CANNOT MAKE AN ENEMY OUT OF MING. THEY ARE SIMPLY TOO POWERFUL.
THANK YOU, ABDUL.
MY QUEEN.

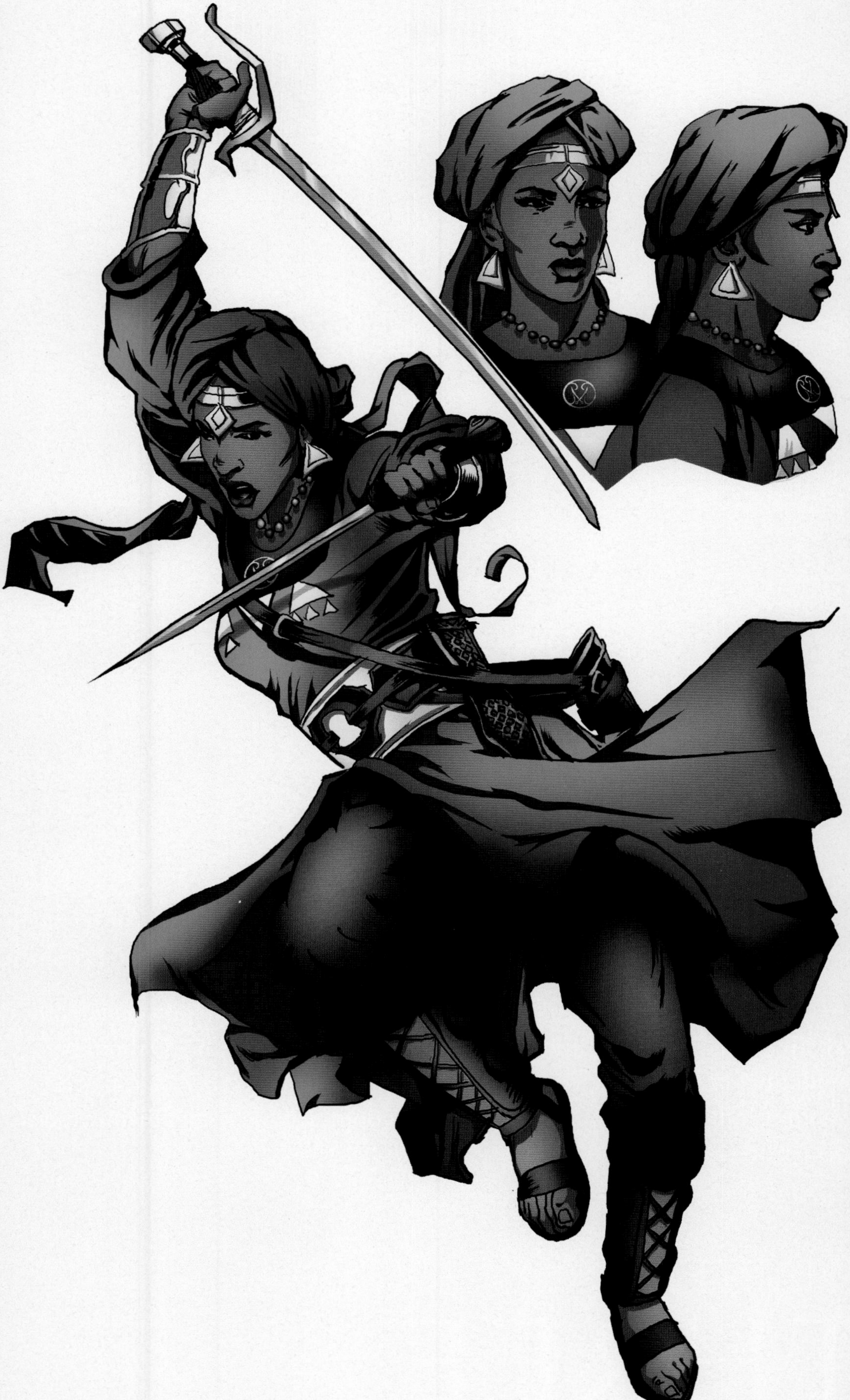

END OF CHAPTER TWO

SON
EMPIR
A
FON
PROVINCE
GREAT WEST RIV
LAKE
FON

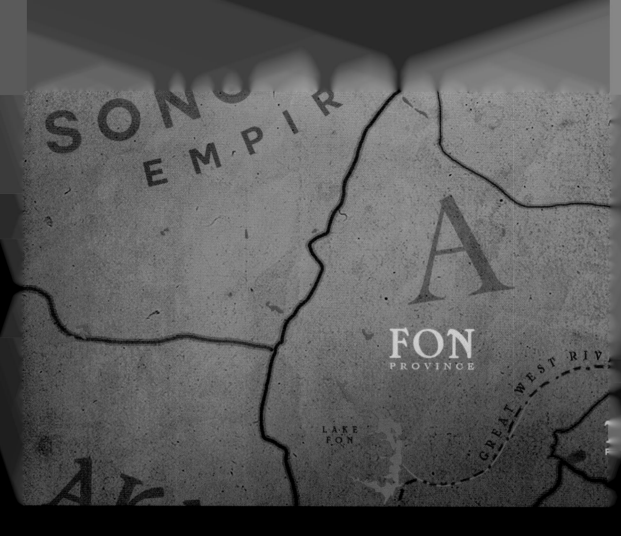

THE FON PROVINCE

The Fon Province is located to the west of the City of Azzaz. Its access to rare raw materials like gold and ivory make it the richest of the five provinces. Chief Dogbari currently governs the Fon Province.

Fun Fact: The creation of the Fon Province takes inspiration from the real life Fon People, of whom's history is linked to the Dahomey Kingdom. Located in a region that is now present-day Benin, the Dahomey kingdom was an African kingdom that existed from about 600 - 1894.

CHAPTER THREE

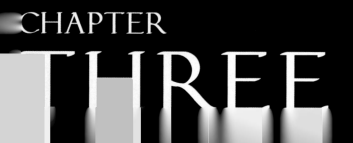

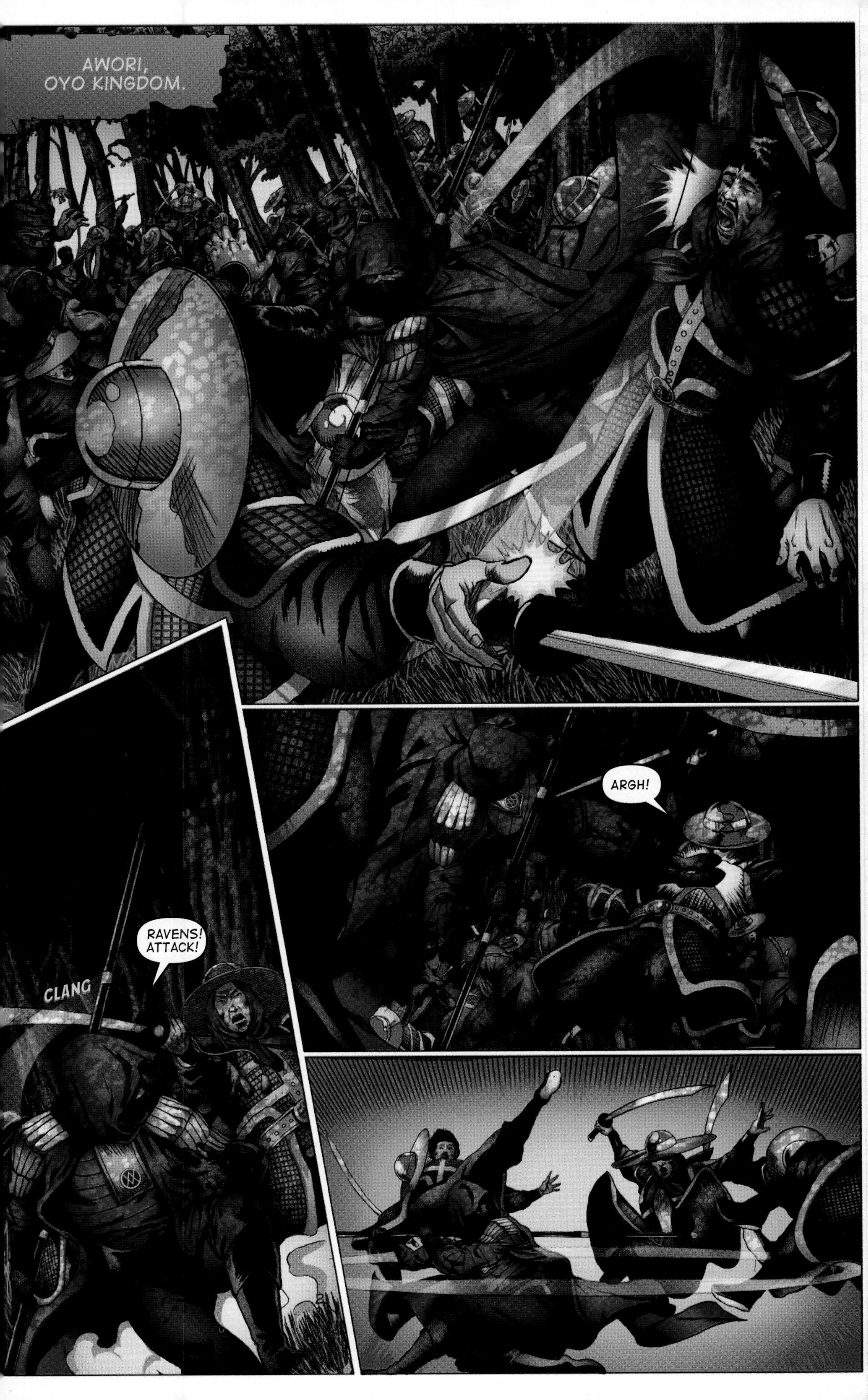
AWORI,
OYO KINGDOM.
ARGH!
RAVENS! ATTACK!
CLANG

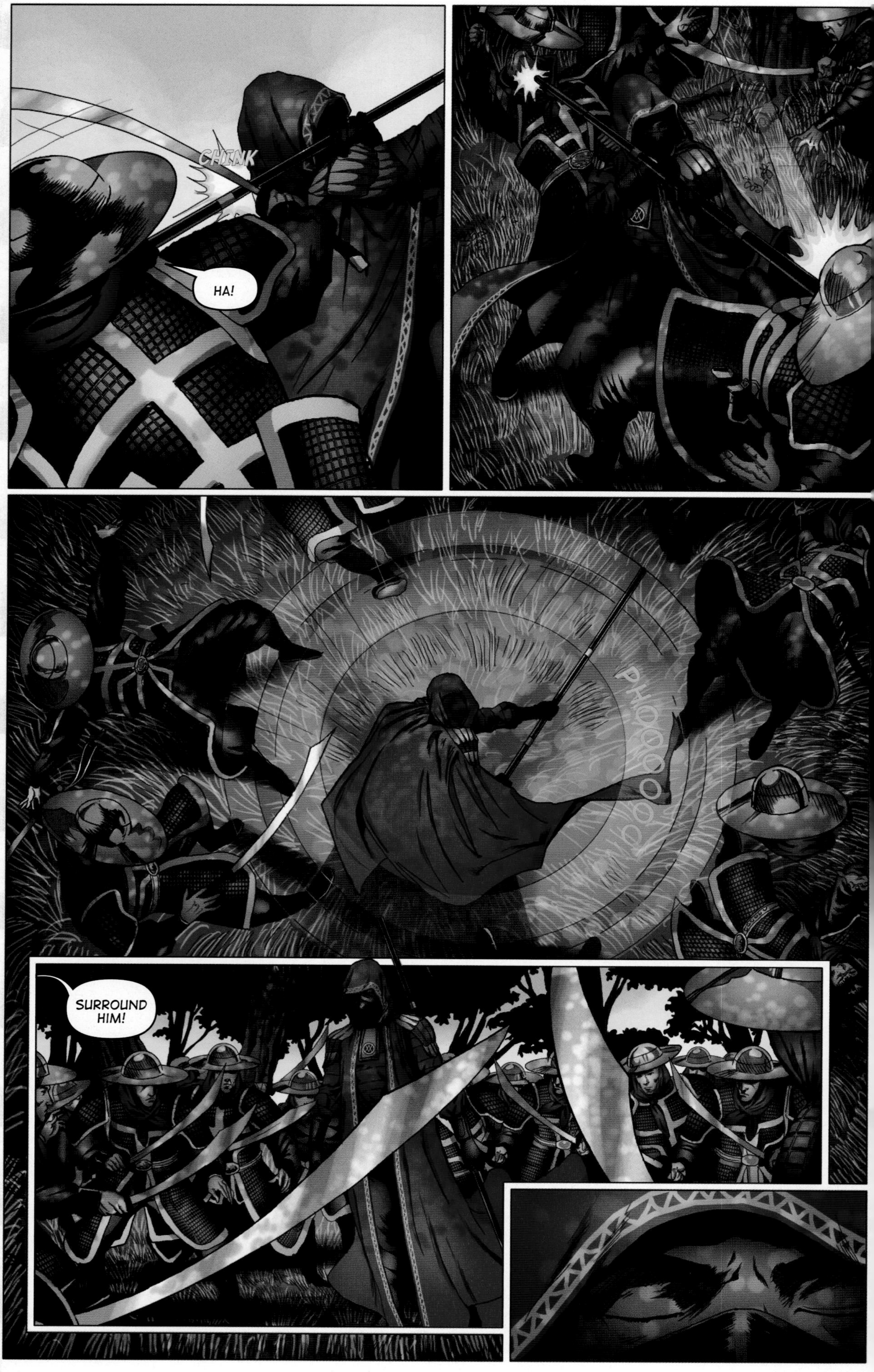
CHINK
HA!
PHOOOOOOO
SURROUND HIM!

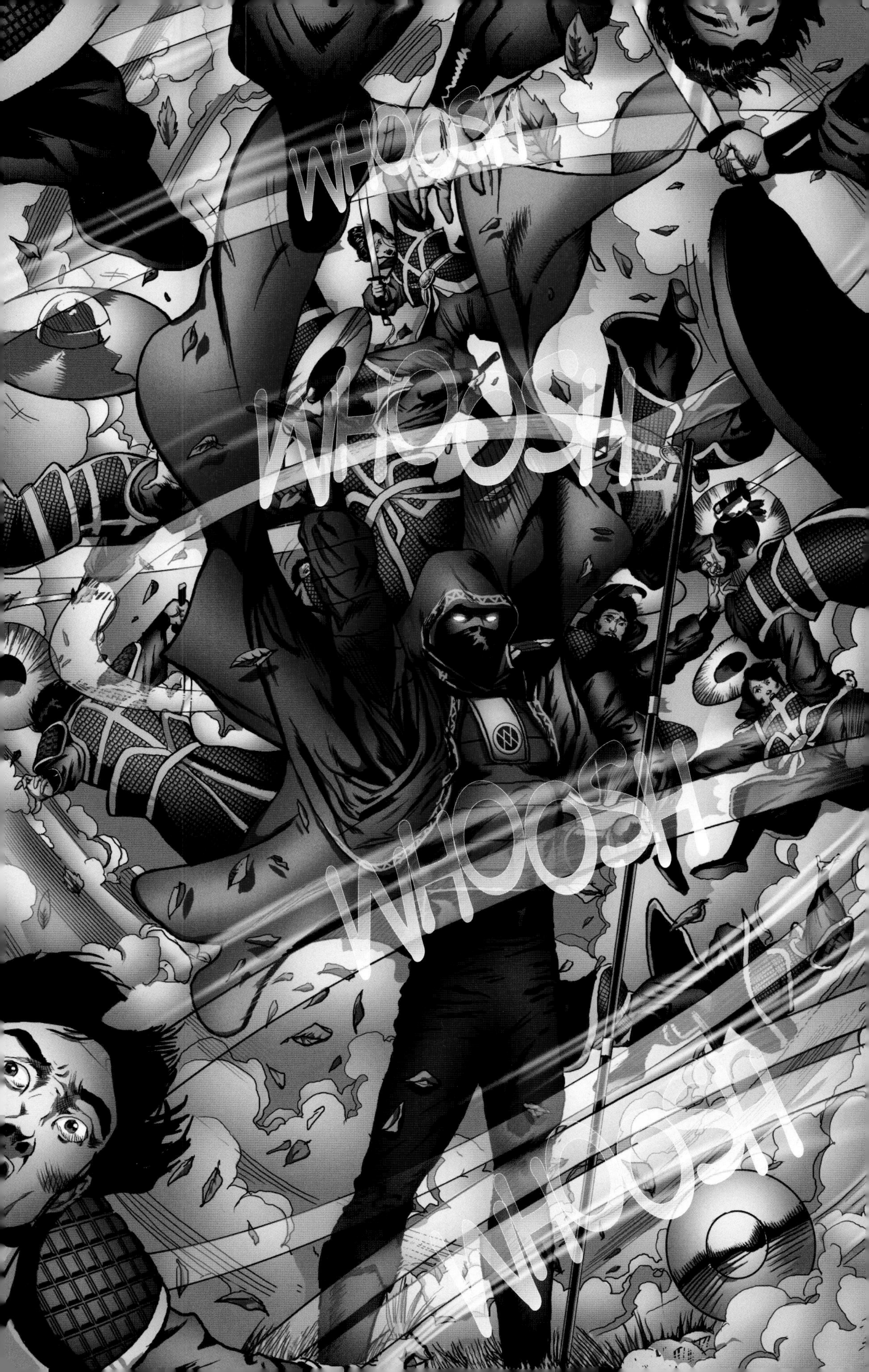
WHOOSH
WHOOSH
WHOOSH
WHOOSH

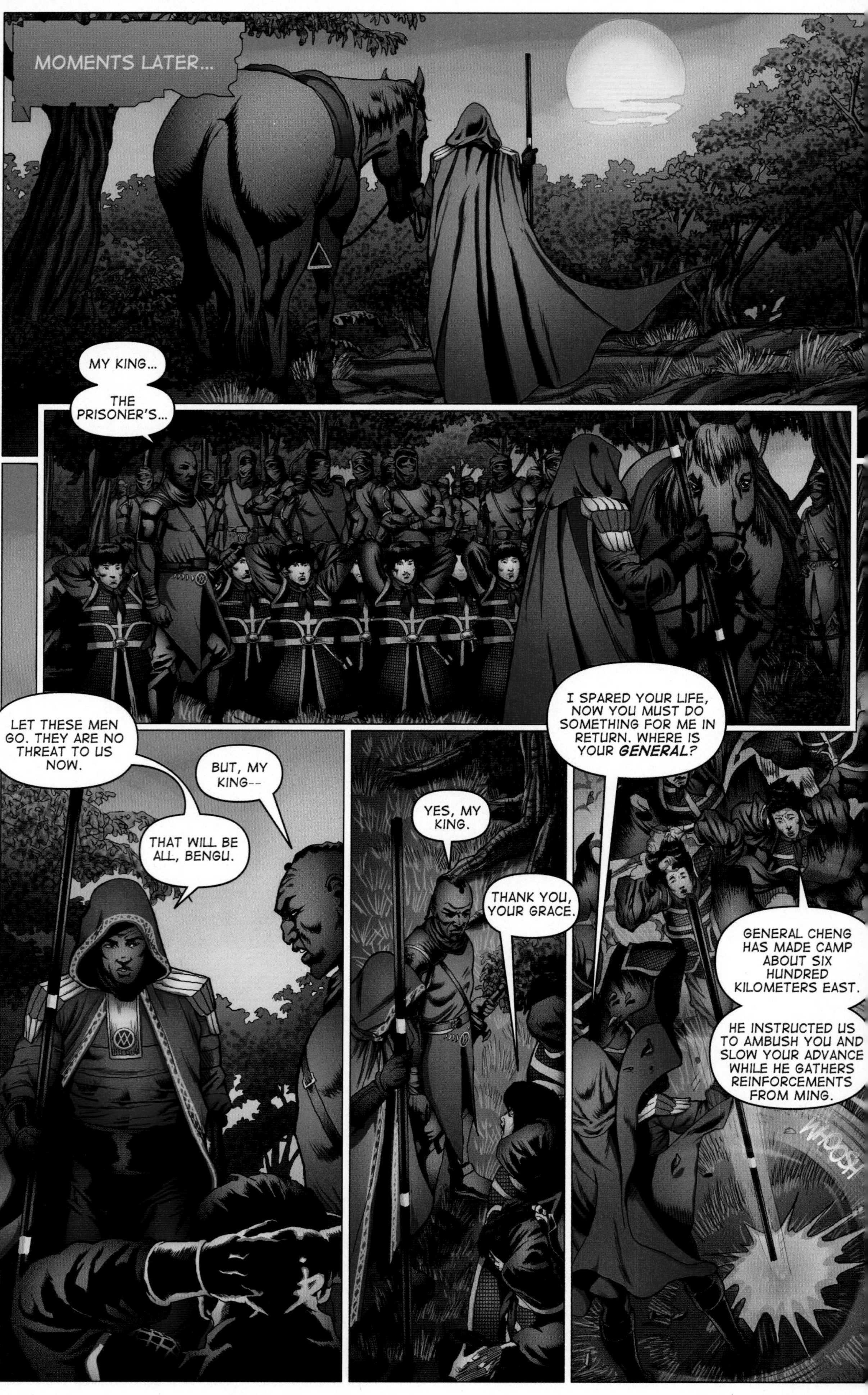
MOMENTS LATER...
MY KING...
THE PRISONER'S...
LET THESE MEN GO. THEY ARE NO THREAT TO US NOW.
BUT, MY KING--
THAT WILL BE ALL, BENGU.
YES, MY KING.
THANK YOU, YOUR GRACE.
I SPARED YOUR LIFE, NOW YOU MUST DO SOMETHING FOR ME IN RETURN. WHERE IS YOUR *GENERAL*?
GENERAL CHENG HAS MADE CAMP ABOUT SIX HUNDRED KILOMETERS EAST.
HE INSTRUCTED US TO AMBUSH YOU AND SLOW YOUR ADVANCE WHILE HE GATHERS REINFORCEMENTS FROM MING.
WHOOSH

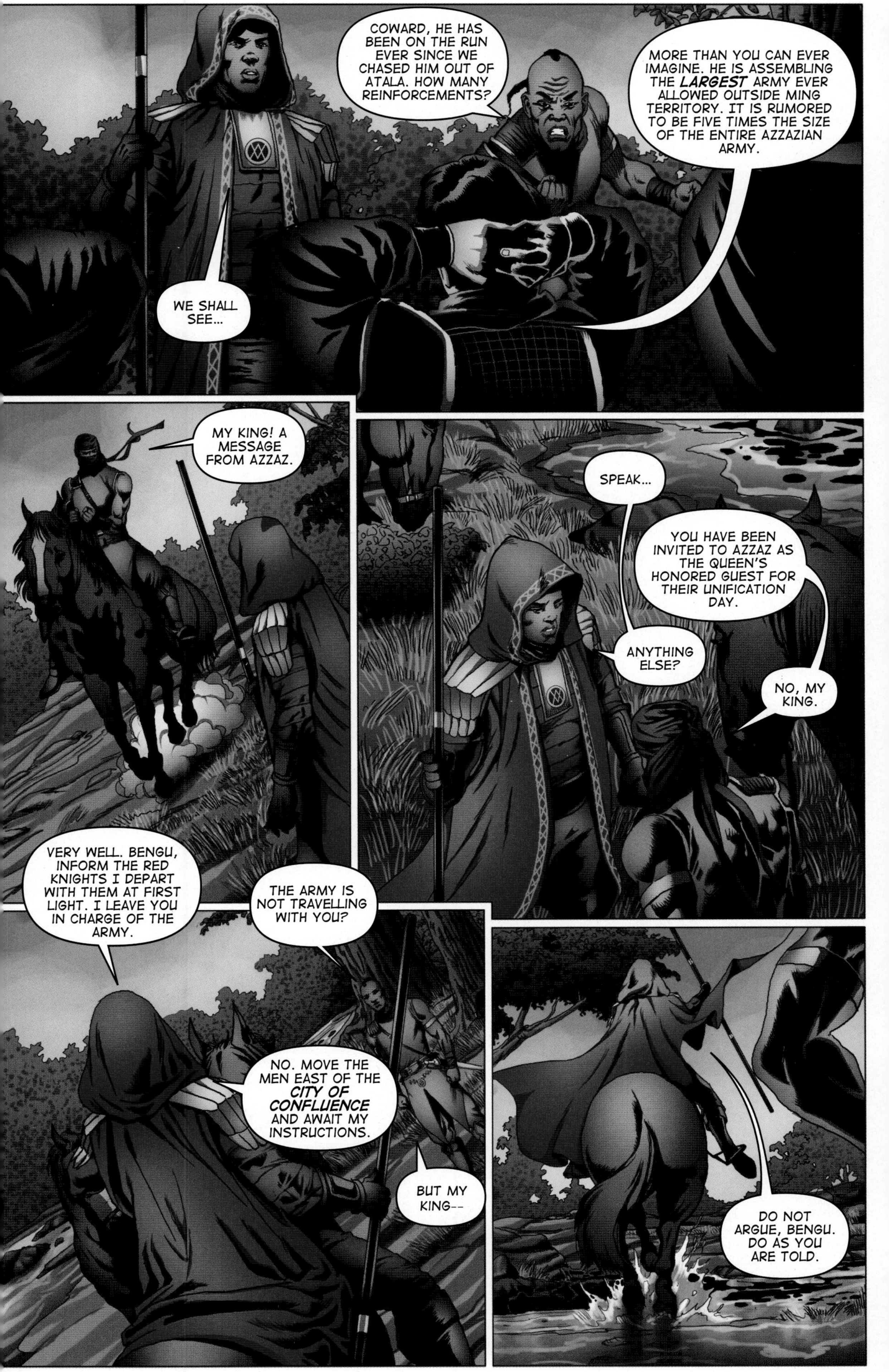
COWARD, HE HAS BEEN ON THE RUN EVER SINCE WE CHASED HIM OUT OF ATALA. HOW MANY REINFORCEMENTS?
MORE THAN YOU CAN EVER IMAGINE. HE IS ASSEMBLING THE LARGEST ARMY EVER ALLOWED OUTSIDE MING TERRITORY. IT IS RUMORED TO BE FIVE TIMES THE SIZE OF THE ENTIRE AZZAZIAN ARMY.
WE SHALL SEE...
MY KING! A MESSAGE FROM AZZAZ.
SPEAK...
YOU HAVE BEEN INVITED TO AZZAZ AS THE QUEEN'S HONORED GUEST FOR THEIR UNIFICATION DAY.
ANYTHING ELSE?
NO, MY KING.
VERY WELL. BENGU, INFORM THE RED KNIGHTS I DEPART WITH THEM AT FIRST LIGHT. I LEAVE YOU IN CHARGE OF THE ARMY.
THE ARMY IS NOT TRAVELLING WITH YOU?
NO. MOVE THE MEN EAST OF THE CITY OF CONFLUENCE AND AWAIT MY INSTRUCTIONS.
BUT MY KING--
DO NOT ARGUE, BENGU. DO AS YOU ARE TOLD.

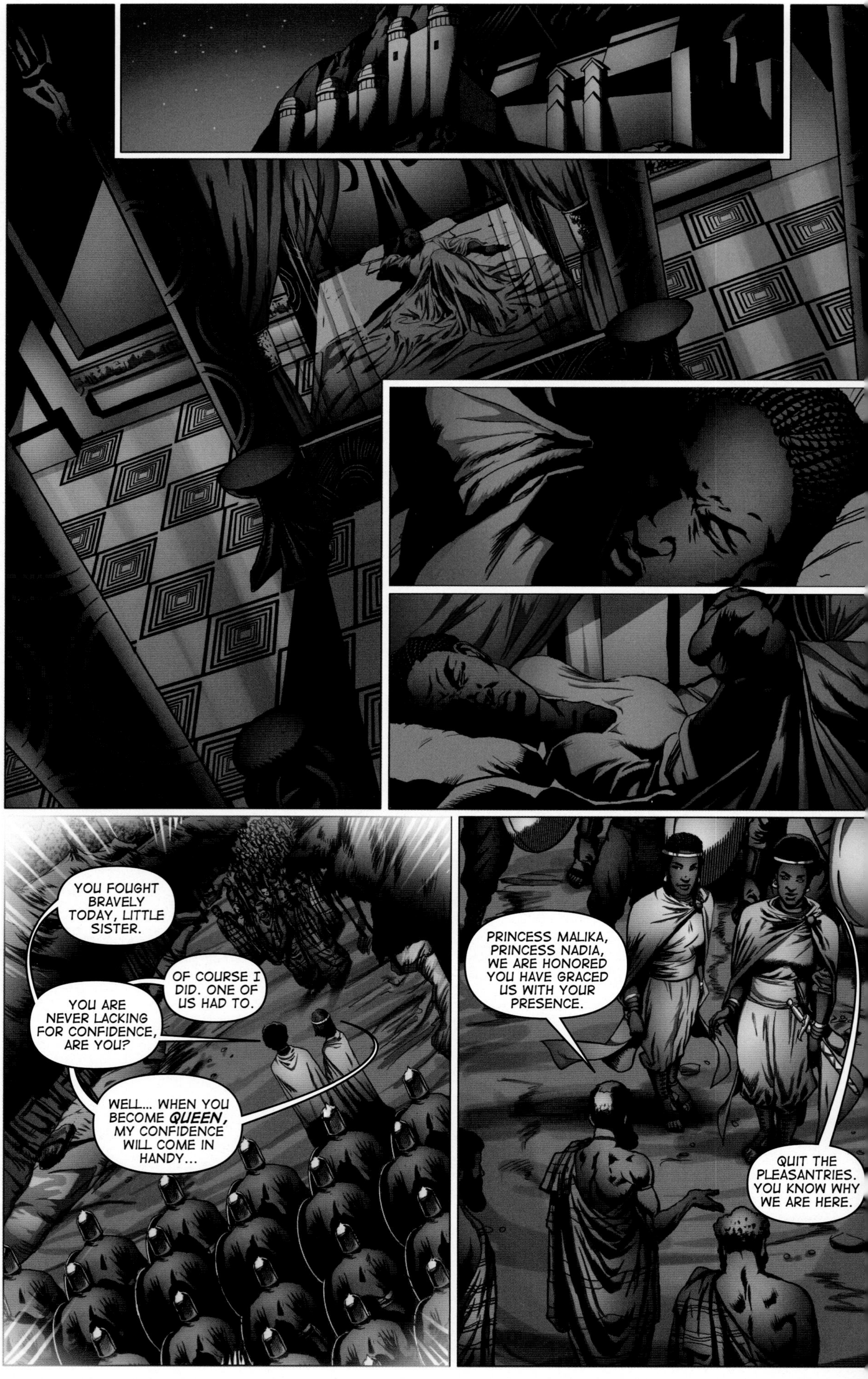
YOU FOUGHT BRAVELY TODAY, LITTLE SISTER.
OF COURSE I DID. ONE OF US HAD TO.
YOU ARE NEVER LACKING FOR CONFIDENCE, ARE YOU?
WELL... WHEN YOU BECOME QUEEN, MY CONFIDENCE WILL COME IN HANDY...
PRINCESS MALIKA, PRINCESS NADIA, WE ARE HONORED YOU HAVE GRACED US WITH YOUR PRESENCE.
QUIT THE PLEASANTRIES. YOU KNOW WHY WE ARE HERE.

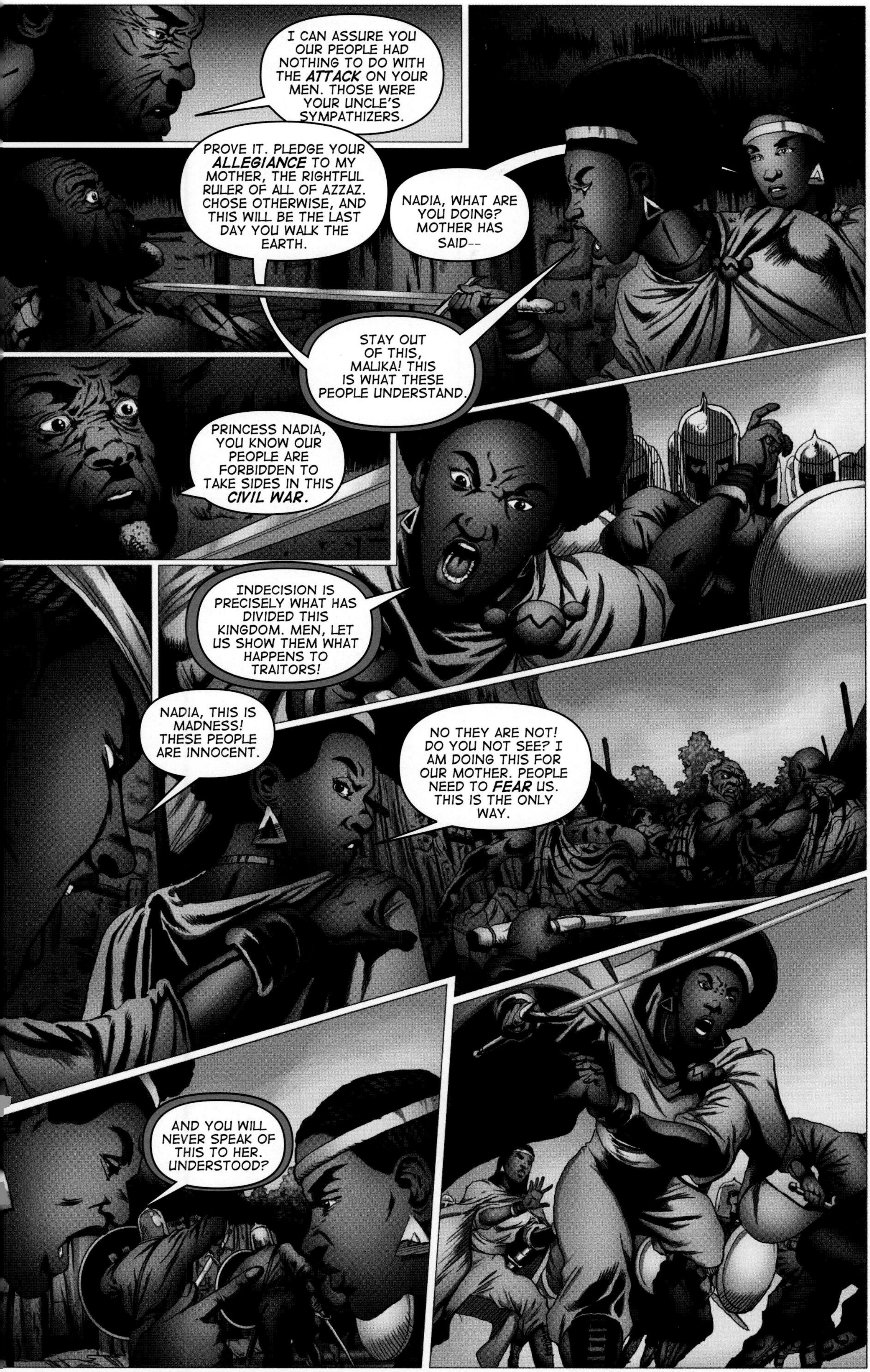
I CAN ASSURE YOU OUR PEOPLE HAD NOTHING TO DO WITH THE ATTACK ON YOUR MEN. THOSE WERE YOUR UNCLE'S SYMPATHIZERS.
PROVE IT. PLEDGE YOUR ALLEGIANCE TO MY MOTHER, THE RIGHTFUL RULER OF ALL OF AZZAZ. CHOSE OTHERWISE, AND THIS WILL BE THE LAST DAY YOU WALK THE EARTH.
NADIA, WHAT ARE YOU DOING? MOTHER HAS SAID--
STAY OUT OF THIS, MALIKA! THIS IS WHAT THESE PEOPLE UNDERSTAND.
PRINCESS NADIA, YOU KNOW OUR PEOPLE ARE FORBIDDEN TO TAKE SIDES IN THIS CIVIL WAR.
INDECISION IS PRECISELY WHAT HAS DIVIDED THIS KINGDOM. MEN, LET US SHOW THEM WHAT HAPPENS TO TRAITORS!
NADIA, THIS IS MADNESS! THESE PEOPLE ARE INNOCENT.
NO THEY ARE NOT! DO YOU NOT SEE? I AM DOING THIS FOR OUR MOTHER. PEOPLE NEED TO FEAR US. THIS IS THE ONLY WAY.
AND YOU WILL NEVER SPEAK OF THIS TO HER. UNDERSTOOD?

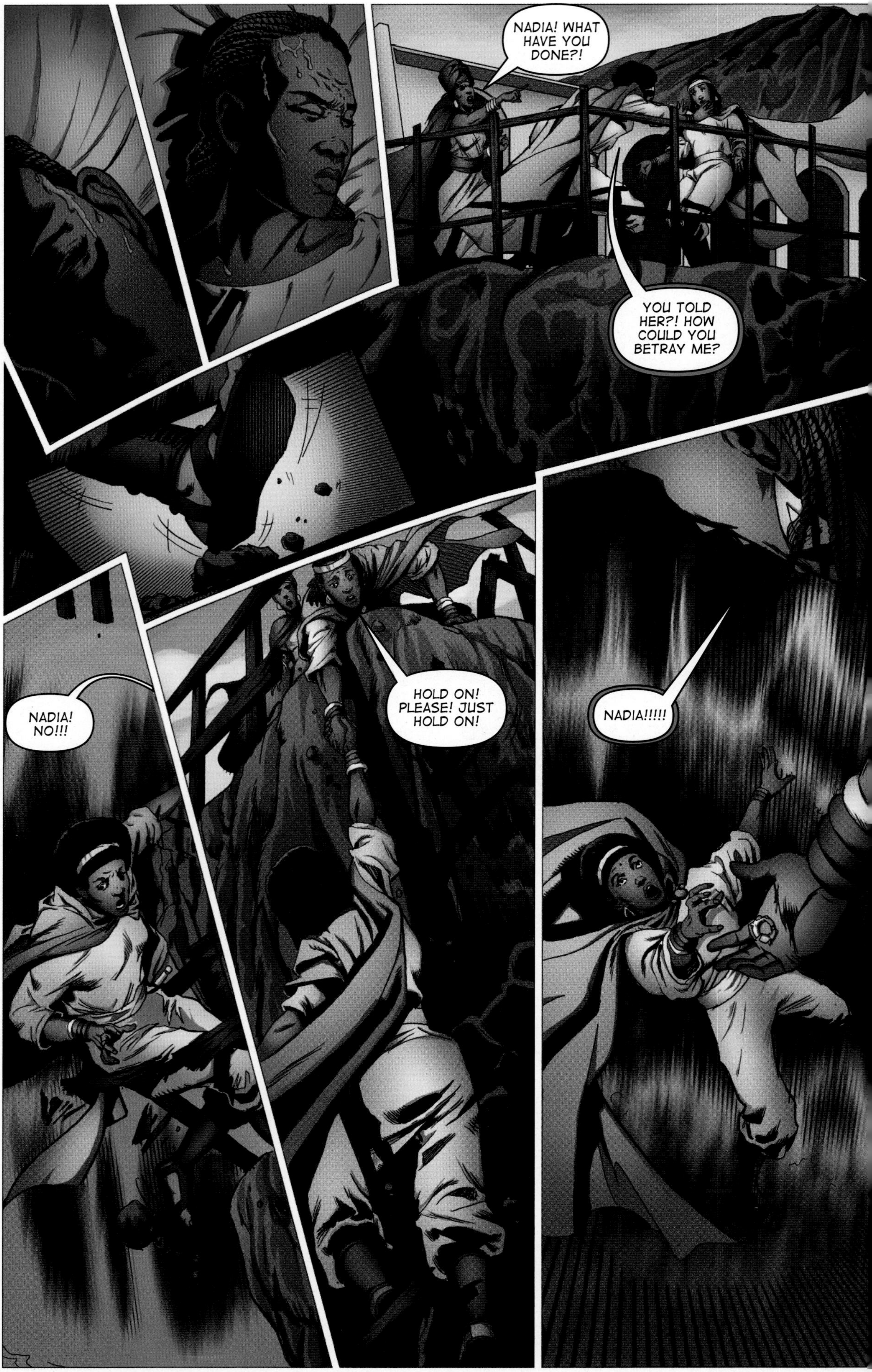
NADIA! WHAT HAVE YOU DONE?!
YOU TOLD HER?! HOW COULD YOU BETRAY ME?
NADIA! NO!!!
HOLD ON! PLEASE! JUST HOLD ON!
NADIA!!!!!

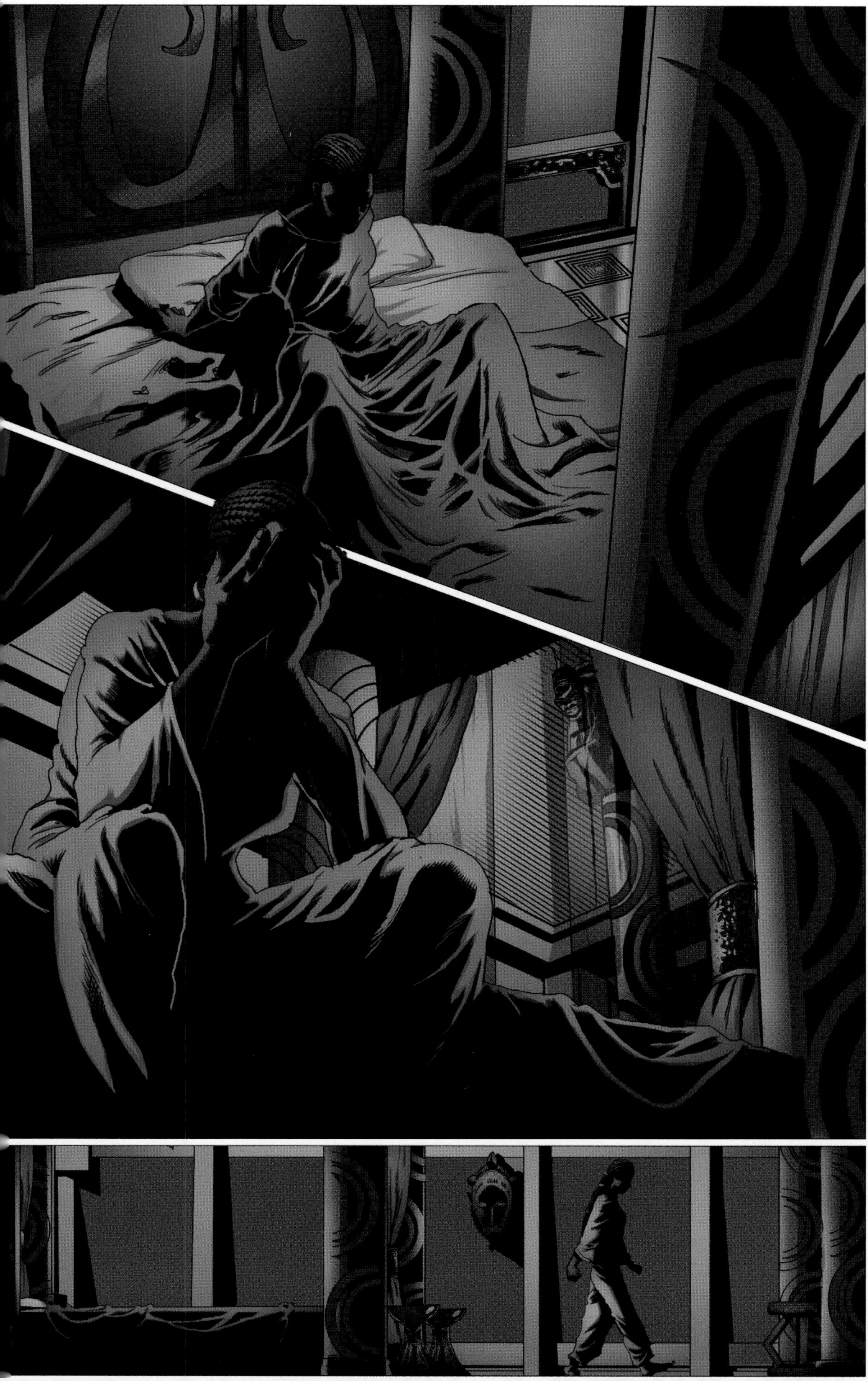

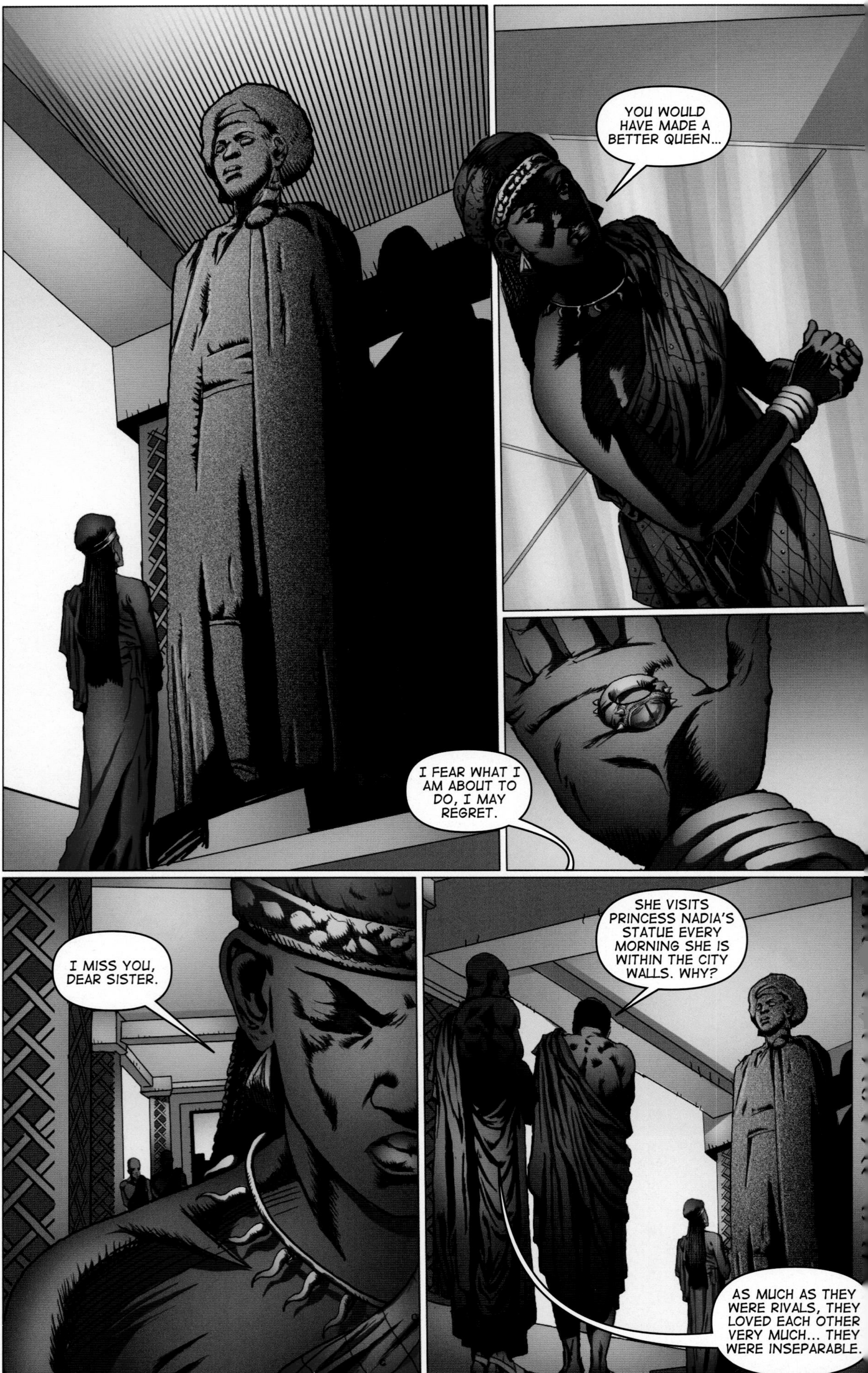
YOU WOULD HAVE MADE A BETTER QUEEN...
I FEAR WHAT I AM ABOUT TO DO, I MAY REGRET.
I MISS YOU, DEAR SISTER.
SHE VISITS PRINCESS NADIA'S STATUE EVERY MORNING SHE IS WITHIN THE CITY WALLS. WHY?
AS MUCH AS THEY WERE RIVALS, THEY LOVED EACH OTHER VERY MUCH... THEY WERE INSEPARABLE.

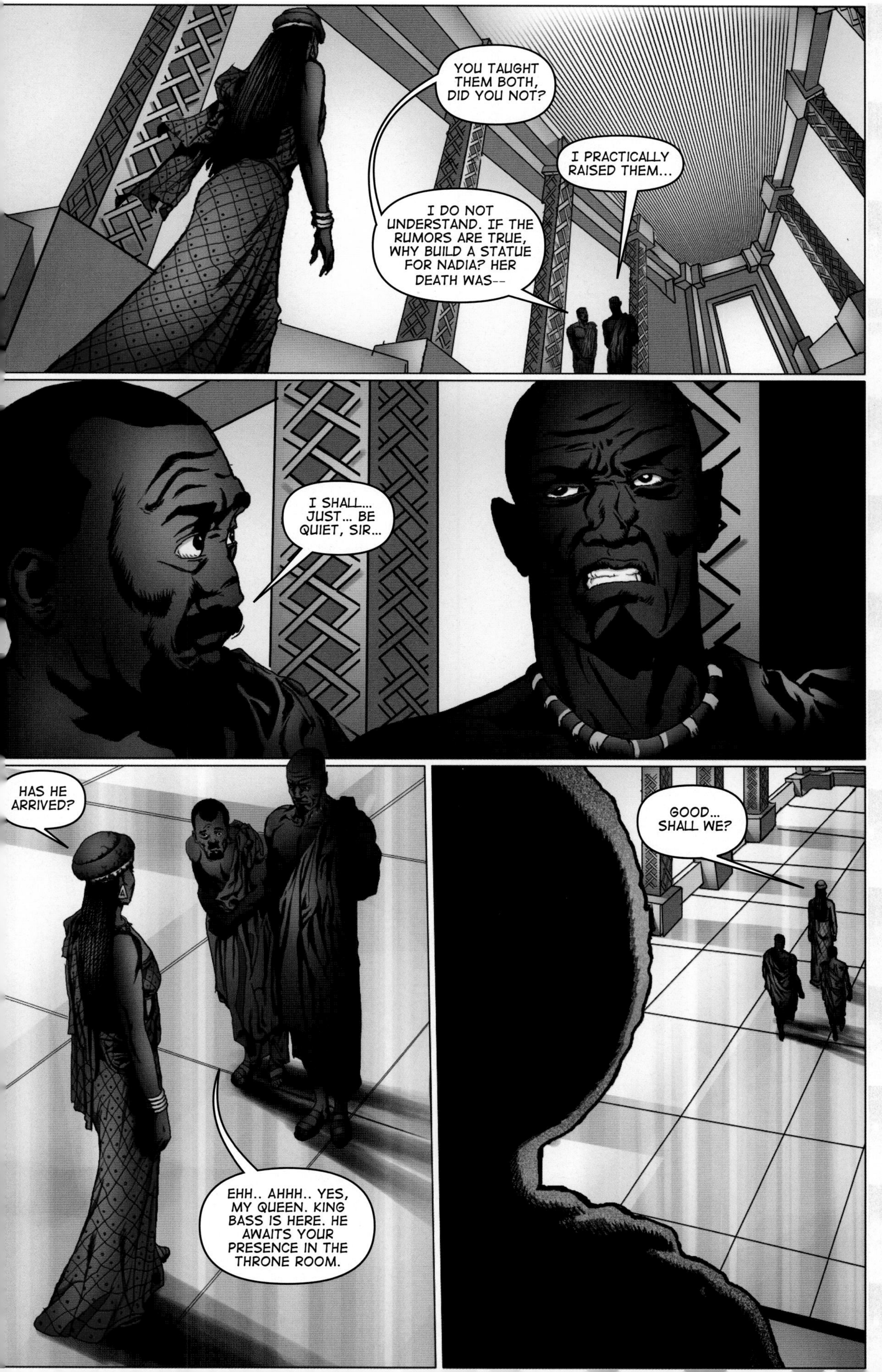
YOU TAUGHT THEM BOTH, DID YOU NOT?
I PRACTICALLY RAISED THEM...
I DO NOT UNDERSTAND. IF THE RUMORS ARE TRUE, WHY BUILD A STATUE FOR NADIA? HER DEATH WAS--
I SHALL... JUST... BE QUIET, SIR...
HAS HE ARRIVED?
EHH.. AHHH.. YES, MY QUEEN. KING BASS IS HERE. HE AWAITS YOUR PRESENCE IN THE THRONE ROOM.
GOOD... SHALL WE?

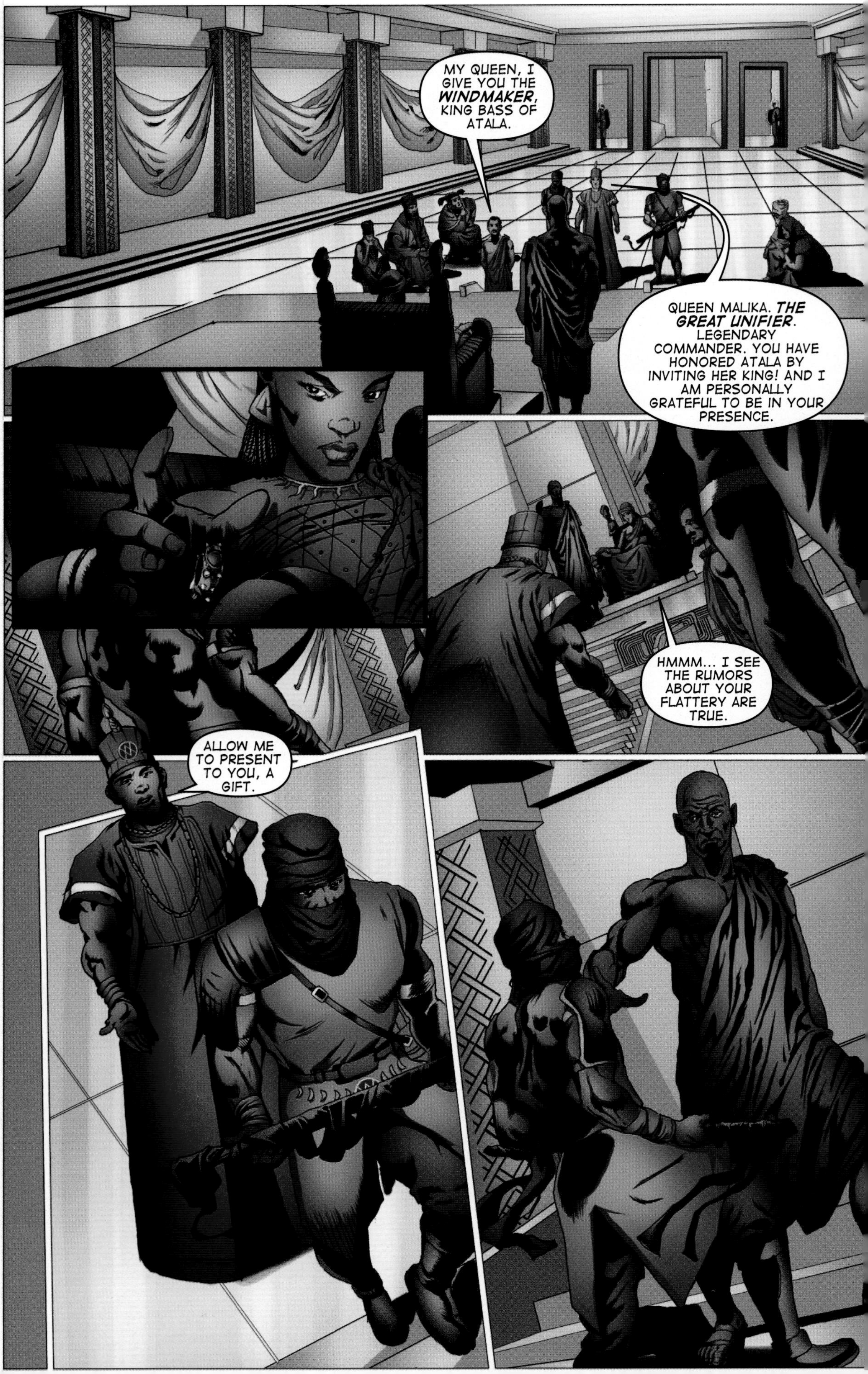
MY QUEEN, I GIVE YOU THE **WINDMAKER**, KING BASS OF ATALA.
QUEEN MALIKA. ***THE GREAT UNIFIER***. LEGENDARY COMMANDER. YOU HAVE HONORED ATALA BY INVITING HER KING! AND I AM PERSONALLY GRATEFUL TO BE IN YOUR PRESENCE.
HMMM... I SEE THE RUMORS ABOUT YOUR FLATTERY ARE TRUE.
ALLOW ME TO PRESENT TO YOU, A GIFT.

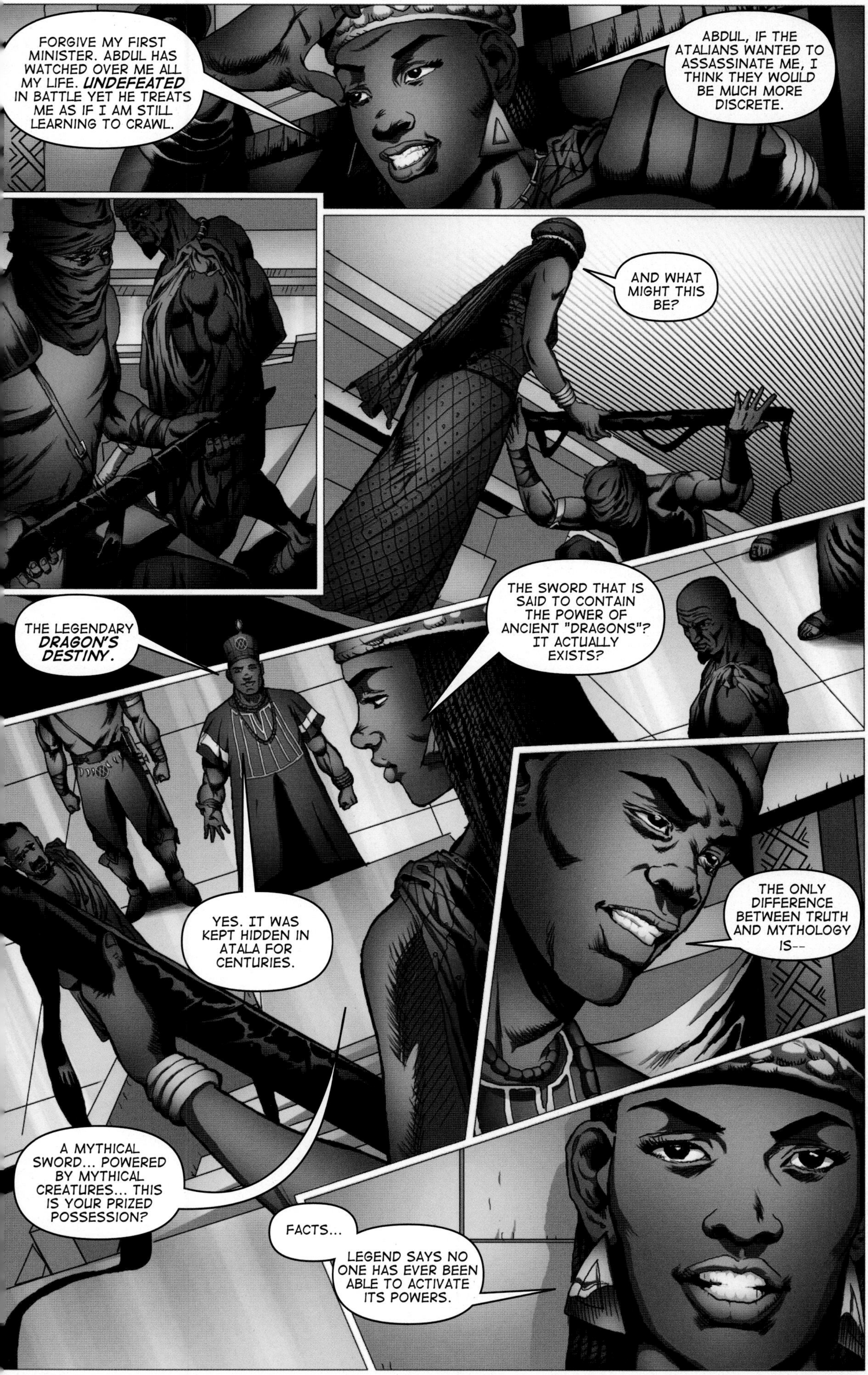
FORGIVE MY FIRST MINISTER. ABDUL HAS WATCHED OVER ME ALL MY LIFE. *UNDEFEATED* IN BATTLE YET HE TREATS ME AS IF I AM STILL LEARNING TO CRAWL.
ABDUL, IF THE ATALIANS WANTED TO ASSASSINATE ME, I THINK THEY WOULD BE MUCH MORE DISCRETE.
AND WHAT MIGHT THIS BE?
THE LEGENDARY *DRAGON'S DESTINY*.
THE SWORD THAT IS SAID TO CONTAIN THE POWER OF ANCIENT "DRAGONS"? IT ACTUALLY EXISTS?
YES. IT WAS KEPT HIDDEN IN ATALA FOR CENTURIES.
THE ONLY DIFFERENCE BETWEEN TRUTH AND MYTHOLOGY IS--
A MYTHICAL SWORD... POWERED BY MYTHICAL CREATURES... THIS IS YOUR PRIZED POSSESSION?
FACTS...
LEGEND SAYS NO ONE HAS EVER BEEN ABLE TO ACTIVATE ITS POWERS.

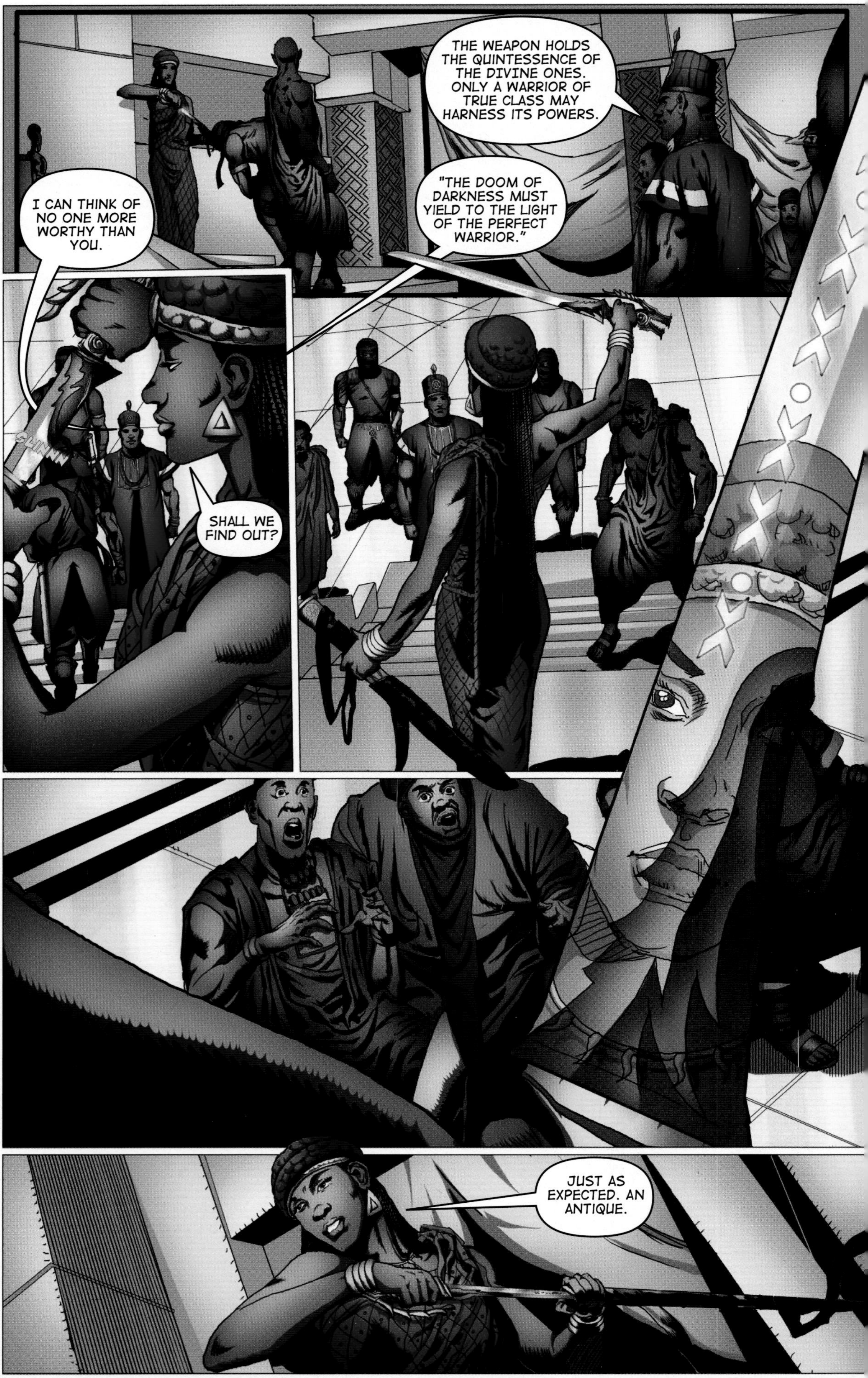
THE WEAPON HOLDS THE QUINTESSENCE OF THE DIVINE ONES. ONLY A WARRIOR OF TRUE CLASS MAY HARNESS ITS POWERS.
I CAN THINK OF NO ONE MORE WORTHY THAN YOU.
"THE DOOM OF DARKNESS MUST YIELD TO THE LIGHT OF THE PERFECT WARRIOR."
SLINNN
SHALL WE FIND OUT?
JUST AS EXPECTED. AN ANTIQUE.

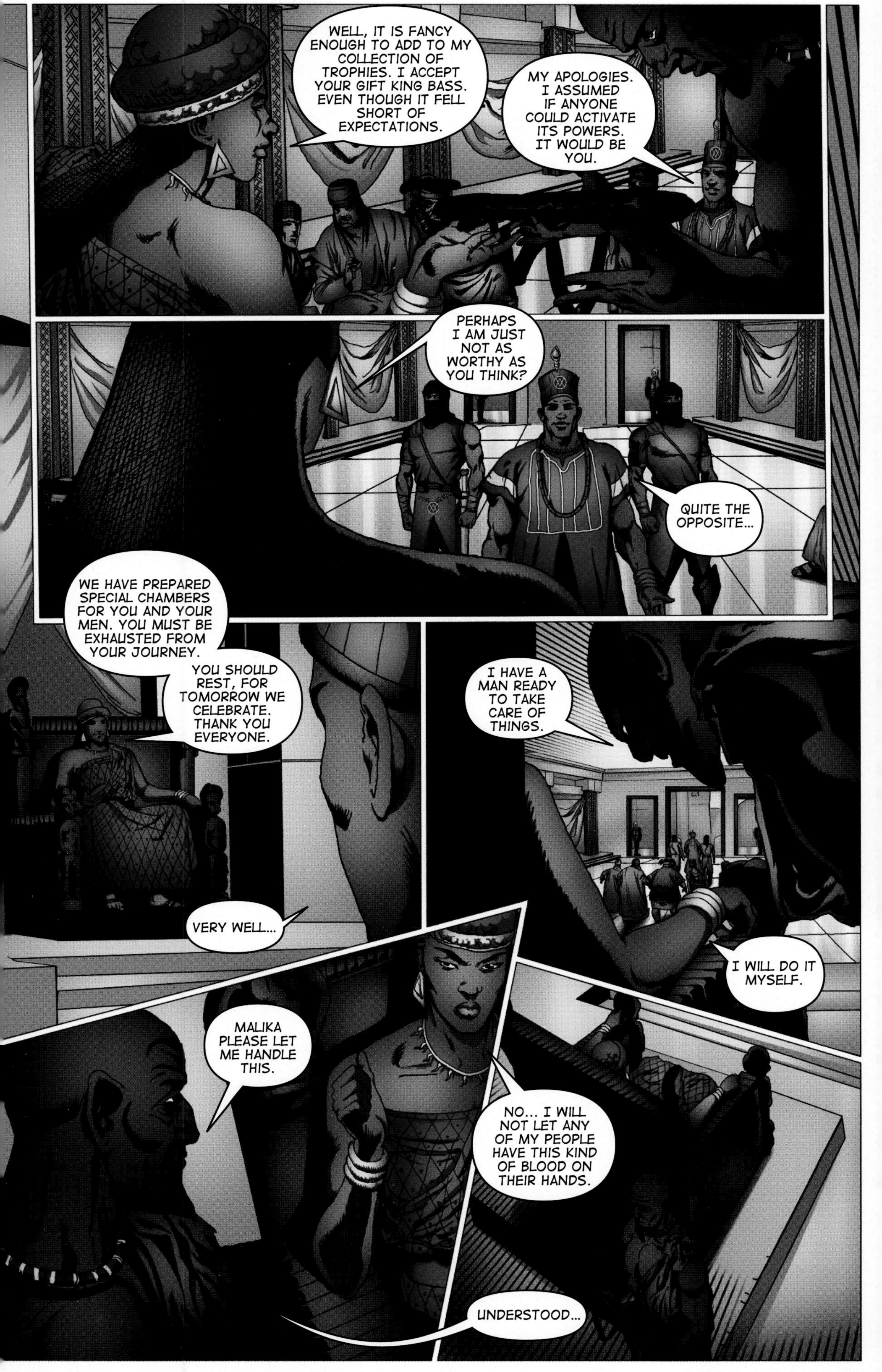
WELL, IT IS FANCY ENOUGH TO ADD TO MY COLLECTION OF TROPHIES. I ACCEPT YOUR GIFT KING BASS. EVEN THOUGH IT FELL SHORT OF EXPECTATIONS.
MY APOLOGIES. I ASSUMED IF ANYONE COULD ACTIVATE ITS POWERS. IT WOULD BE YOU.
PERHAPS I AM JUST NOT AS WORTHY AS YOU THINK?
QUITE THE OPPOSITE...
WE HAVE PREPARED SPECIAL CHAMBERS FOR YOU AND YOUR MEN. YOU MUST BE EXHAUSTED FROM YOUR JOURNEY.
YOU SHOULD REST, FOR TOMORROW WE CELEBRATE. THANK YOU EVERYONE.
VERY WELL...
I HAVE A MAN READY TO TAKE CARE OF THINGS.
I WILL DO IT MYSELF.
MALIKA PLEASE LET ME HANDLE THIS.
NO... I WILL NOT LET ANY OF MY PEOPLE HAVE THIS KIND OF BLOOD ON THEIR HANDS.
UNDERSTOOD...

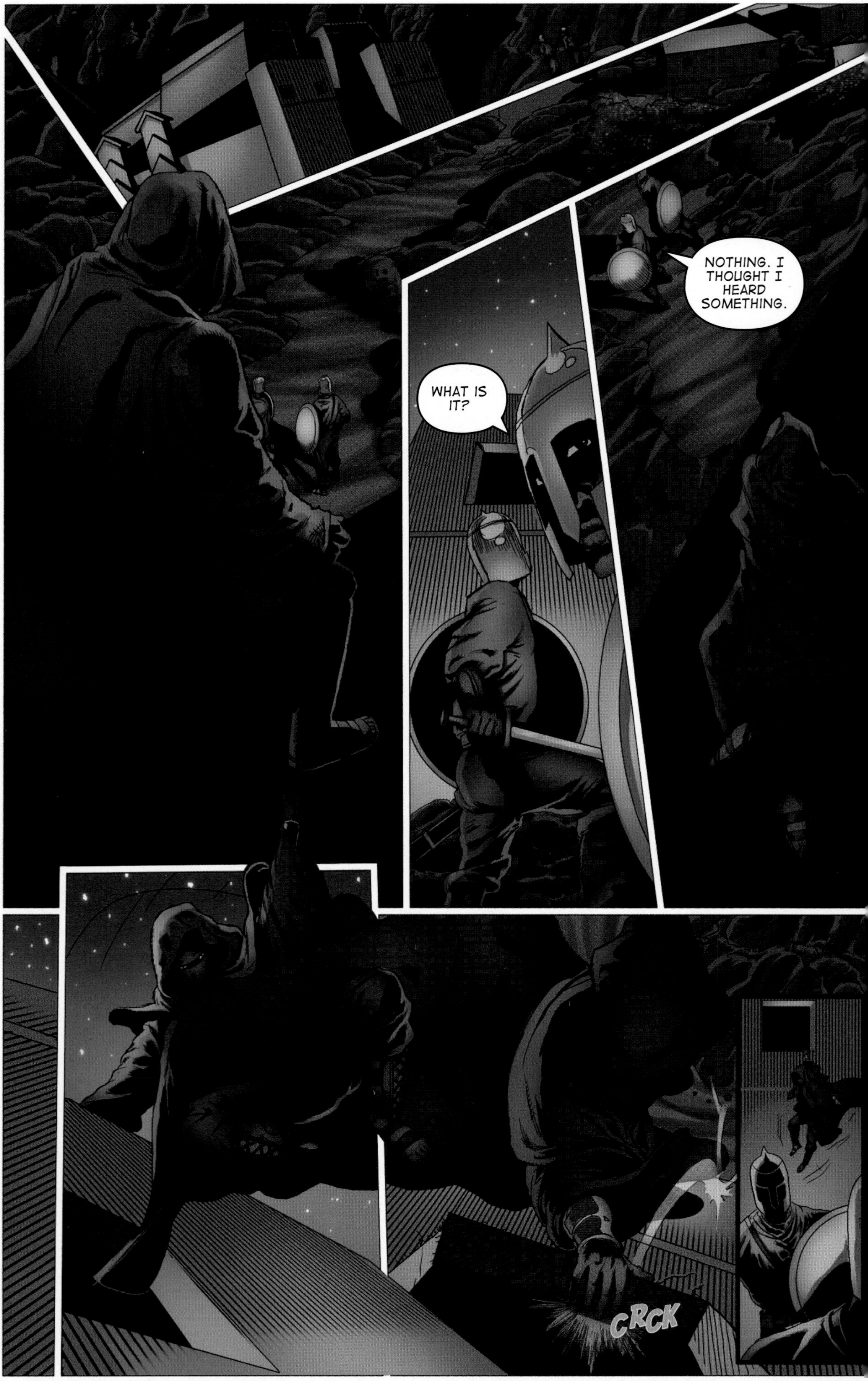
WHAT IS IT?
NOTHING. I THOUGHT I HEARD SOMETHING.
CRCK

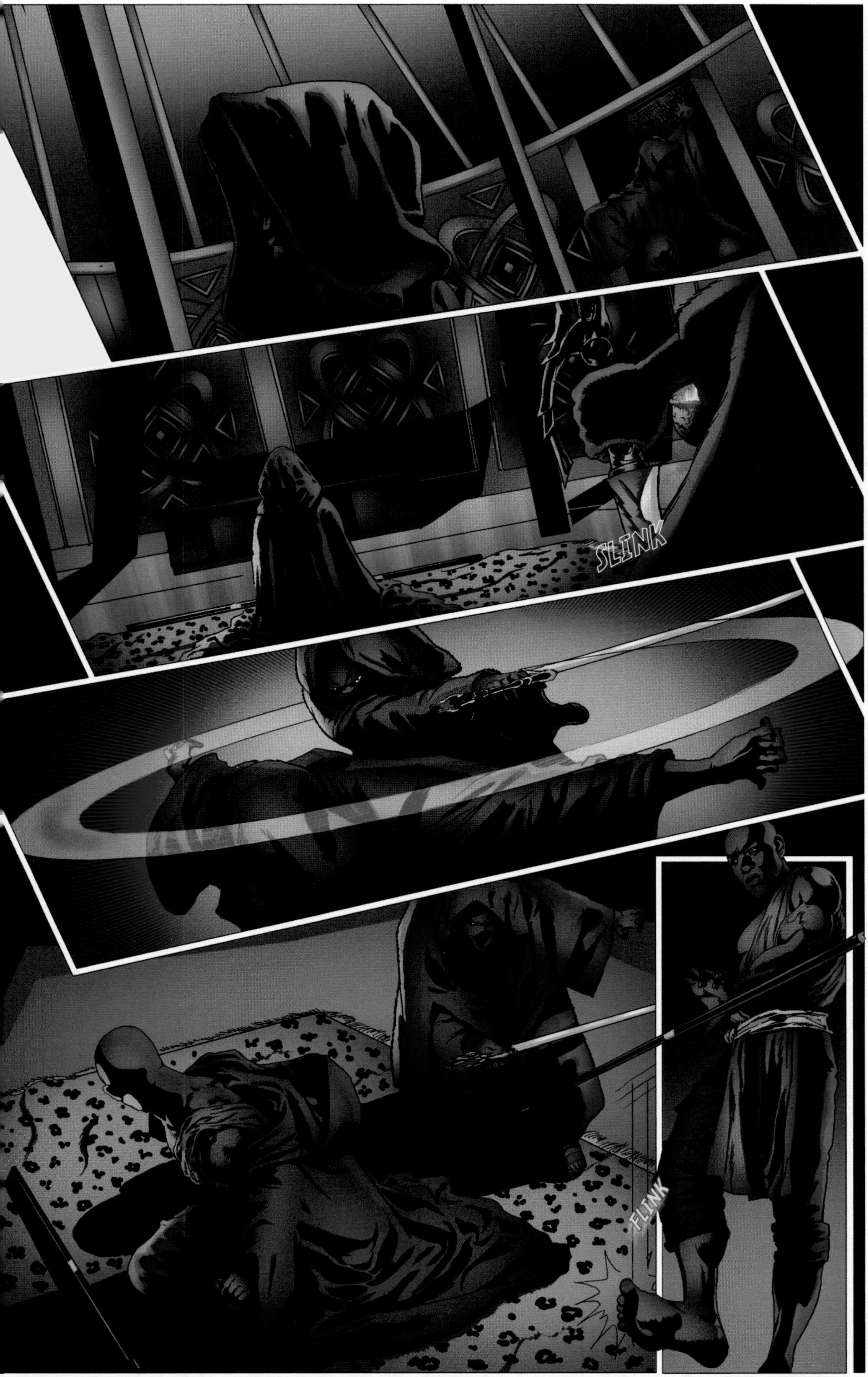
SLINK
FLINK

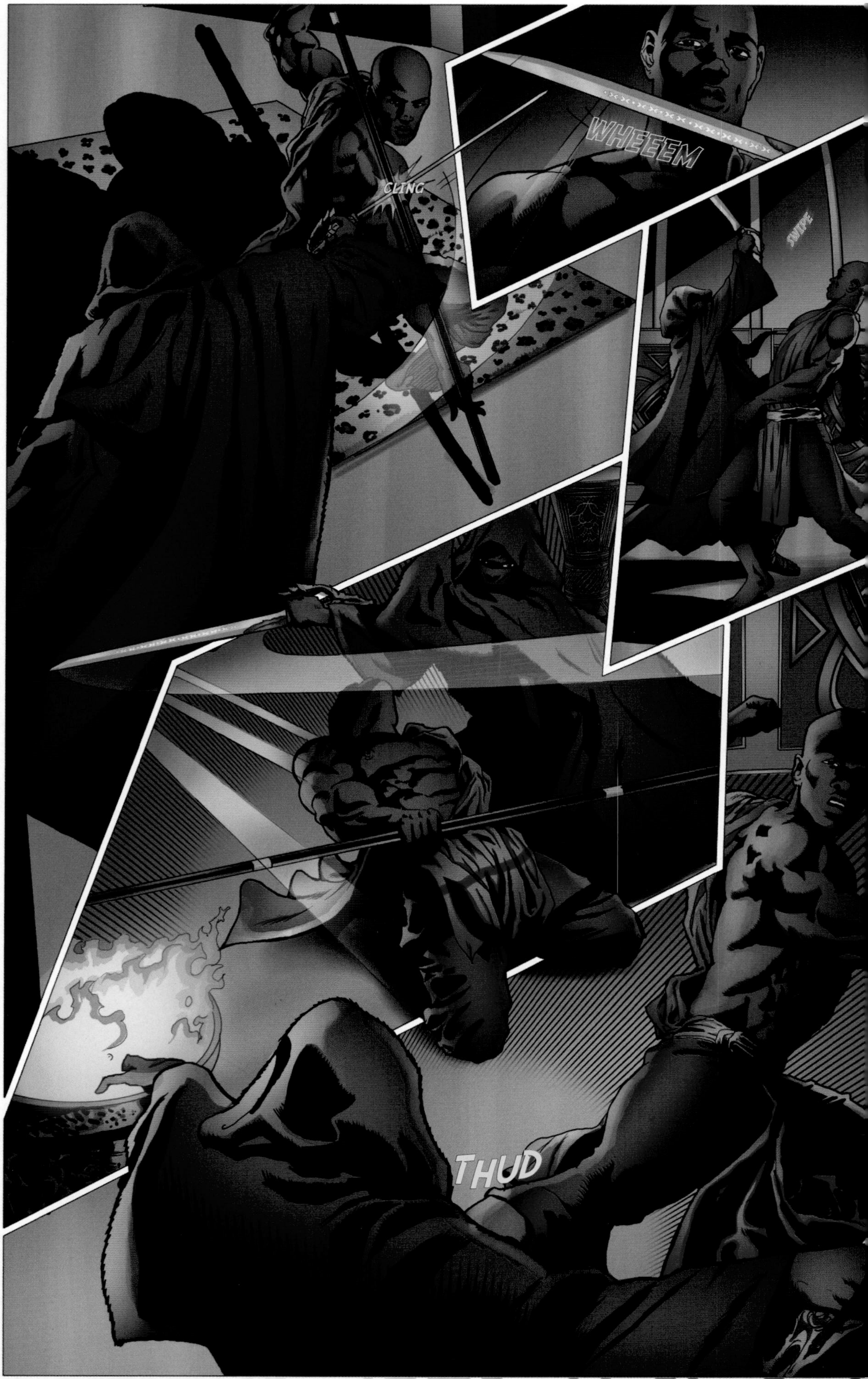
CLING
WHEEEM
SWIPE
THUD

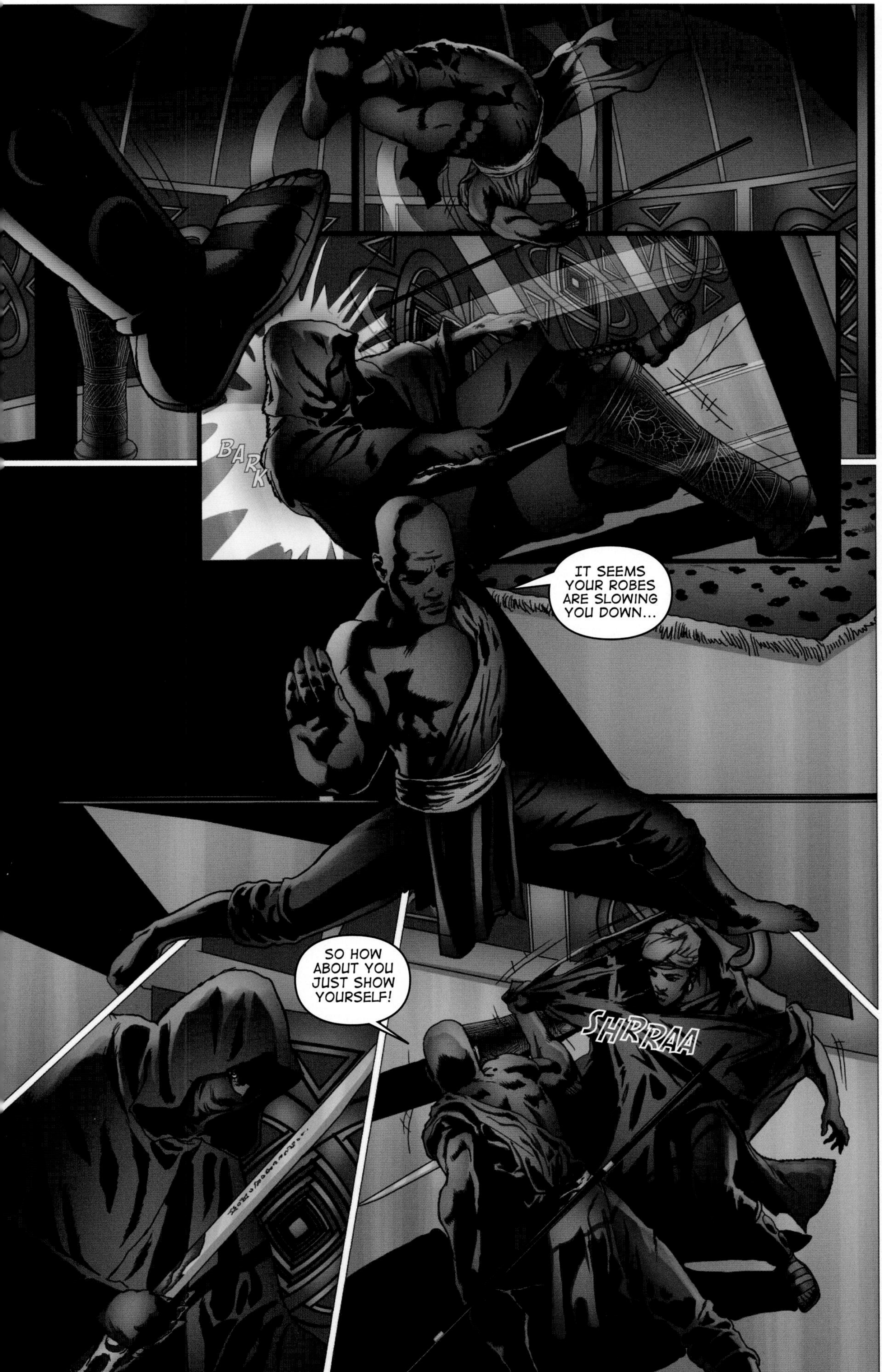
BARK
IT SEEMS YOUR ROBES ARE SLOWING YOU DOWN...
SO HOW ABOUT YOU JUST SHOW YOURSELF!
SHRRAA

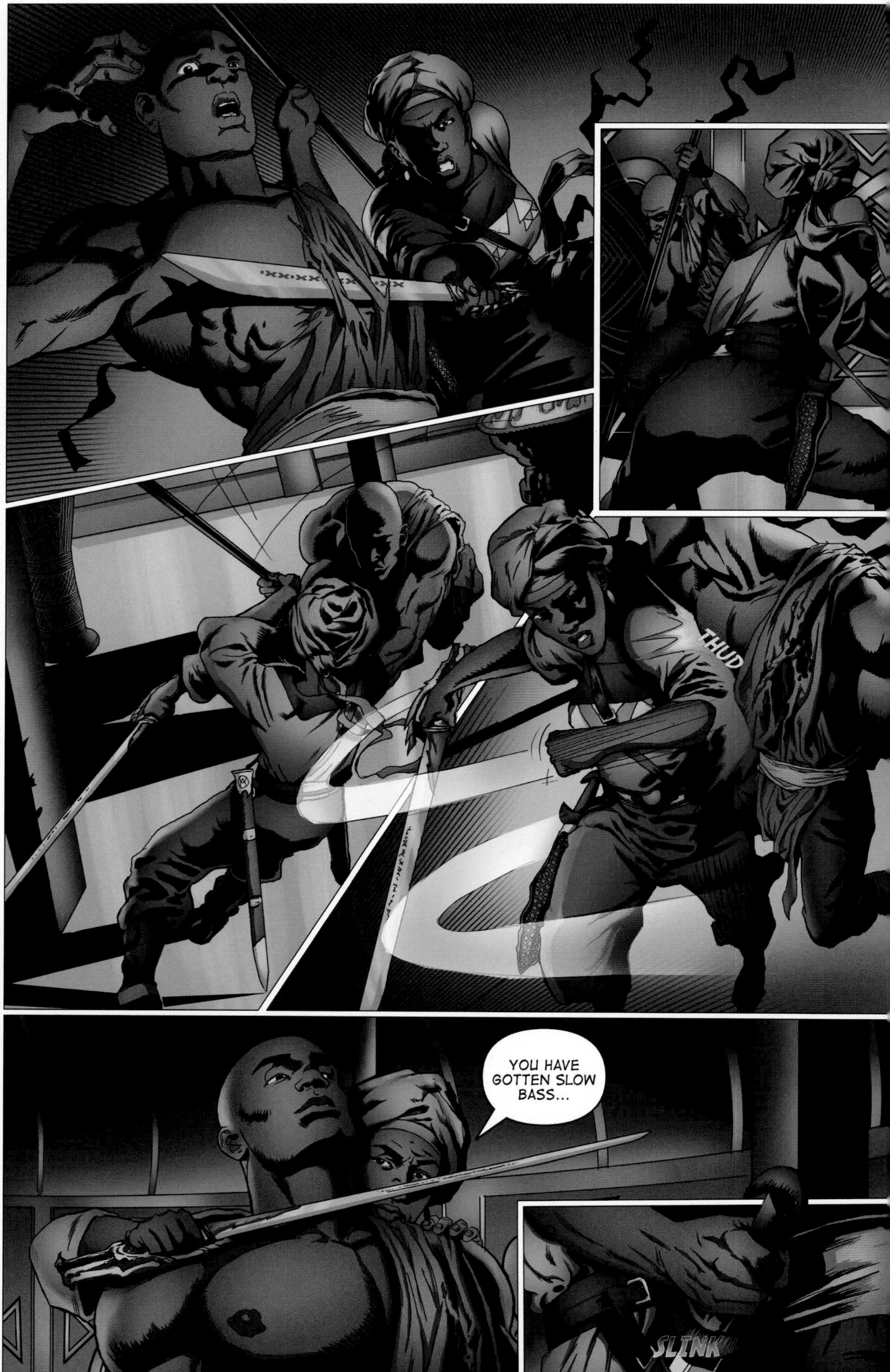
THUD
YOU HAVE GOTTEN SLOW BASS...
SLINK

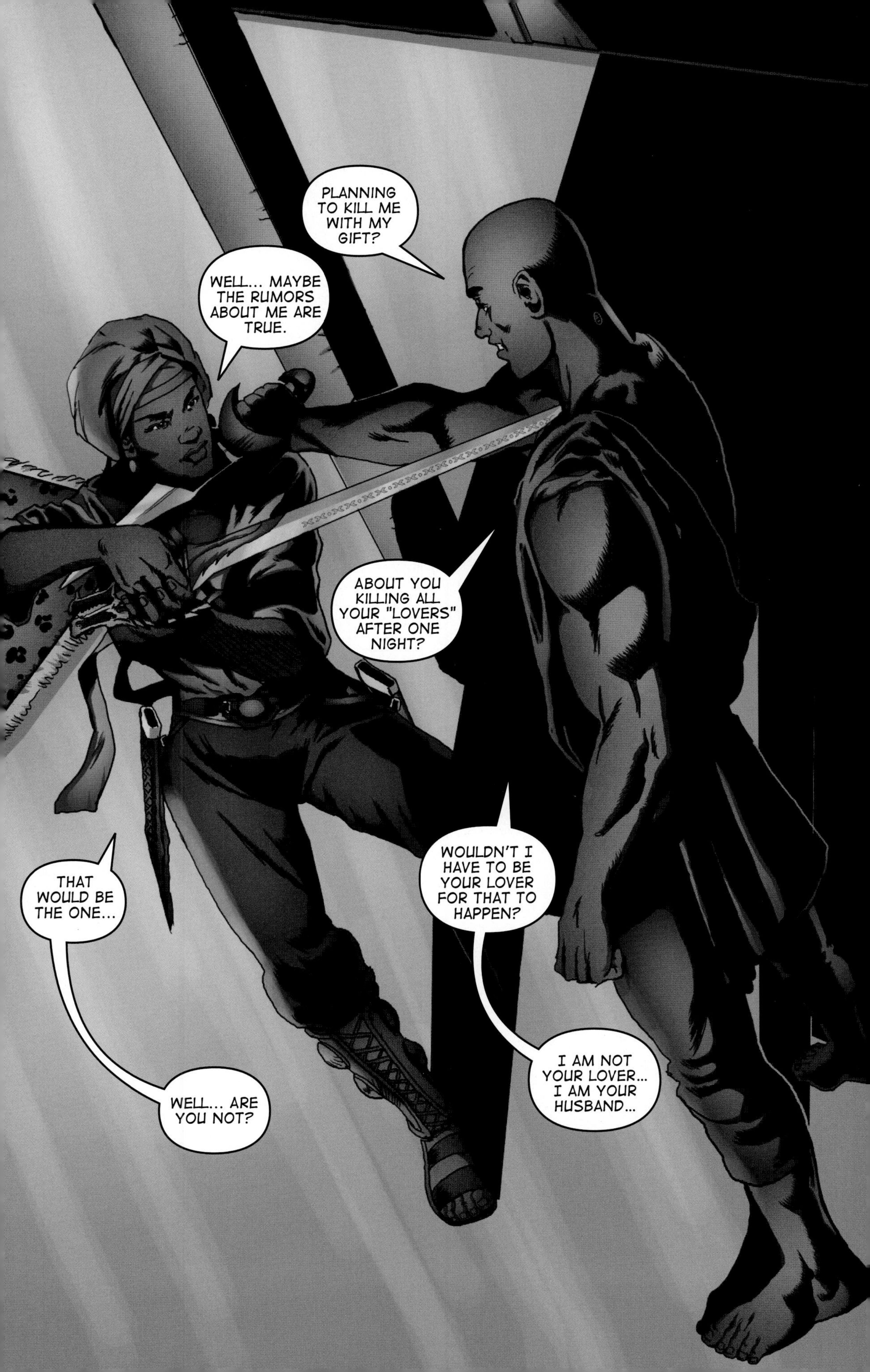
PLANNING TO KILL ME WITH MY GIFT?
WELL... MAYBE THE RUMORS ABOUT ME ARE TRUE.
ABOUT YOU KILLING ALL YOUR "LOVERS" AFTER ONE NIGHT?
THAT WOULD BE THE ONE...
WELL... ARE YOU NOT?
WOULDN'T I HAVE TO BE YOUR LOVER FOR THAT TO HAPPEN?
I AM NOT YOUR LOVER... I AM YOUR HUSBAND...

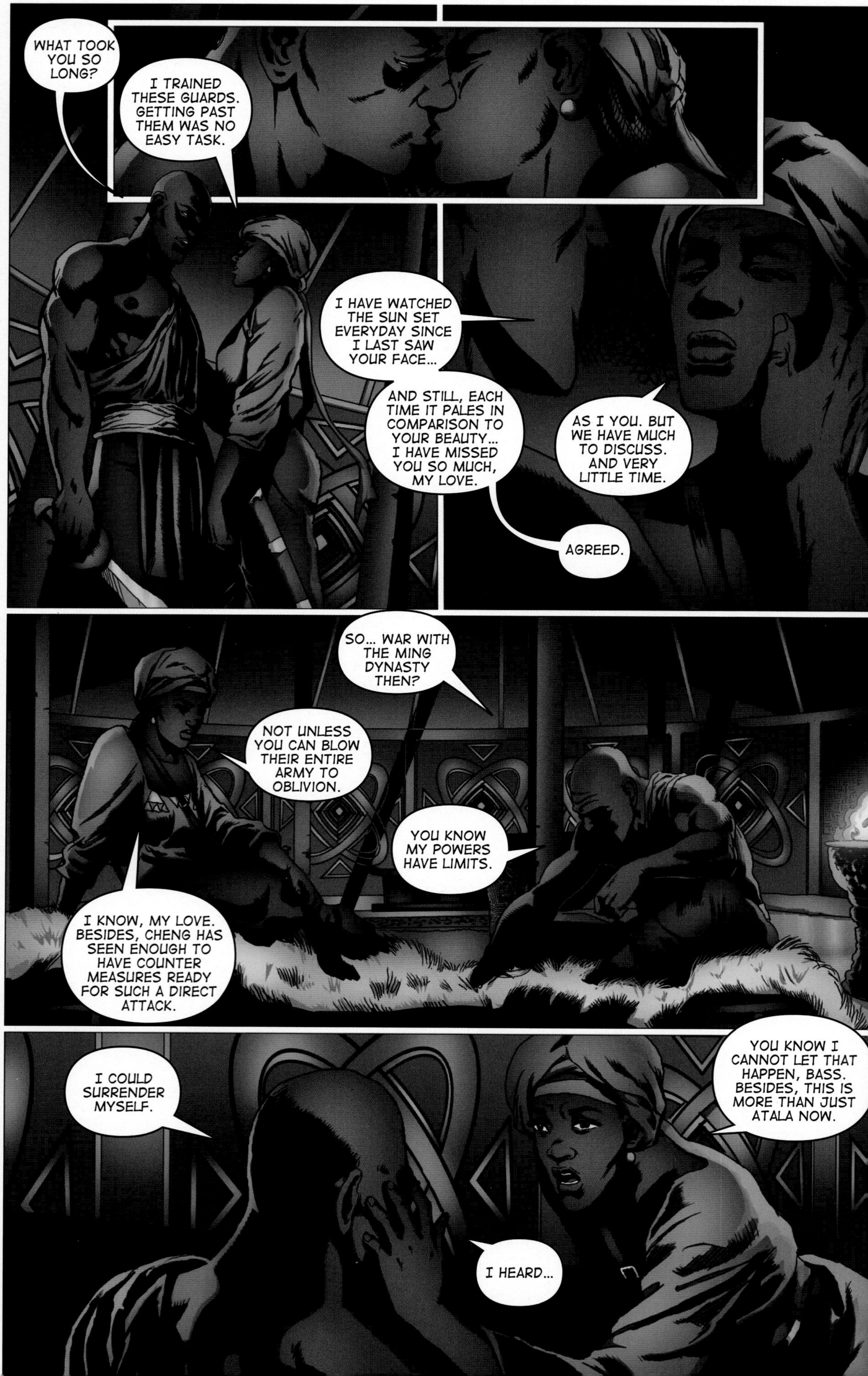
WHAT TOOK YOU SO LONG?
I TRAINED THESE GUARDS. GETTING PAST THEM WAS NO EASY TASK.
I HAVE WATCHED THE SUN SET EVERYDAY SINCE I LAST SAW YOUR FACE...
AND STILL, EACH TIME IT PALES IN COMPARISON TO YOUR BEAUTY... I HAVE MISSED YOU SO MUCH, MY LOVE.
AS I YOU. BUT WE HAVE MUCH TO DISCUSS. AND VERY LITTLE TIME.
AGREED.
SO... WAR WITH THE MING DYNASTY THEN?
NOT UNLESS YOU CAN BLOW THEIR ENTIRE ARMY TO OBLIVION.
YOU KNOW MY POWERS HAVE LIMITS.
I KNOW, MY LOVE. BESIDES, CHENG HAS SEEN ENOUGH TO HAVE COUNTER MEASURES READY FOR SUCH A DIRECT ATTACK.
I COULD SURRENDER MYSELF.
YOU KNOW I CANNOT LET THAT HAPPEN, BASS. BESIDES, THIS IS MORE THAN JUST ATALA NOW.
I HEARD...

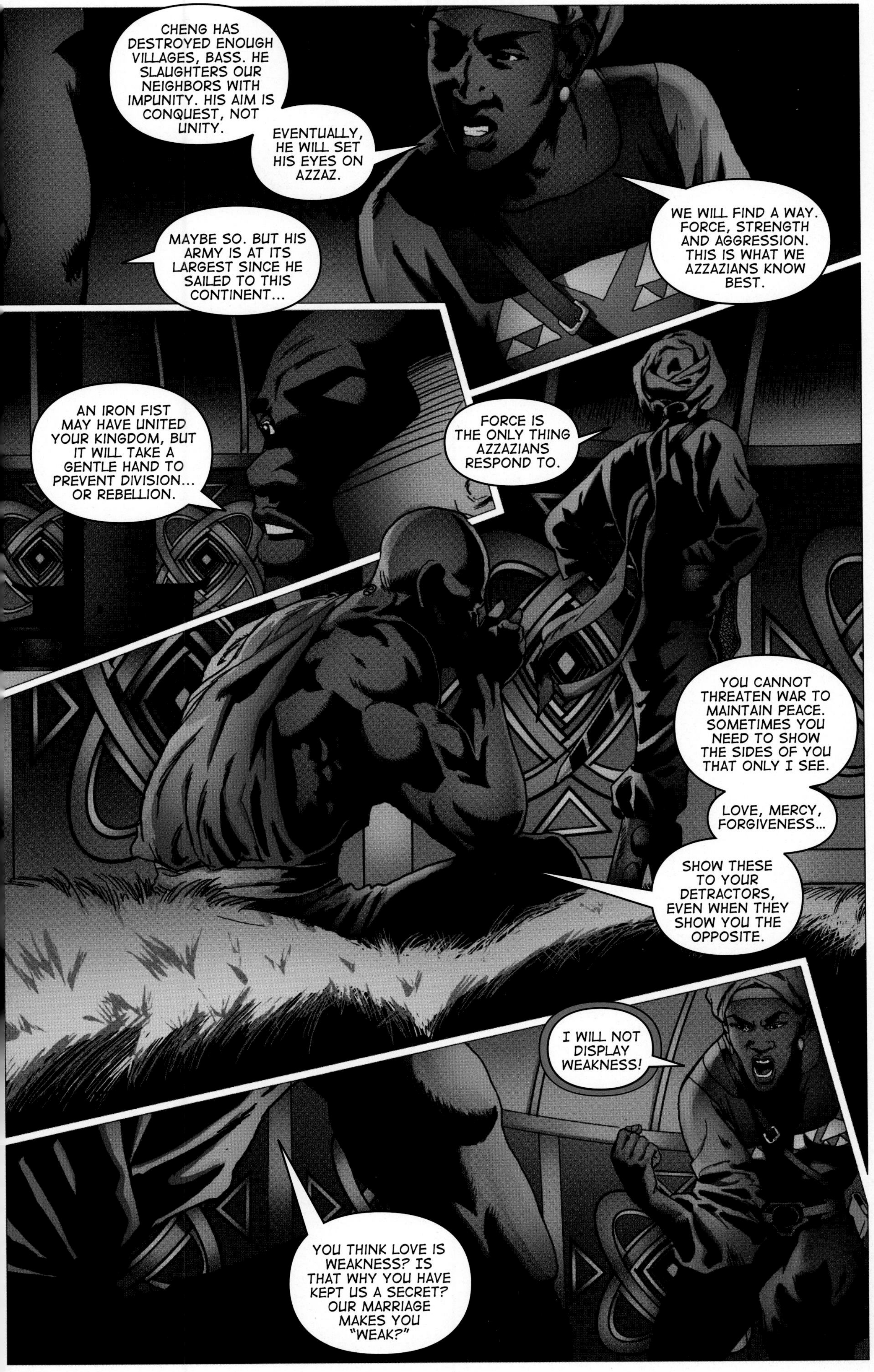
CHENG HAS DESTROYED ENOUGH VILLAGES, BASS. HE SLAUGHTERS OUR NEIGHBORS WITH IMPUNITY. HIS AIM IS CONQUEST, NOT UNITY.
EVENTUALLY, HE WILL SET HIS EYES ON AZZAZ.
MAYBE SO. BUT HIS ARMY IS AT ITS LARGEST SINCE HE SAILED TO THIS CONTINENT...
WE WILL FIND A WAY. FORCE, STRENGTH AND AGGRESSION. THIS IS WHAT WE AZZAZIANS KNOW BEST.
AN IRON FIST MAY HAVE UNITED YOUR KINGDOM, BUT IT WILL TAKE A GENTLE HAND TO PREVENT DIVISION... OR REBELLION.
FORCE IS THE ONLY THING AZZAZIANS RESPOND TO.
YOU CANNOT THREATEN WAR TO MAINTAIN PEACE. SOMETIMES YOU NEED TO SHOW THE SIDES OF YOU THAT ONLY I SEE.
LOVE, MERCY, FORGIVENESS...
SHOW THESE TO YOUR DETRACTORS, EVEN WHEN THEY SHOW YOU THE OPPOSITE.
I WILL NOT DISPLAY WEAKNESS!
YOU THINK LOVE IS WEAKNESS? IS THAT WHY YOU HAVE KEPT US A SECRET? OUR MARRIAGE MAKES YOU "WEAK?"

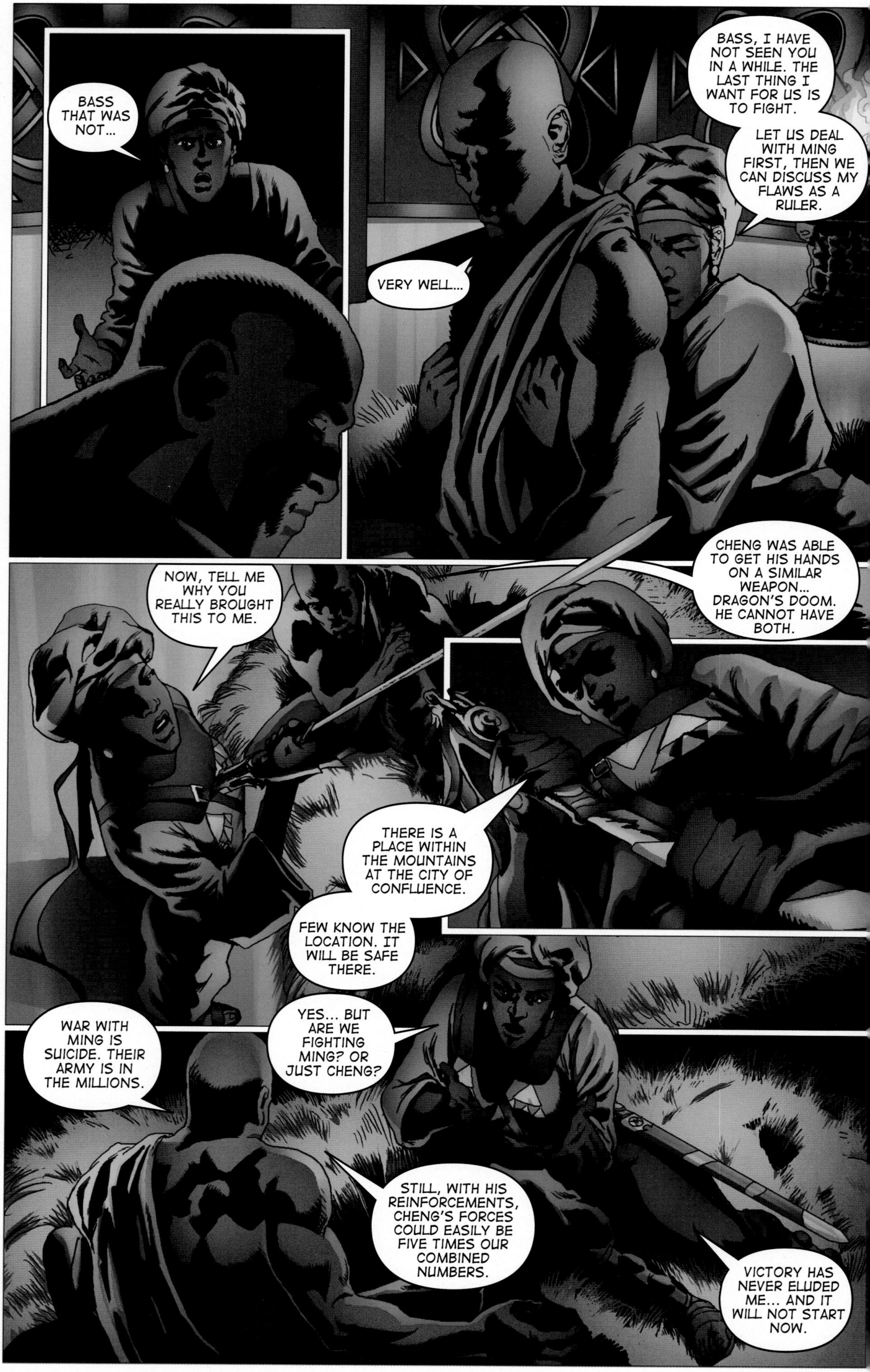
BASS THAT WAS NOT...
BASS, I HAVE NOT SEEN YOU IN A WHILE. THE LAST THING I WANT FOR US IS TO FIGHT.
LET US DEAL WITH MING FIRST, THEN WE CAN DISCUSS MY FLAWS AS A RULER.
VERY WELL...
NOW, TELL ME WHY YOU REALLY BROUGHT THIS TO ME.
CHENG WAS ABLE TO GET HIS HANDS ON A SIMILAR WEAPON... DRAGON'S DOOM. HE CANNOT HAVE BOTH.
THERE IS A PLACE WITHIN THE MOUNTAINS AT THE CITY OF CONFLUENCE.
FEW KNOW THE LOCATION. IT WILL BE SAFE THERE.
WAR WITH MING IS SUICIDE. THEIR ARMY IS IN THE MILLIONS.
YES... BUT ARE WE FIGHTING MING? OR JUST CHENG?
STILL, WITH HIS REINFORCEMENTS, CHENG'S FORCES COULD EASILY BE FIVE TIMES OUR COMBINED NUMBERS.
VICTORY HAS NEVER ELUDED ME... AND IT WILL NOT START NOW.

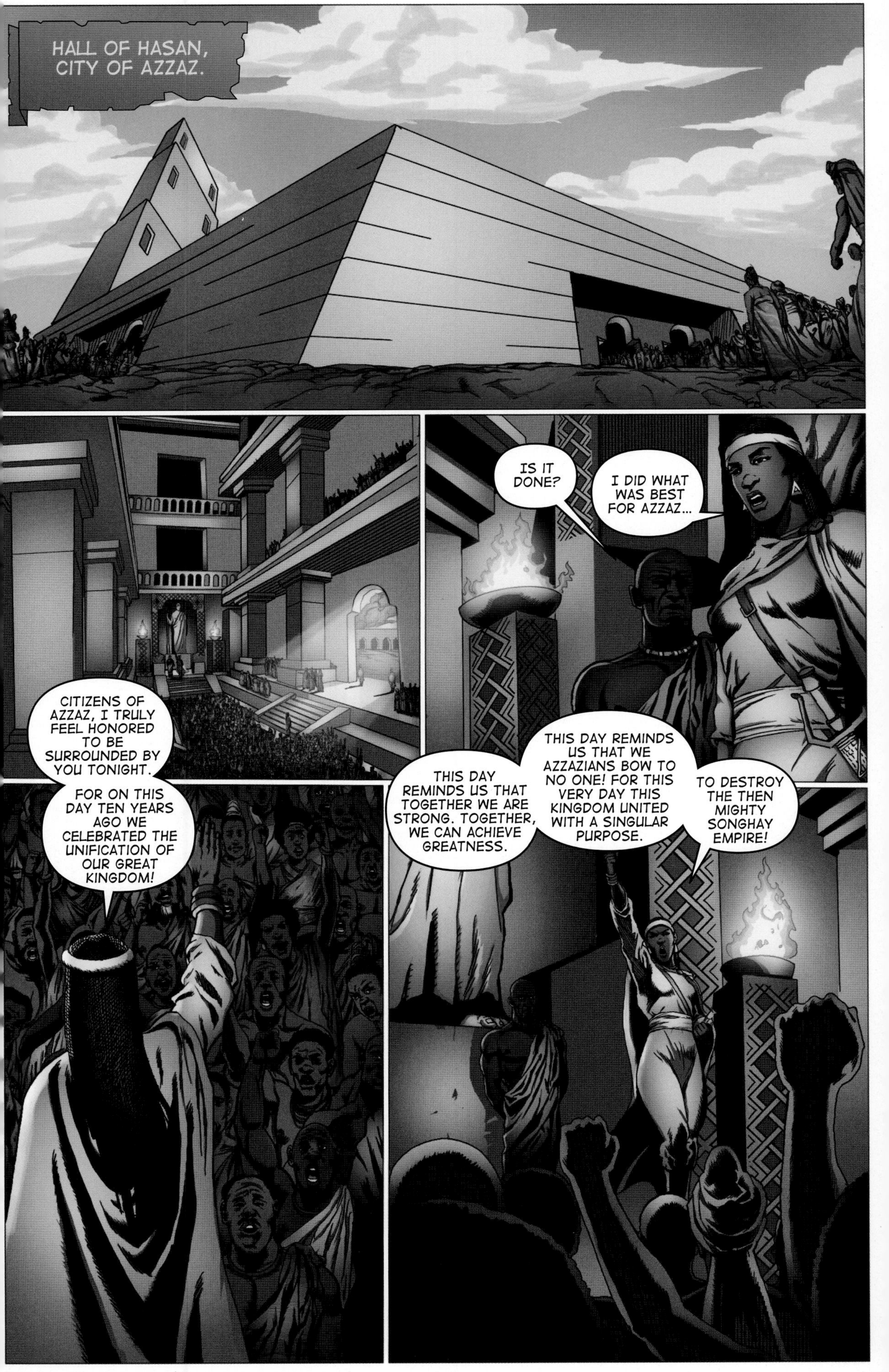
HALL OF HASAN, CITY OF AZZAZ.
IS IT DONE?
I DID WHAT WAS BEST FOR AZZAZ...
CITIZENS OF AZZAZ, I TRULY FEEL HONORED TO BE SURROUNDED BY YOU TONIGHT.
FOR ON THIS DAY TEN YEARS AGO WE CELEBRATED THE UNIFICATION OF OUR GREAT KINGDOM!
THIS DAY REMINDS US THAT TOGETHER WE ARE STRONG. TOGETHER, WE CAN ACHIEVE GREATNESS.
THIS DAY REMINDS US THAT WE AZZAZIANS BOW TO NO ONE! FOR THIS VERY DAY THIS KINGDOM UNITED WITH A SINGULAR PURPOSE.
TO DESTROY THE THEN MIGHTY SONGHAY EMPIRE!

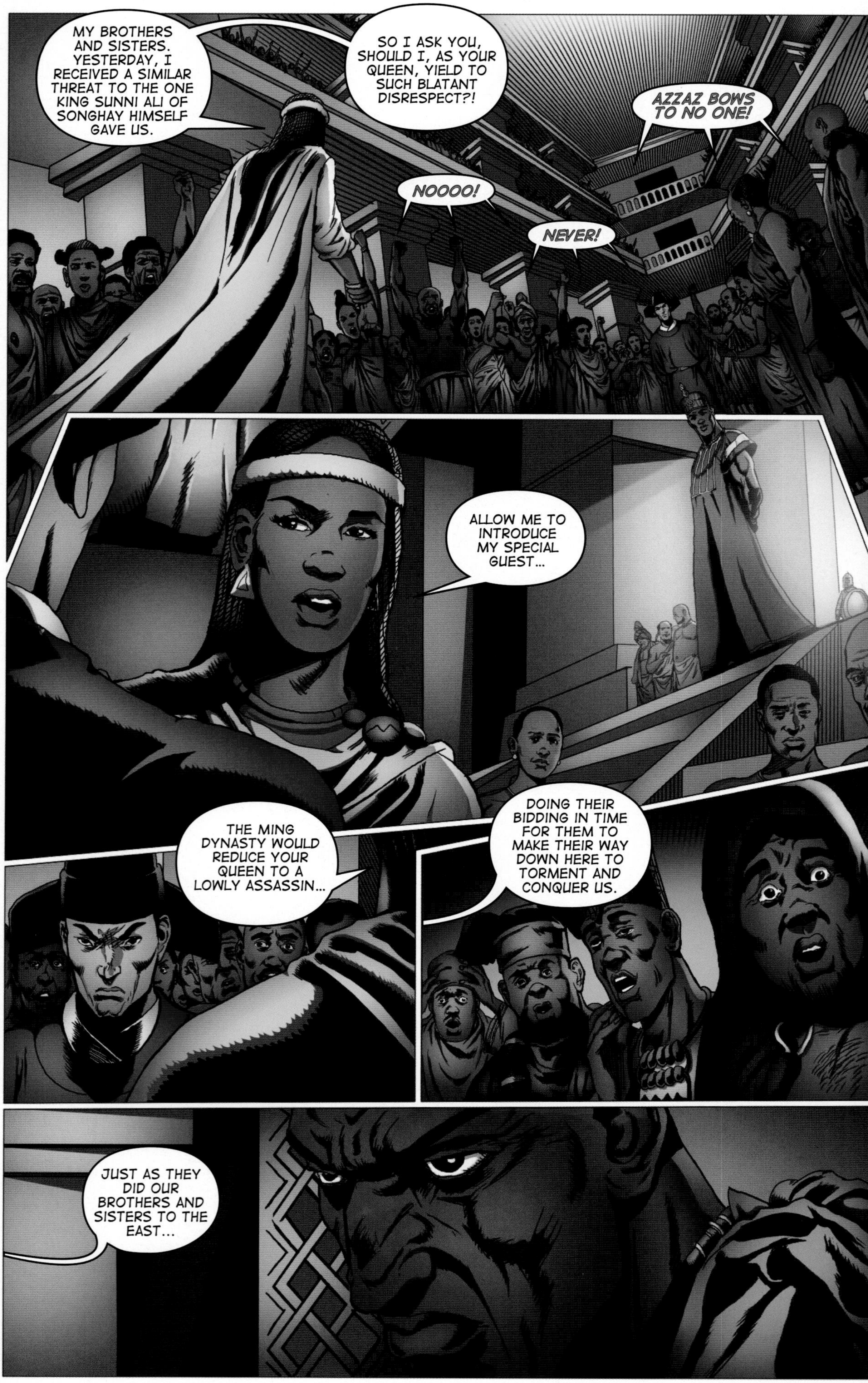
MY BROTHERS AND SISTERS. YESTERDAY, I RECEIVED A SIMILAR THREAT TO THE ONE KING SUNNI ALI OF SONGHAY HIMSELF GAVE US.
SO I ASK YOU, SHOULD I, AS YOUR QUEEN, YIELD TO SUCH BLATANT DISRESPECT?!
AZZAZ BOWS TO NO ONE!
NOOOO!
NEVER!
ALLOW ME TO INTRODUCE MY SPECIAL GUEST...
THE MING DYNASTY WOULD REDUCE YOUR QUEEN TO A LOWLY ASSASSIN...
DOING THEIR BIDDING IN TIME FOR THEM TO MAKE THEIR WAY DOWN HERE TO TORMENT AND CONQUER US.
JUST AS THEY DID OUR BROTHERS AND SISTERS TO THE EAST...

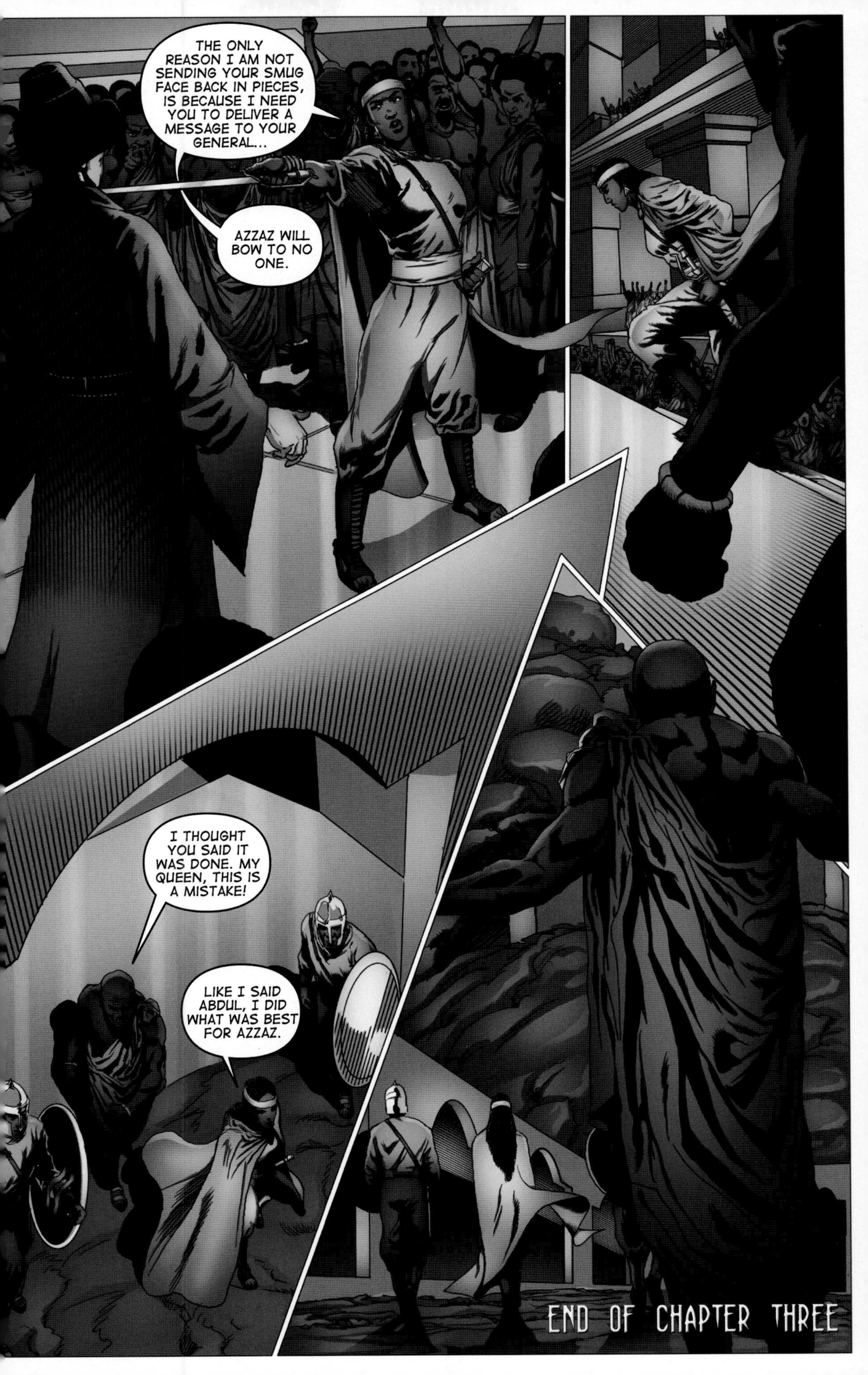
THE ONLY REASON I AM NOT SENDING YOUR SMUG FACE BACK IN PIECES, IS BECAUSE I NEED YOU TO DELIVER A MESSAGE TO YOUR GENERAL...
AZZAZ WILL BOW TO NO ONE.
I THOUGHT YOU SAID IT WAS DONE. MY QUEEN, THIS IS A MISTAKE!
LIKE I SAID ABDUL, I DID WHAT WAS BEST FOR AZZAZ.
END OF CHAPTER THREE

GREAT WEST RIVER
TRADE ROUTE
NUPE
PROVINCE
CITY OF
AZZAZ
OYO
KINGDOM
CITY OF
CONFLUENCE
BENIN
KINGDOM
AWORI

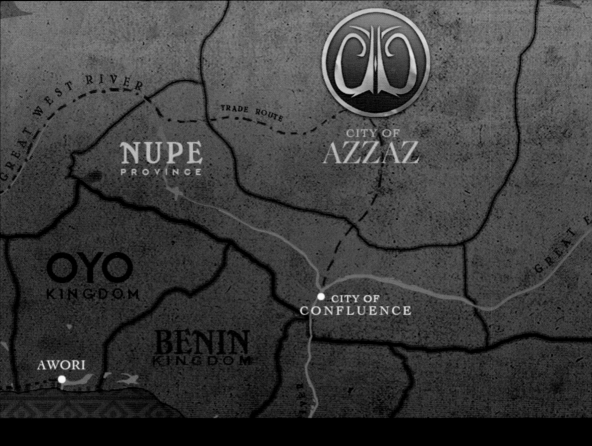

THE NUPE PROVINCE

The Nupe Province, located to the south of the City of Azzaz, is bordered by the Oyo, Benin and Nri Kingdoms to the south of the empire. Its capital, the City of Confluence (also called "The City of Three Rivers"), is the center of all trade for all merchants, towns, kingdoms and empires in all of West Africa. Chief Jimada currently governs the Nupe Province.

Fun Fact: The creation of the Nupe Province takes inspiration from the real life Nupe People, an ethnic group located in both central and northern parts of Nigeria (Niger, Kwara, and Kogi). Nupe Province's "City of Confluence" takes inspiration from Lokoja, a city located in Kogi state Nigeria where the two river's: Niger and Benue form a confluence.

CHAPTER FOUR

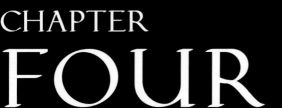

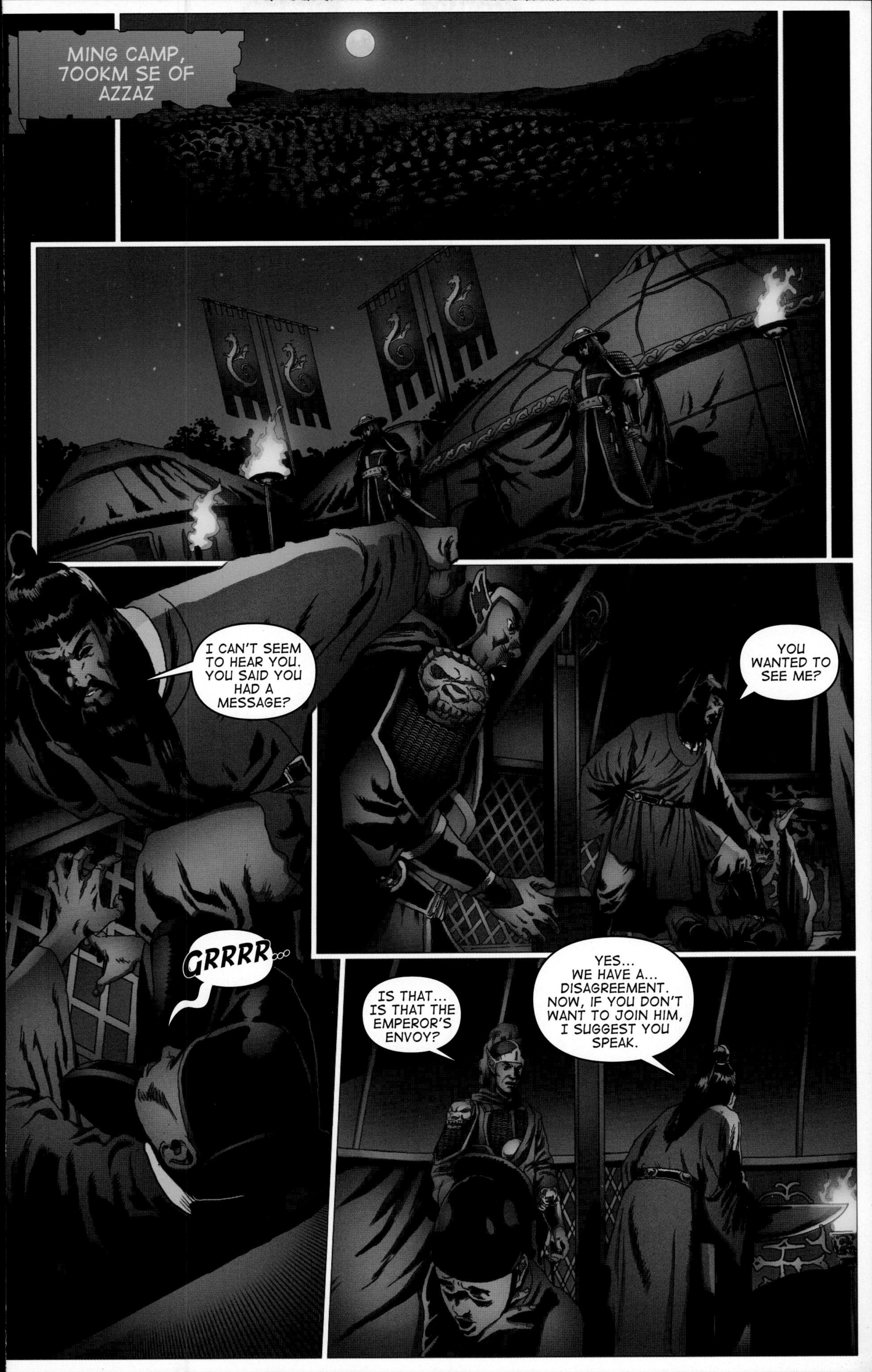
MING CAMP, 700KM SE OF AZZAZ
I CAN'T SEEM TO HEAR YOU. YOU SAID YOU HAD A MESSAGE?
YOU WANTED TO SEE ME?
GRRRR...
IS THAT... IS THAT THE EMPEROR'S ENVOY?
YES... WE HAVE A... DISAGREEMENT. NOW, IF YOU DON'T WANT TO JOIN HIM, I SUGGEST YOU SPEAK.

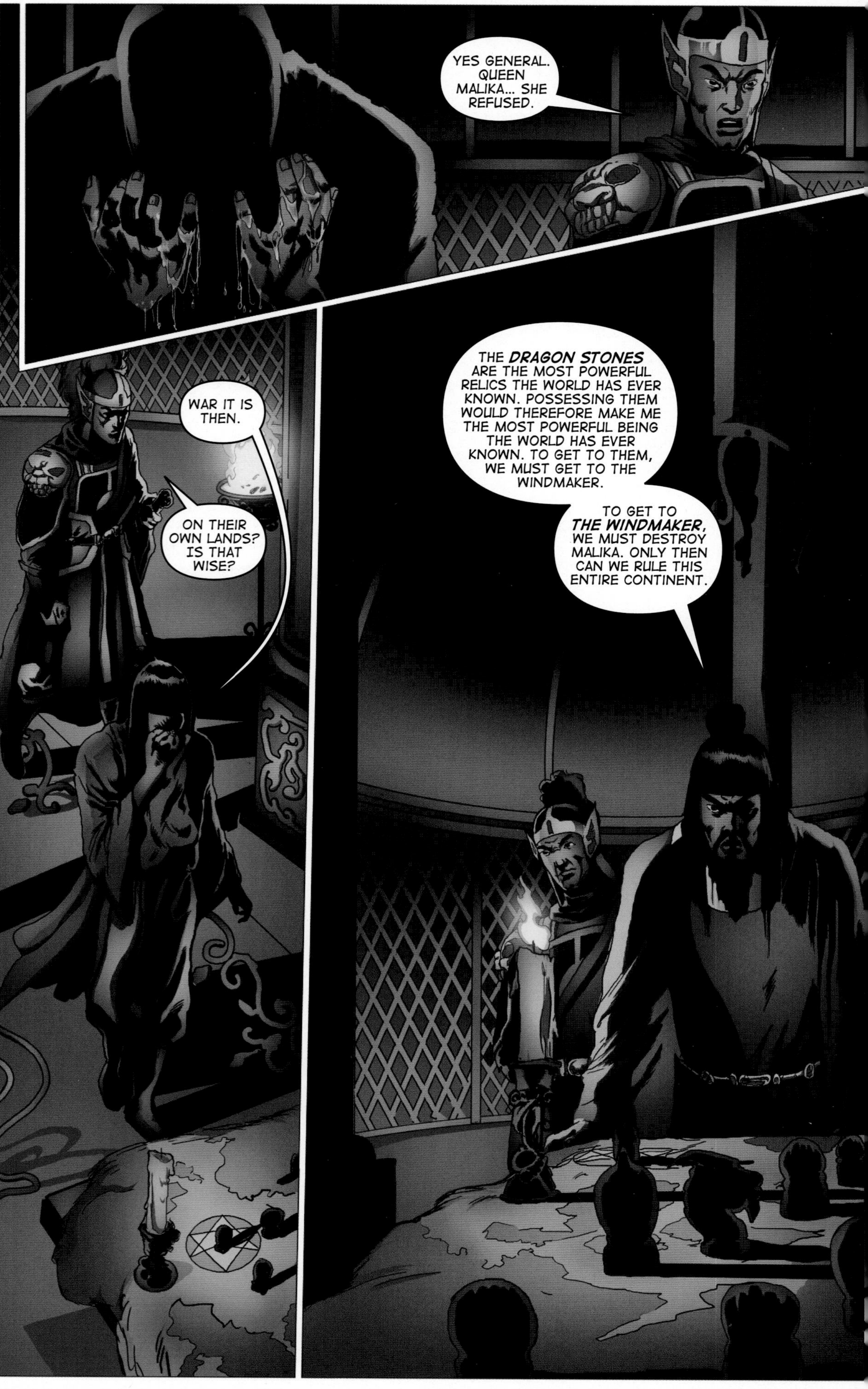
YES GENERAL. QUEEN MALIKA... SHE REFUSED.
WAR IT IS THEN.
ON THEIR OWN LANDS? IS THAT WISE?
THE **DRAGON STONES** ARE THE MOST POWERFUL RELICS THE WORLD HAS EVER KNOWN. POSSESSING THEM WOULD THEREFORE MAKE ME THE MOST POWERFUL BEING THE WORLD HAS EVER KNOWN. TO GET TO THEM, WE MUST GET TO THE WINDMAKER.
TO GET TO **THE WINDMAKER,** WE MUST DESTROY MALIKA. ONLY THEN CAN WE RULE THIS ENTIRE CONTINENT.

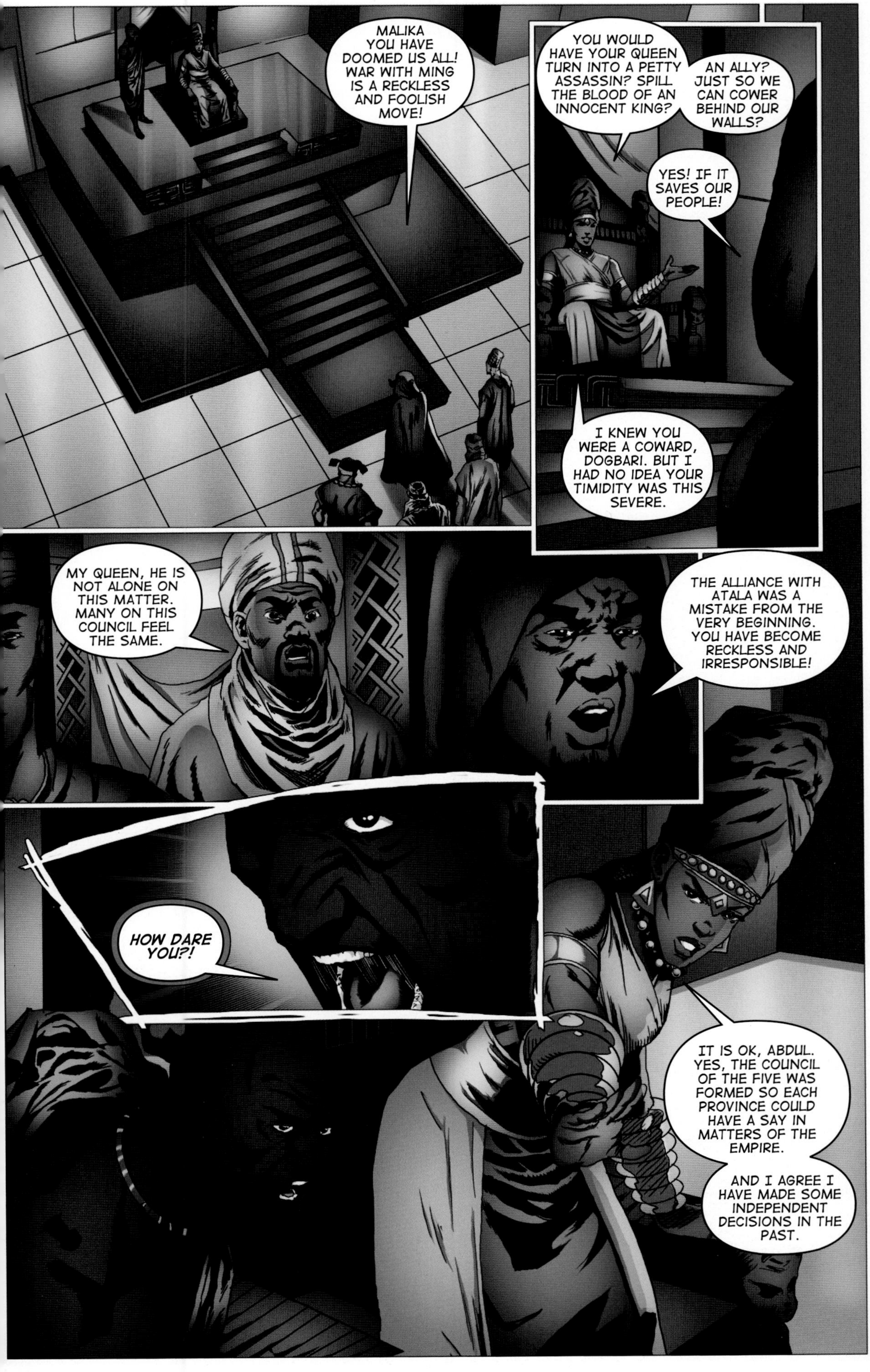
MALIKA YOU HAVE DOOMED US ALL! WAR WITH MING IS A RECKLESS AND FOOLISH MOVE!
YOU WOULD HAVE YOUR QUEEN TURN INTO A PETTY ASSASSIN? SPILL THE BLOOD OF AN INNOCENT KING?
AN ALLY? JUST SO WE CAN COWER BEHIND OUR WALLS?
YES! IF IT SAVES OUR PEOPLE!
I KNEW YOU WERE A COWARD, DOGBARI. BUT I HAD NO IDEA YOUR TIMIDITY WAS THIS SEVERE.
MY QUEEN, HE IS NOT ALONE ON THIS MATTER. MANY ON THIS COUNCIL FEEL THE SAME.
THE ALLIANCE WITH ATALA WAS A MISTAKE FROM THE VERY BEGINNING. YOU HAVE BECOME RECKLESS AND IRRESPONSIBLE!
HOW DARE YOU?!
IT IS OK, ABDUL. YES, THE COUNCIL OF THE FIVE WAS FORMED SO EACH PROVINCE COULD HAVE A SAY IN MATTERS OF THE EMPIRE.
AND I AGREE I HAVE MADE SOME INDEPENDENT DECISIONS IN THE PAST.

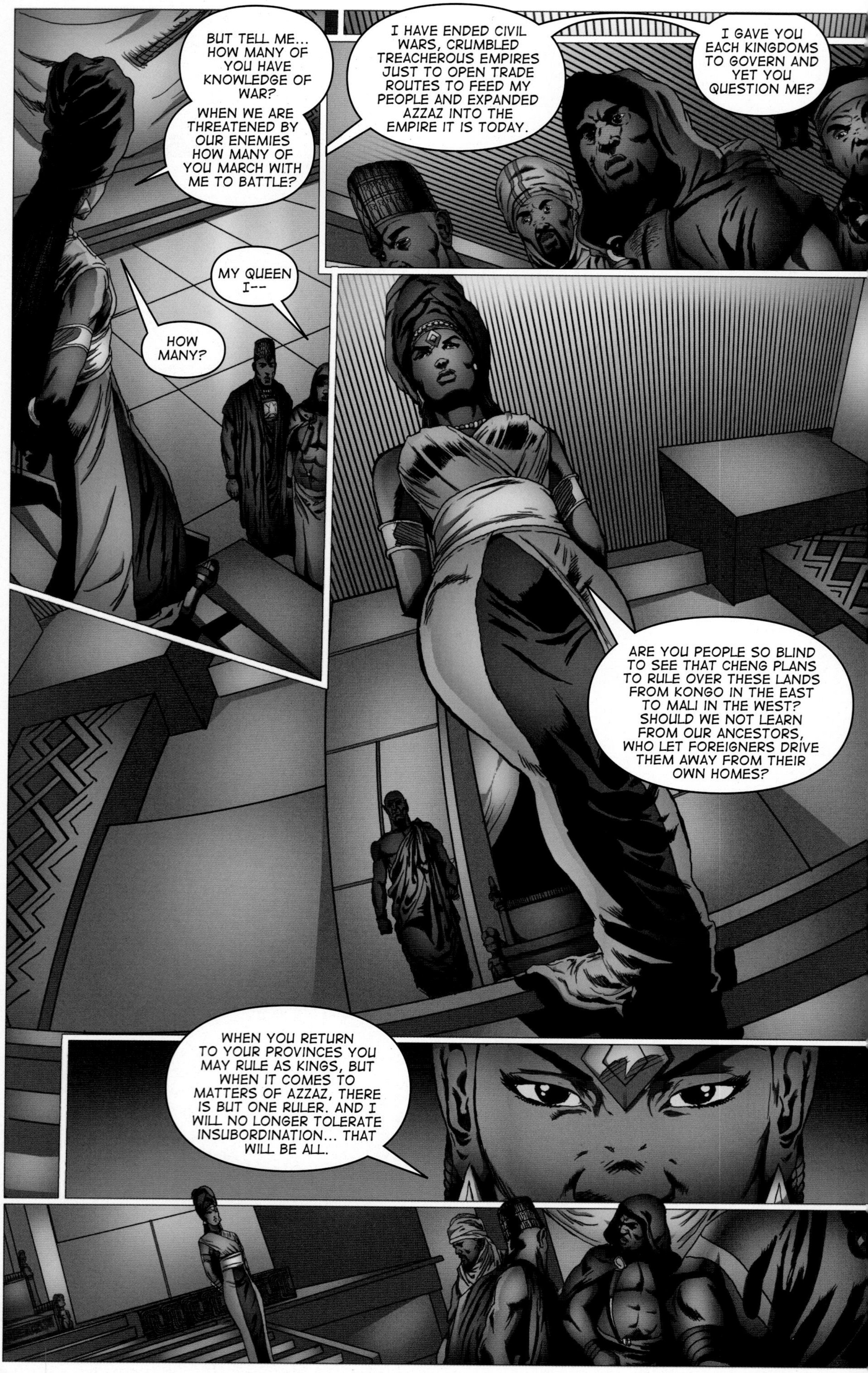
BUT TELL ME... HOW MANY OF YOU HAVE KNOWLEDGE OF WAR?
WHEN WE ARE THREATENED BY OUR ENEMIES HOW MANY OF YOU MARCH WITH ME TO BATTLE?
I HAVE ENDED CIVIL WARS, CRUMBLED TREACHEROUS EMPIRES JUST TO OPEN TRADE ROUTES TO FEED MY PEOPLE AND EXPANDED AZZAZ INTO THE EMPIRE IT IS TODAY.
I GAVE YOU EACH KINGDOMS TO GOVERN AND YET YOU QUESTION ME?
MY QUEEN I--
HOW MANY?
ARE YOU PEOPLE SO BLIND TO SEE THAT CHENG PLANS TO RULE OVER THESE LANDS FROM KONGO IN THE EAST TO MALI IN THE WEST? SHOULD WE NOT LEARN FROM OUR ANCESTORS, WHO LET FOREIGNERS DRIVE THEM AWAY FROM THEIR OWN HOMES?
WHEN YOU RETURN TO YOUR PROVINCES YOU MAY RULE AS KINGS, BUT WHEN IT COMES TO MATTERS OF AZZAZ, THERE IS BUT ONE RULER. AND I WILL NO LONGER TOLERATE INSUBORDINATION... THAT WILL BE ALL.

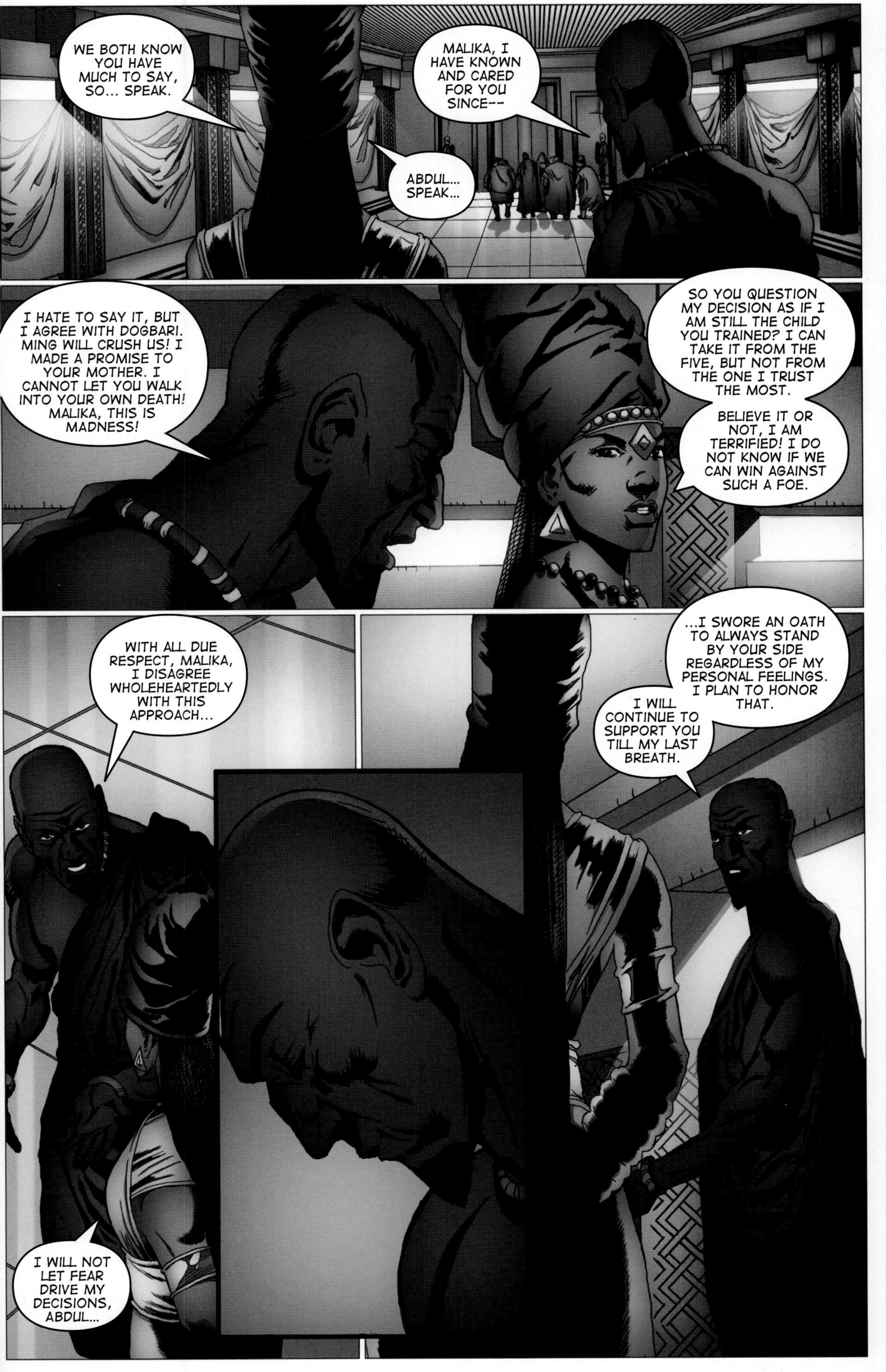
WE BOTH KNOW YOU HAVE MUCH TO SAY, SO... SPEAK.
MALIKA, I HAVE KNOWN AND CARED FOR YOU SINCE--
ABDUL... SPEAK...
I HATE TO SAY IT, BUT I AGREE WITH DOGBARI. MING WILL CRUSH US! I MADE A PROMISE TO YOUR MOTHER. I CANNOT LET YOU WALK INTO YOUR OWN DEATH! MALIKA, THIS IS MADNESS!
SO YOU QUESTION MY DECISION AS IF I AM STILL THE CHILD YOU TRAINED? I CAN TAKE IT FROM THE FIVE, BUT NOT FROM THE ONE I TRUST THE MOST.
BELIEVE IT OR NOT, I AM TERRIFIED! I DO NOT KNOW IF WE CAN WIN AGAINST SUCH A FOE.
WITH ALL DUE RESPECT, MALIKA, I DISAGREE WHOLEHEARTEDLY WITH THIS APPROACH...
I WILL NOT LET FEAR DRIVE MY DECISIONS, ABDUL...
...I SWORE AN OATH TO ALWAYS STAND BY YOUR SIDE REGARDLESS OF MY PERSONAL FEELINGS. I PLAN TO HONOR THAT.
I WILL CONTINUE TO SUPPORT YOU TILL MY LAST BREATH.

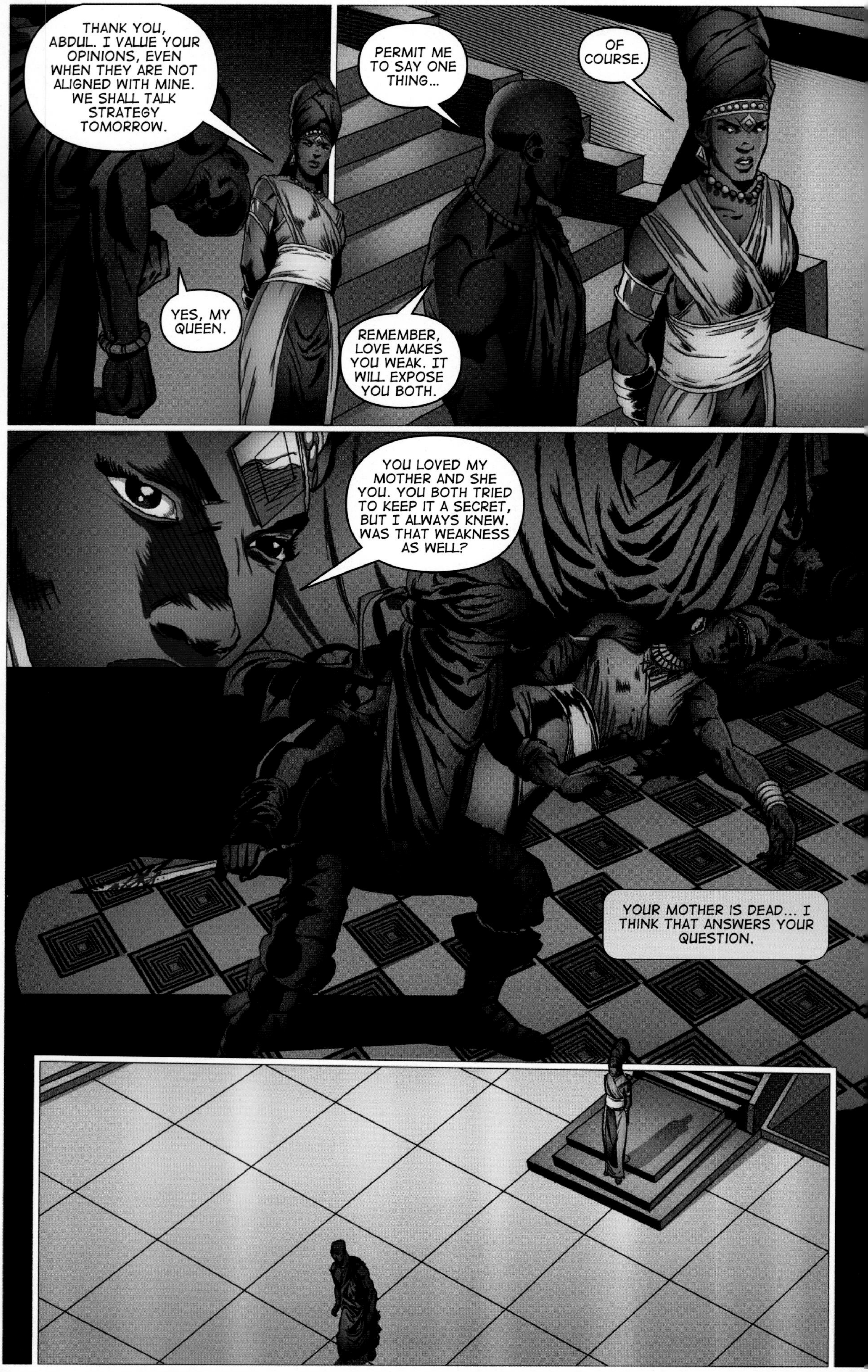
THANK YOU, ABDUL. I VALUE YOUR OPINIONS, EVEN WHEN THEY ARE NOT ALIGNED WITH MINE. WE SHALL TALK STRATEGY TOMORROW.
YES, MY QUEEN.
PERMIT ME TO SAY ONE THING...
OF COURSE.
REMEMBER, LOVE MAKES YOU WEAK. IT WILL EXPOSE YOU BOTH.
YOU LOVED MY MOTHER AND SHE YOU. YOU BOTH TRIED TO KEEP IT A SECRET, BUT I ALWAYS KNEW. WAS THAT WEAKNESS AS WELL?
YOUR MOTHER IS DEAD... I THINK THAT ANSWERS YOUR QUESTION.

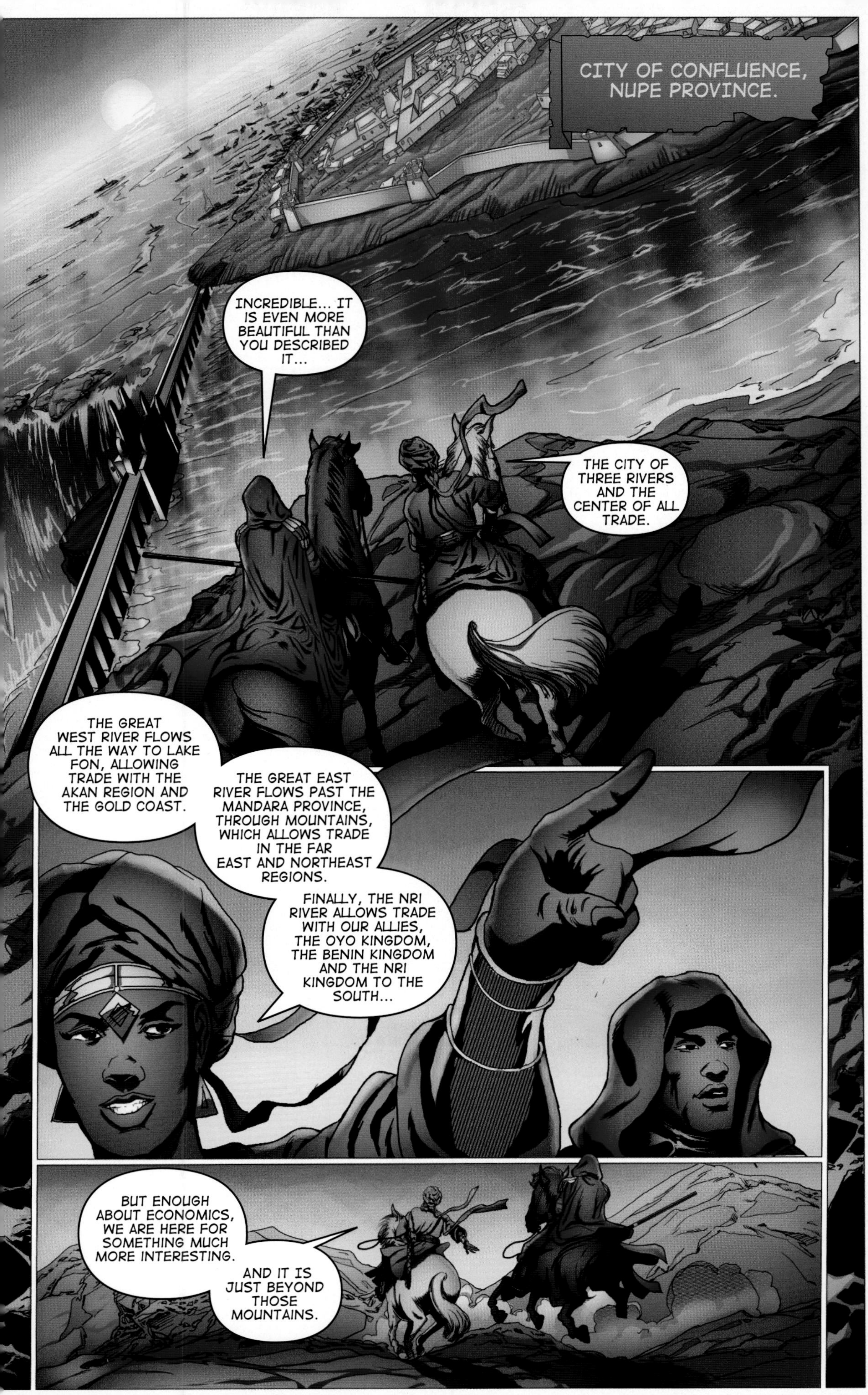
CITY OF CONFLUENCE, NUPE PROVINCE.
INCREDIBLE... IT IS EVEN MORE BEAUTIFUL THAN YOU DESCRIBED IT...
THE CITY OF THREE RIVERS AND THE CENTER OF ALL TRADE.
THE GREAT WEST RIVER FLOWS ALL THE WAY TO LAKE FON, ALLOWING TRADE WITH THE AKAN REGION AND THE GOLD COAST.
THE GREAT EAST RIVER FLOWS PAST THE MANDARA PROVINCE, THROUGH MOUNTAINS, WHICH ALLOWS TRADE IN THE FAR EAST AND NORTHEAST REGIONS.
FINALLY, THE NRI RIVER ALLOWS TRADE WITH OUR ALLIES, THE OYO KINGDOM, THE BENIN KINGDOM AND THE NRI KINGDOM TO THE SOUTH...
BUT ENOUGH ABOUT ECONOMICS, WE ARE HERE FOR SOMETHING MUCH MORE INTERESTING.
AND IT IS JUST BEYOND THOSE MOUNTAINS.

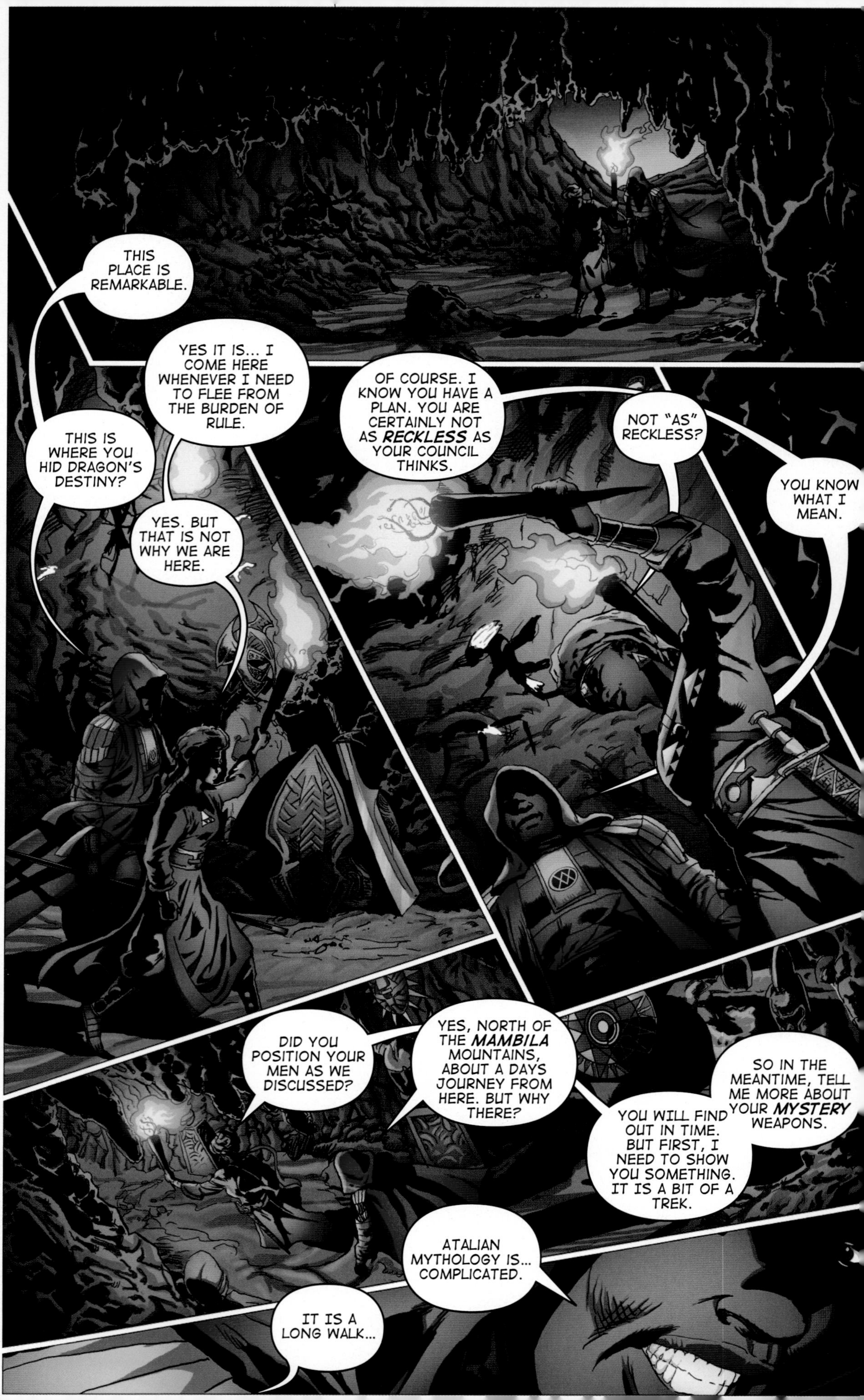
THIS PLACE IS REMARKABLE.
YES IT IS... I COME HERE WHENEVER I NEED TO FLEE FROM THE BURDEN OF RULE.
THIS IS WHERE YOU HID DRAGON'S DESTINY?
YES. BUT THAT IS NOT WHY WE ARE HERE.
OF COURSE. I KNOW YOU HAVE A PLAN. YOU ARE CERTAINLY NOT AS RECKLESS AS YOUR COUNCIL THINKS.
NOT "AS" RECKLESS?
YOU KNOW WHAT I MEAN.
DID YOU POSITION YOUR MEN AS WE DISCUSSED?
YES, NORTH OF THE MAMBILA MOUNTAINS, ABOUT A DAYS JOURNEY FROM HERE. BUT WHY THERE?
YOU WILL FIND OUT IN TIME. BUT FIRST, I NEED TO SHOW YOU SOMETHING. IT IS A BIT OF A TREK.
SO IN THE MEANTIME, TELL ME MORE ABOUT YOUR MYSTERY WEAPONS.
ATALIAN MYTHOLOGY IS... COMPLICATED.
IT IS A LONG WALK...

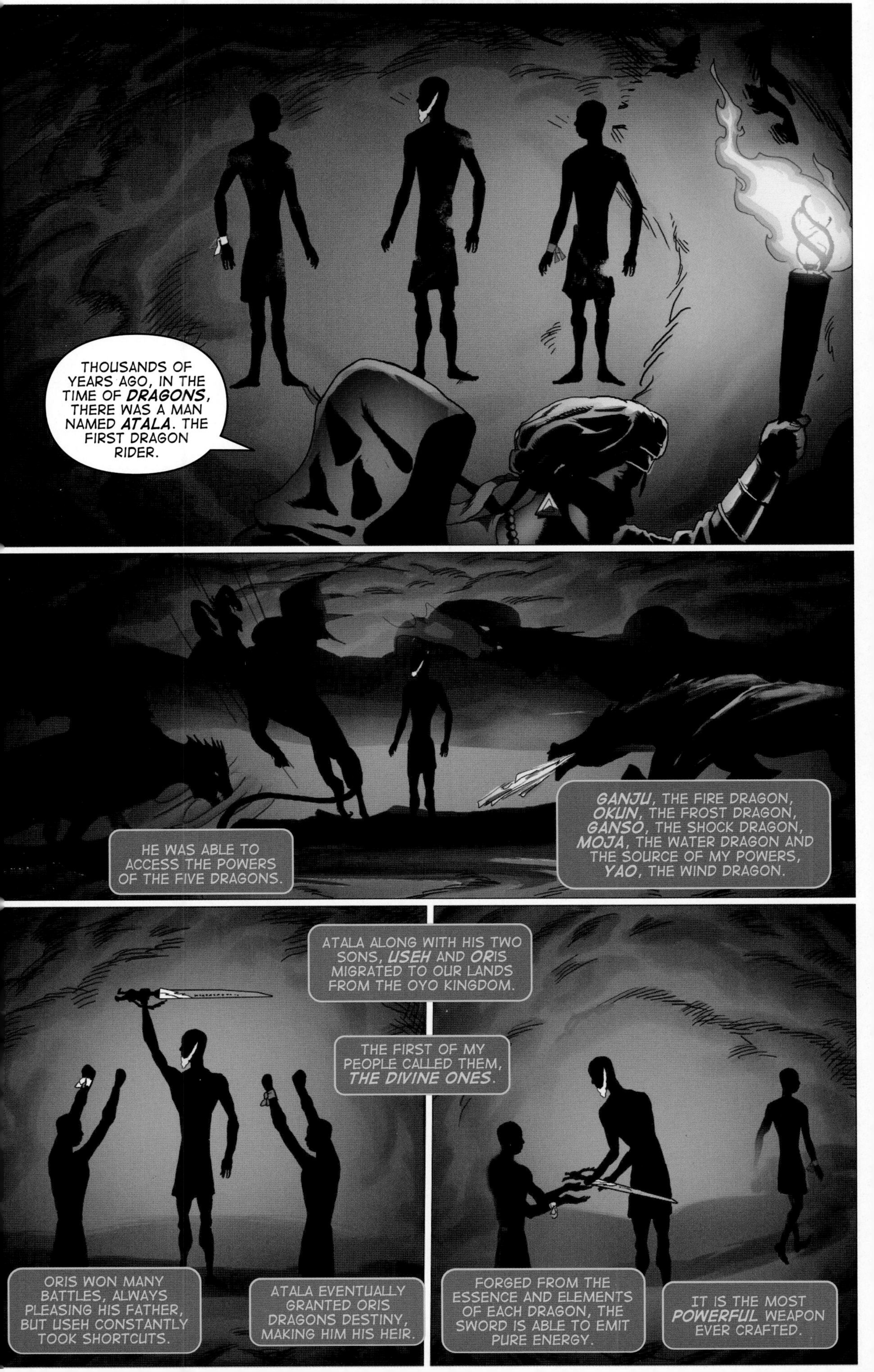
THOUSANDS OF YEARS AGO, IN THE TIME OF DRAGONS, THERE WAS A MAN NAMED ATALA. THE FIRST DRAGON RIDER.
HE WAS ABLE TO ACCESS THE POWERS OF THE FIVE DRAGONS.
GANJU, THE FIRE DRAGON, OKUN, THE FROST DRAGON, GANSO, THE SHOCK DRAGON, MOJA, THE WATER DRAGON AND THE SOURCE OF MY POWERS, YAO, THE WIND DRAGON.
ATALA ALONG WITH HIS TWO SONS, USEH AND ORIS MIGRATED TO OUR LANDS FROM THE OYO KINGDOM.
THE FIRST OF MY PEOPLE CALLED THEM, THE DIVINE ONES.
ORIS WON MANY BATTLES, ALWAYS PLEASING HIS FATHER, BUT USEH CONSTANTLY TOOK SHORTCUTS.
ATALA EVENTUALLY GRANTED ORIS DRAGONS DESTINY, MAKING HIM HIS HEIR.
FORGED FROM THE ESSENCE AND ELEMENTS OF EACH DRAGON, THE SWORD IS ABLE TO EMIT PURE ENERGY.
IT IS THE MOST POWERFUL WEAPON EVER CRAFTED.

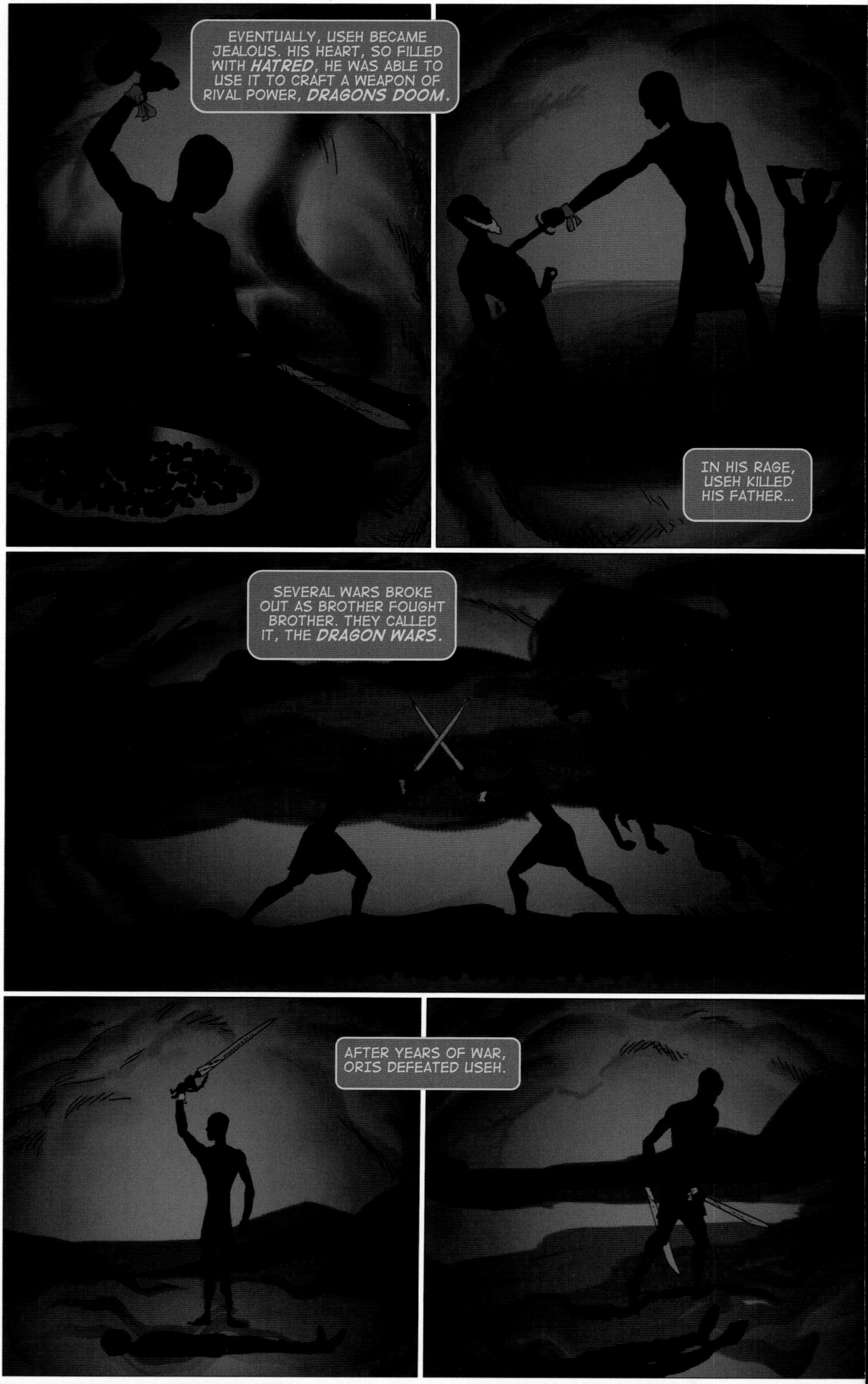
EVENTUALLY, USEH BECAME JEALOUS. HIS HEART, SO FILLED WITH HATRED, HE WAS ABLE TO USE IT TO CRAFT A WEAPON OF RIVAL POWER, DRAGONS DOOM.
IN HIS RAGE, USEH KILLED HIS FATHER...
SEVERAL WARS BROKE OUT AS BROTHER FOUGHT BROTHER. THEY CALLED IT, THE DRAGON WARS.
AFTER YEARS OF WAR, ORIS DEFEATED USEH.

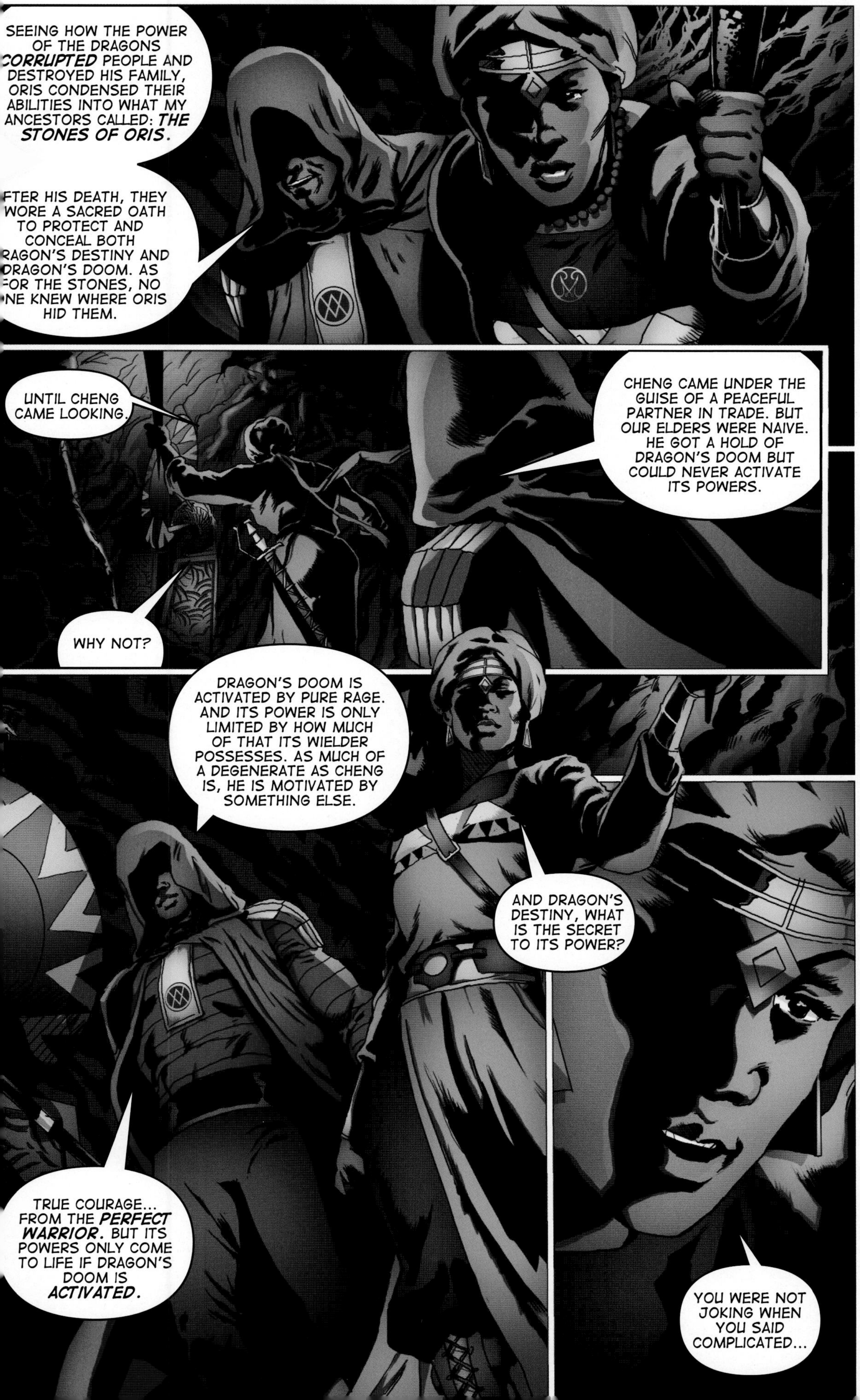

SEEING HOW THE POWER OF THE DRAGONS *CORRUPTED* PEOPLE AND DESTROYED HIS FAMILY, ORIS CONDENSED THEIR ABILITIES INTO WHAT MY ANCESTORS CALLED: *THE STONES OF ORIS*.
FTER HIS DEATH, THEY WORE A SACRED OATH TO PROTECT AND CONCEAL BOTH RAGON'S DESTINY AND DRAGON'S DOOM. AS FOR THE STONES, NO NE KNEW WHERE ORIS HID THEM.
UNTIL CHENG CAME LOOKING.
CHENG CAME UNDER THE GUISE OF A PEACEFUL PARTNER IN TRADE. BUT OUR ELDERS WERE NAIVE. HE GOT A HOLD OF DRAGON'S DOOM BUT COULD NEVER ACTIVATE ITS POWERS.
WHY NOT?
DRAGON'S DOOM IS ACTIVATED BY PURE RAGE. AND ITS POWER IS ONLY LIMITED BY HOW MUCH OF THAT ITS WIELDER POSSESSES. AS MUCH OF A DEGENERATE AS CHENG IS, HE IS MOTIVATED BY SOMETHING ELSE.
AND DRAGON'S DESTINY, WHAT IS THE SECRET TO ITS POWER?
TRUE COURAGE... FROM THE *PERFECT WARRIOR*. BUT ITS POWERS ONLY COME TO LIFE IF DRAGON'S DOOM IS *ACTIVATED*.
YOU WERE NOT JOKING WHEN YOU SAID COMPLICATED...

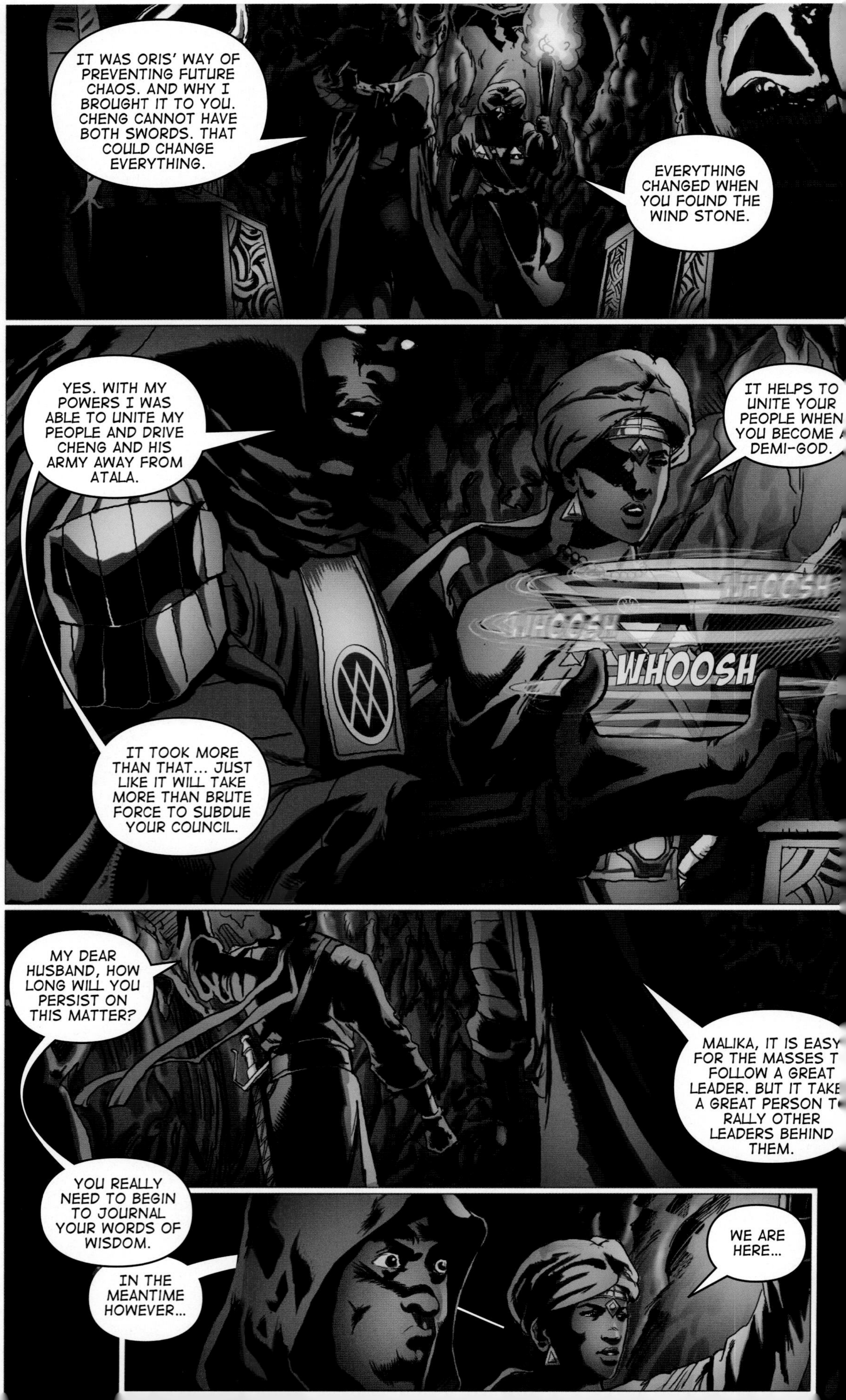

IT WAS ORIS' WAY OF PREVENTING FUTURE CHAOS. AND WHY I BROUGHT IT TO YOU. CHENG CANNOT HAVE BOTH SWORDS. THAT COULD CHANGE EVERYTHING.
EVERYTHING CHANGED WHEN YOU FOUND THE WIND STONE.
YES. WITH MY POWERS I WAS ABLE TO UNITE MY PEOPLE AND DRIVE CHENG AND HIS ARMY AWAY FROM ATALA.
IT HELPS TO UNITE YOUR PEOPLE WHEN YOU BECOME A DEMI-GOD.
WHOOSH
WHOOSH
WHOOSH
IT TOOK MORE THAN THAT... JUST LIKE IT WILL TAKE MORE THAN BRUTE FORCE TO SUBDUE YOUR COUNCIL.
MY DEAR HUSBAND, HOW LONG WILL YOU PERSIST ON THIS MATTER?
MALIKA, IT IS EASY FOR THE MASSES TO FOLLOW A GREAT LEADER. BUT IT TAKES A GREAT PERSON TO RALLY OTHER LEADERS BEHIND THEM.
YOU REALLY NEED TO BEGIN TO JOURNAL YOUR WORDS OF WISDOM.
IN THE MEANTIME HOWEVER...
WE ARE HERE...

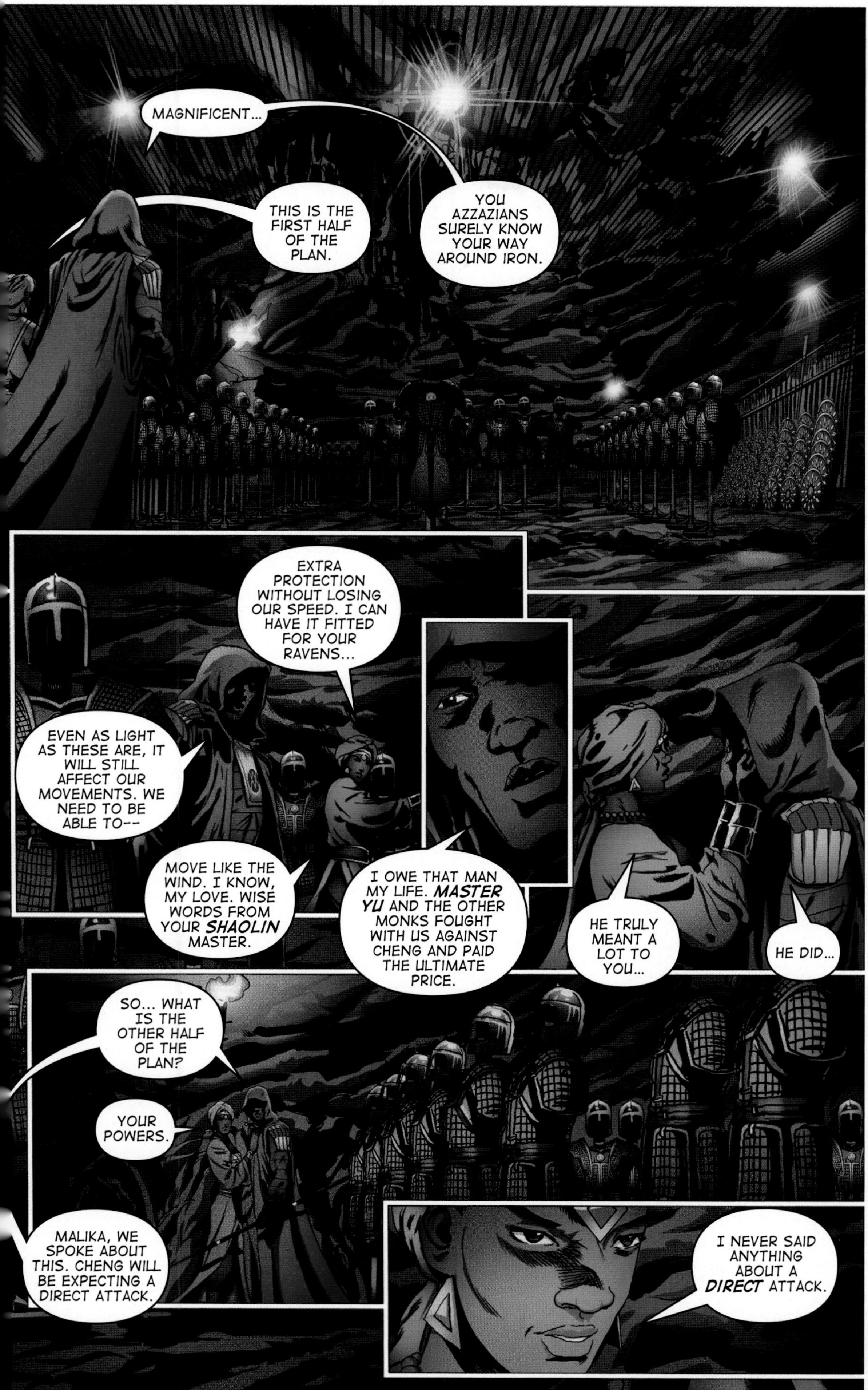
MAGNIFICENT...
THIS IS THE FIRST HALF OF THE PLAN.
YOU AZZAZIANS SURELY KNOW YOUR WAY AROUND IRON.
EXTRA PROTECTION WITHOUT LOSING OUR SPEED. I CAN HAVE IT FITTED FOR YOUR RAVENS...
EVEN AS LIGHT AS THESE ARE, IT WILL STILL AFFECT OUR MOVEMENTS. WE NEED TO BE ABLE TO--
MOVE LIKE THE WIND. I KNOW, MY LOVE. WISE WORDS FROM YOUR *SHAOLIN* MASTER.
I OWE THAT MAN MY LIFE. *MASTER YU* AND THE OTHER MONKS FOUGHT WITH US AGAINST CHENG AND PAID THE ULTIMATE PRICE.
HE TRULY MEANT A LOT TO YOU...
HE DID...
SO... WHAT IS THE OTHER HALF OF THE PLAN?
YOUR POWERS.
MALIKA, WE SPOKE ABOUT THIS. CHENG WILL BE EXPECTING A DIRECT ATTACK.
I NEVER SAID ANYTHING ABOUT A *DIRECT* ATTACK.

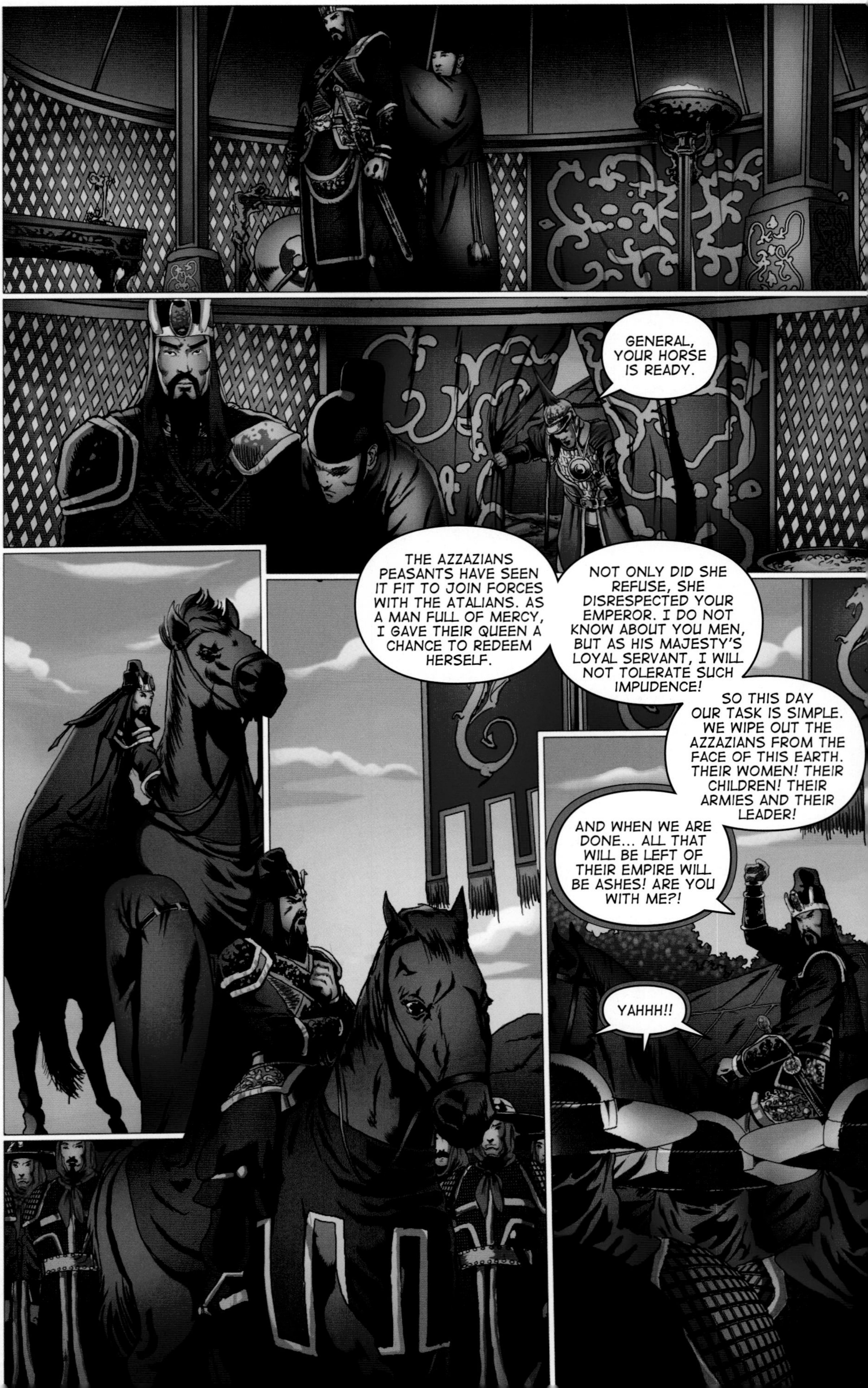
GENERAL, YOUR HORSE IS READY.
THE AZZAZIANS PEASANTS HAVE SEEN IT FIT TO JOIN FORCES WITH THE ATALIANS. AS A MAN FULL OF MERCY, I GAVE THEIR QUEEN A CHANCE TO REDEEM HERSELF.
NOT ONLY DID SHE REFUSE, SHE DISRESPECTED YOUR EMPEROR. I DO NOT KNOW ABOUT YOU MEN, BUT AS HIS MAJESTY'S LOYAL SERVANT, I WILL NOT TOLERATE SUCH IMPUDENCE!
SO THIS DAY OUR TASK IS SIMPLE. WE WIPE OUT THE AZZAZIANS FROM THE FACE OF THIS EARTH. THEIR WOMEN! THEIR CHILDREN! THEIR ARMIES AND THEIR LEADER!
AND WHEN WE ARE DONE... ALL THAT WILL BE LEFT OF THEIR EMPIRE WILL BE ASHES! ARE YOU WITH ME?!
YAHHH!!

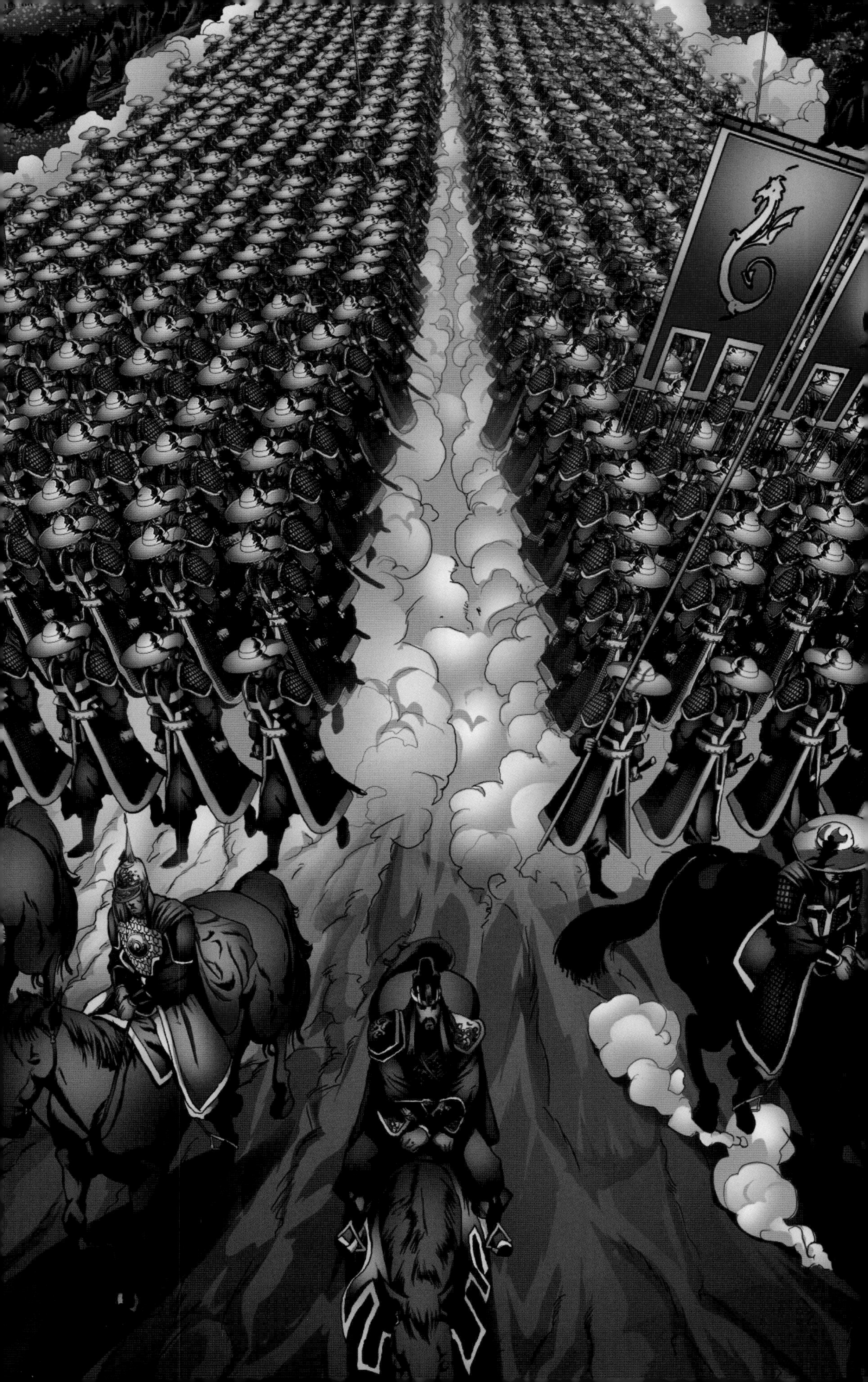

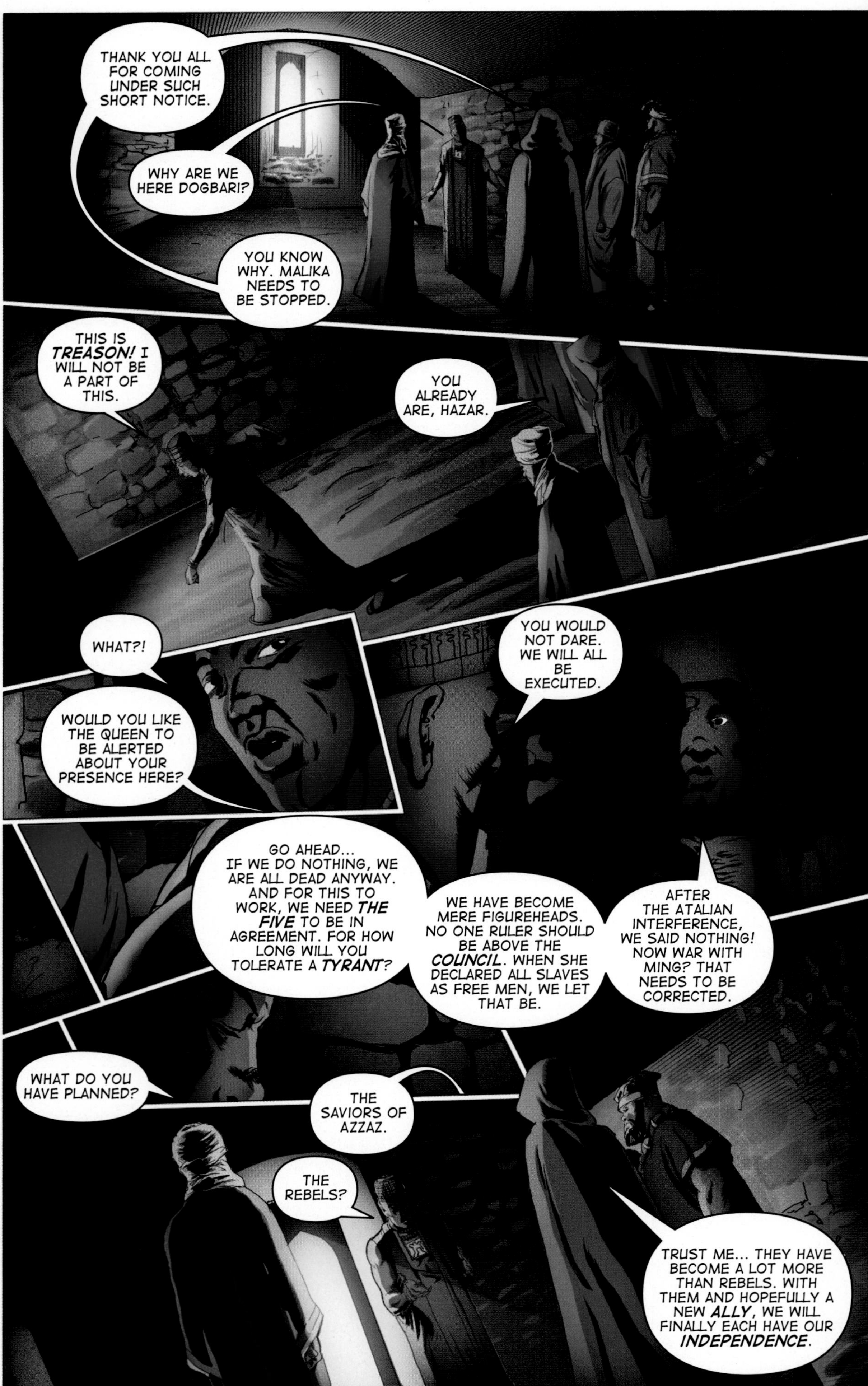
THANK YOU ALL FOR COMING UNDER SUCH SHORT NOTICE.
WHY ARE WE HERE DOGBARI?
YOU KNOW WHY. MALIKA NEEDS TO BE STOPPED.
THIS IS *TREASON!* I WILL NOT BE A PART OF THIS.
YOU ALREADY ARE, HAZAR.
WHAT?!
WOULD YOU LIKE THE QUEEN TO BE ALERTED ABOUT YOUR PRESENCE HERE?
YOU WOULD NOT DARE. WE WILL ALL BE EXECUTED.
GO AHEAD... IF WE DO NOTHING, WE ARE ALL DEAD ANYWAY. AND FOR THIS TO WORK, WE NEED *THE FIVE* TO BE IN AGREEMENT. FOR HOW LONG WILL YOU TOLERATE A *TYRANT*?
WE HAVE BECOME MERE FIGUREHEADS. NO ONE RULER SHOULD BE ABOVE THE *COUNCIL*. WHEN SHE DECLARED ALL SLAVES AS FREE MEN, WE LET THAT BE.
AFTER THE ATALIAN INTERFERENCE, WE SAID NOTHING! NOW WAR WITH MING? THAT NEEDS TO BE CORRECTED.
WHAT DO YOU HAVE PLANNED?
THE SAVIORS OF AZZAZ.
THE REBELS?
TRUST ME... THEY HAVE BECOME A LOT MORE THAN REBELS. WITH THEM AND HOPEFULLY A NEW *ALLY*, WE WILL FINALLY EACH HAVE OUR *INDEPENDENCE*.

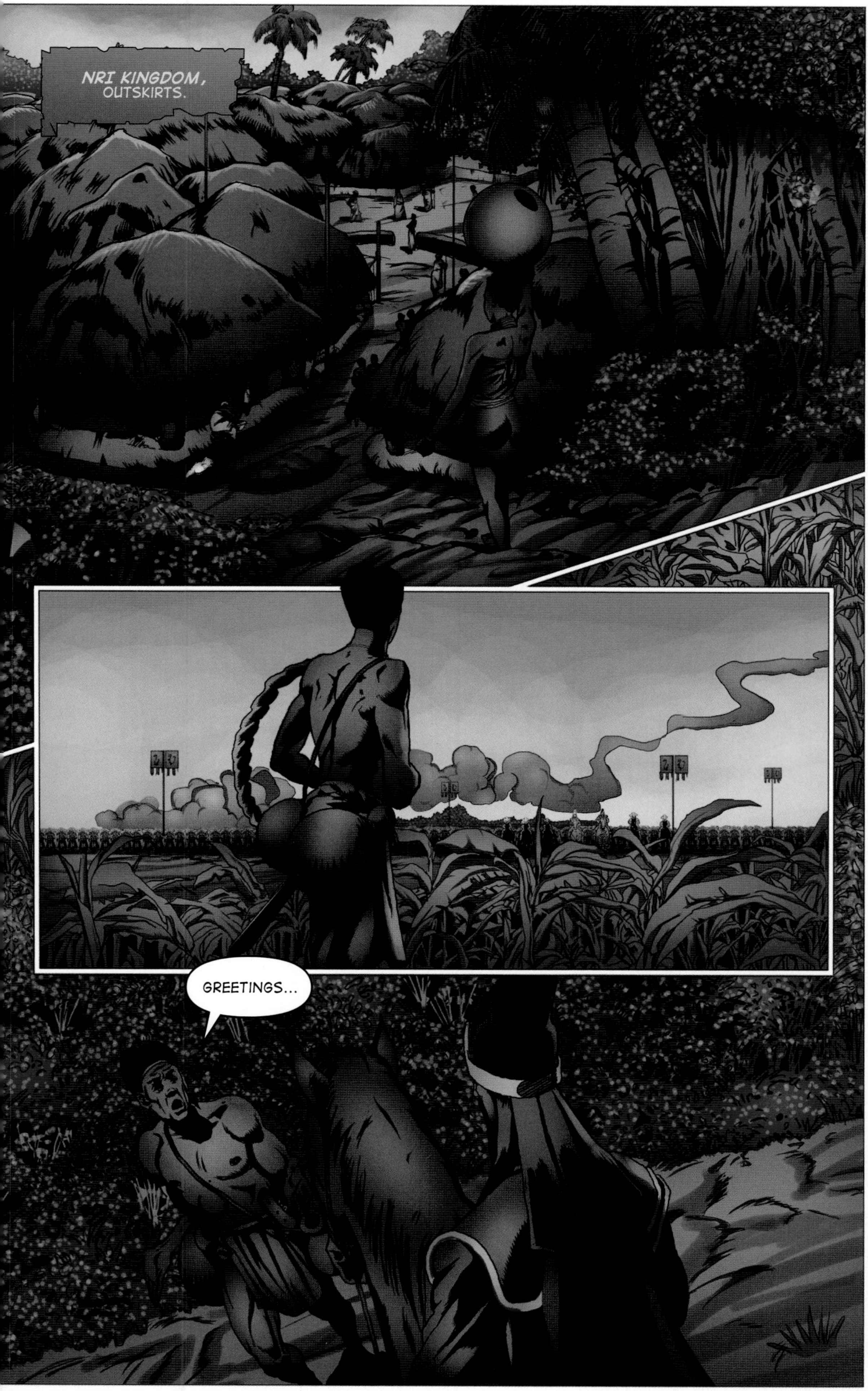
NRI KINGDOM,
OUTSKIRTS.
GREETINGS...

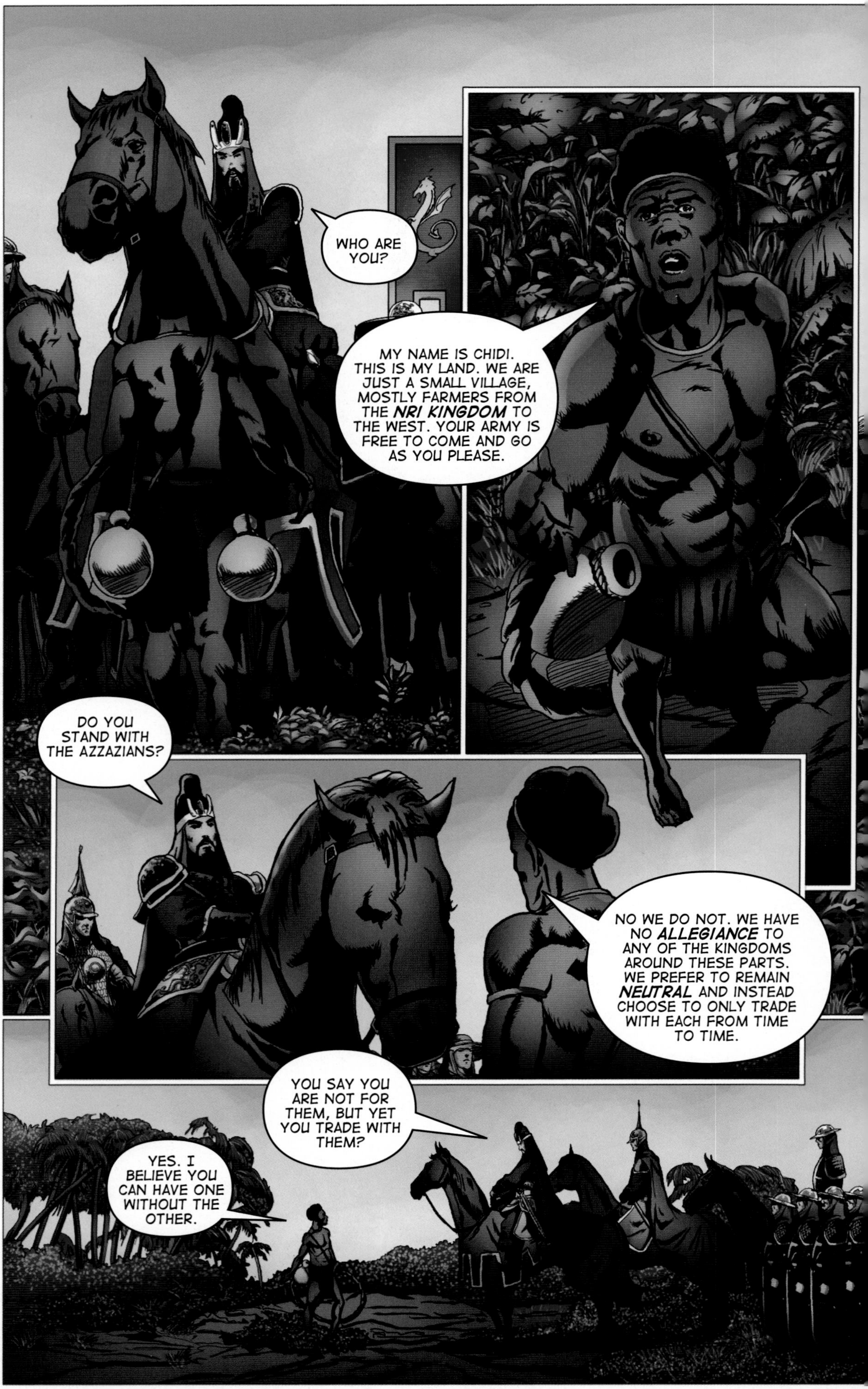
WHO ARE YOU?
MY NAME IS CHIDI. THIS IS MY LAND. WE ARE JUST A SMALL VILLAGE, MOSTLY FARMERS FROM THE NRI KINGDOM TO THE WEST. YOUR ARMY IS FREE TO COME AND GO AS YOU PLEASE.
DO YOU STAND WITH THE AZZAZIANS?
NO WE DO NOT. WE HAVE NO ALLEGIANCE TO ANY OF THE KINGDOMS AROUND THESE PARTS. WE PREFER TO REMAIN NEUTRAL AND INSTEAD CHOOSE TO ONLY TRADE WITH EACH FROM TIME TO TIME.
YOU SAY YOU ARE NOT FOR THEM, BUT YET YOU TRADE WITH THEM?
YES. I BELIEVE YOU CAN HAVE ONE WITHOUT THE OTHER.

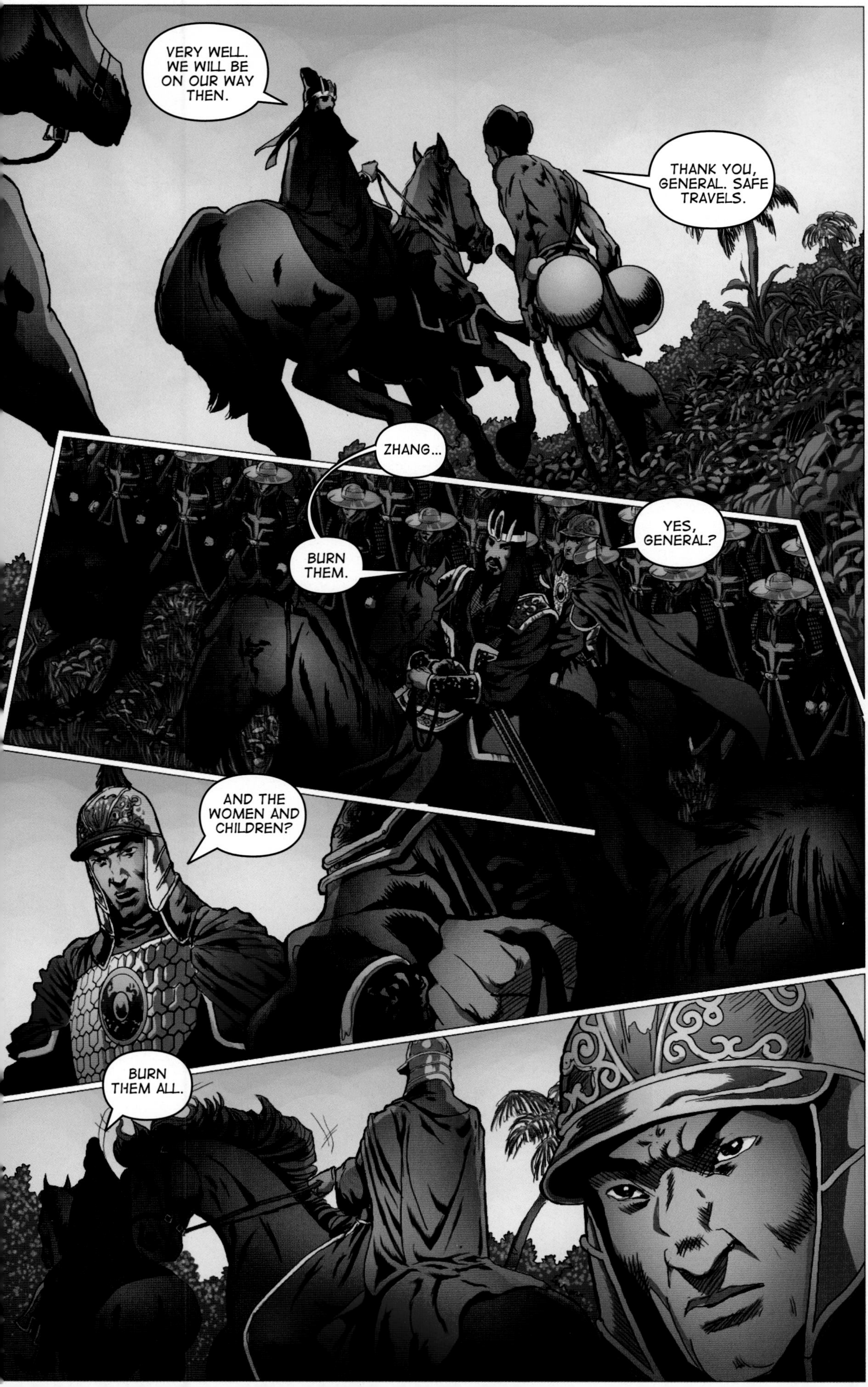
VERY WELL. WE WILL BE ON OUR WAY THEN.
THANK YOU, GENERAL. SAFE TRAVELS.
ZHANG...
YES, GENERAL?
BURN THEM.
AND THE WOMEN AND CHILDREN?
BURN THEM ALL.

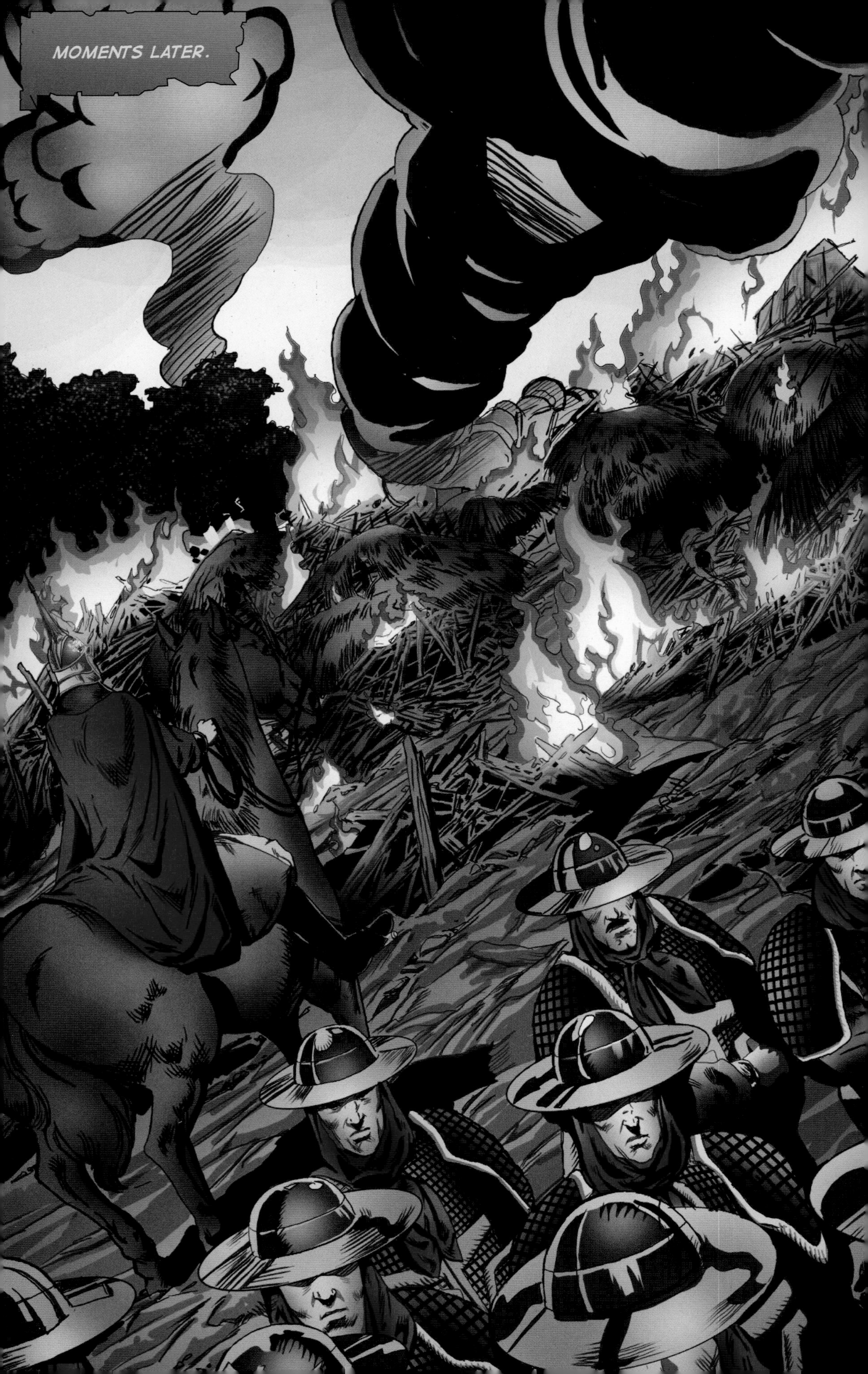
MOMENTS LATER.

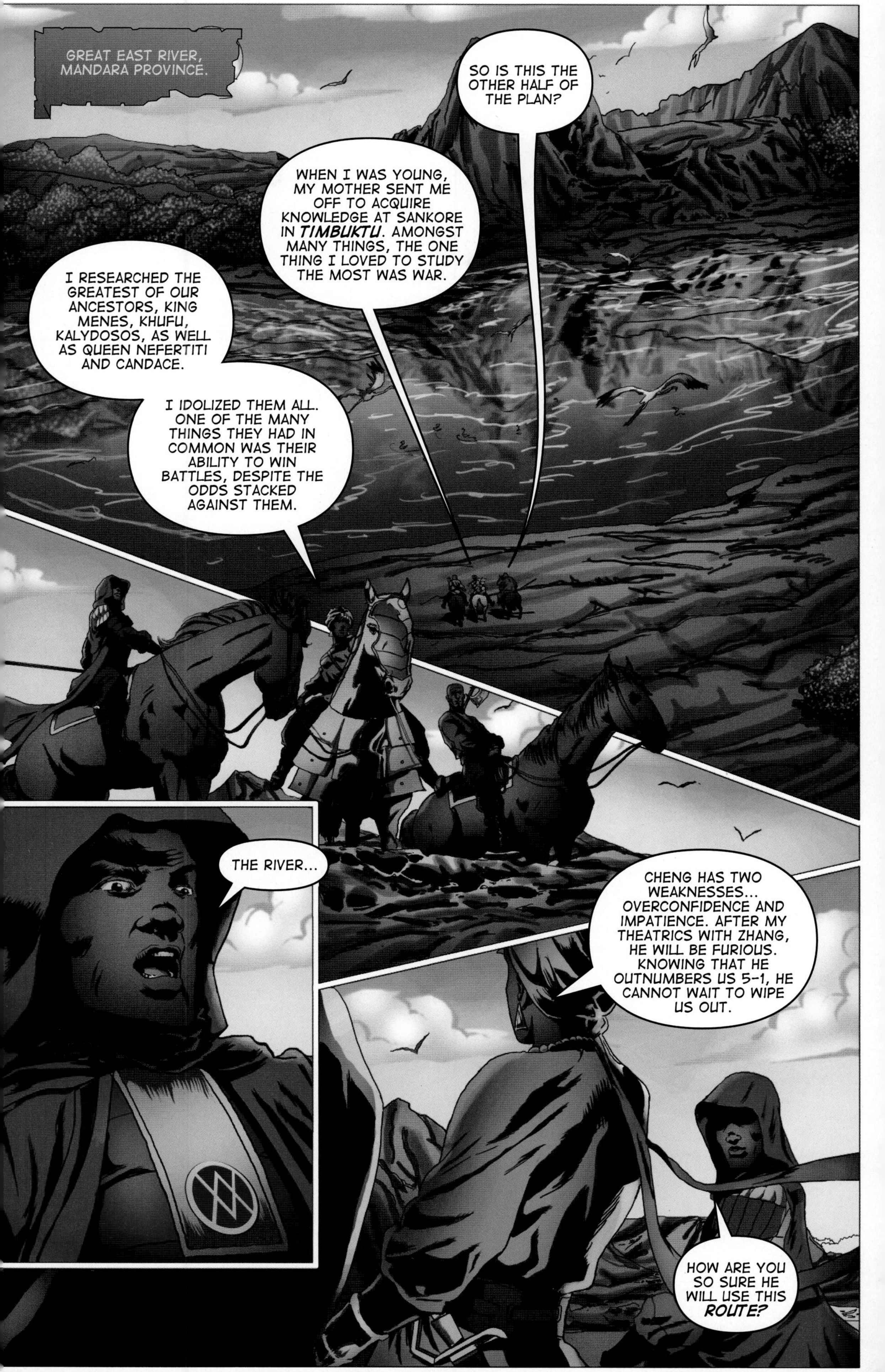
GREAT EAST RIVER, MANDARA PROVINCE.
SO IS THIS THE OTHER HALF OF THE PLAN?
WHEN I WAS YOUNG, MY MOTHER SENT ME OFF TO ACQUIRE KNOWLEDGE AT SANKORE IN TIMBUKTU. AMONGST MANY THINGS, THE ONE THING I LOVED TO STUDY THE MOST WAS WAR.
I RESEARCHED THE GREATEST OF OUR ANCESTORS, KING MENES, KHUFU, KALYDOSOS, AS WELL AS QUEEN NEFERTITI AND CANDACE.
I IDOLIZED THEM ALL. ONE OF THE MANY THINGS THEY HAD IN COMMON WAS THEIR ABILITY TO WIN BATTLES, DESPITE THE ODDS STACKED AGAINST THEM.
THE RIVER...
CHENG HAS TWO WEAKNESSES... OVERCONFIDENCE AND IMPATIENCE. AFTER MY THEATRICS WITH ZHANG, HE WILL BE FURIOUS. KNOWING THAT HE OUTNUMBERS US 5-1, HE CANNOT WAIT TO WIPE US OUT.
HOW ARE YOU SO SURE HE WILL USE THIS ROUTE?

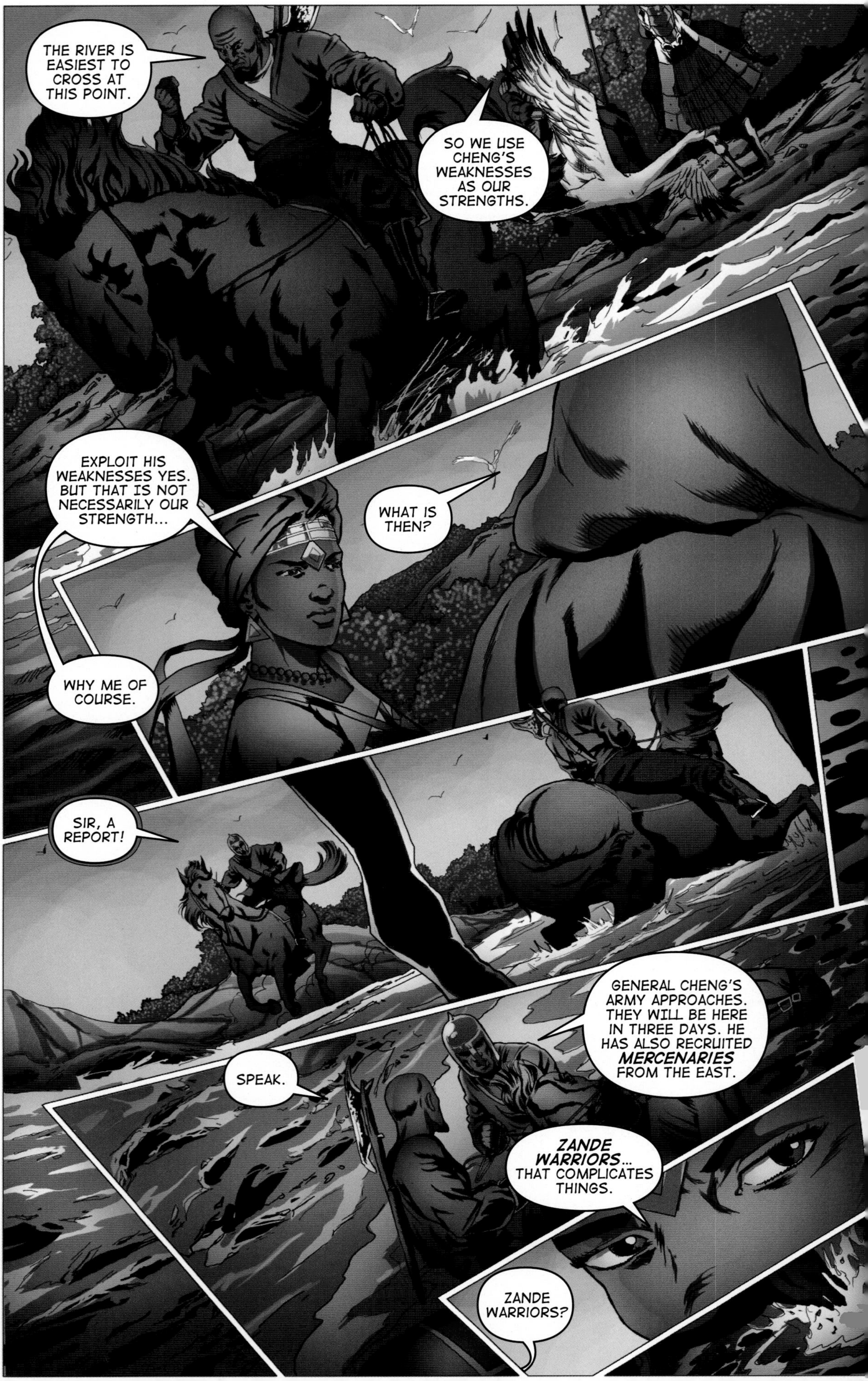
THE RIVER IS EASIEST TO CROSS AT THIS POINT.
SO WE USE CHENG'S WEAKNESSES AS OUR STRENGTHS.
EXPLOIT HIS WEAKNESSES YES. BUT THAT IS NOT NECESSARILY OUR STRENGTH...
WHAT IS THEN?
WHY ME OF COURSE.
SIR, A REPORT!
SPEAK.
GENERAL CHENG'S ARMY APPROACHES. THEY WILL BE HERE IN THREE DAYS. HE HAS ALSO RECRUITED MERCENARIES FROM THE EAST.
ZANDE WARRIORS... THAT COMPLICATES THINGS.
ZANDE WARRIORS?

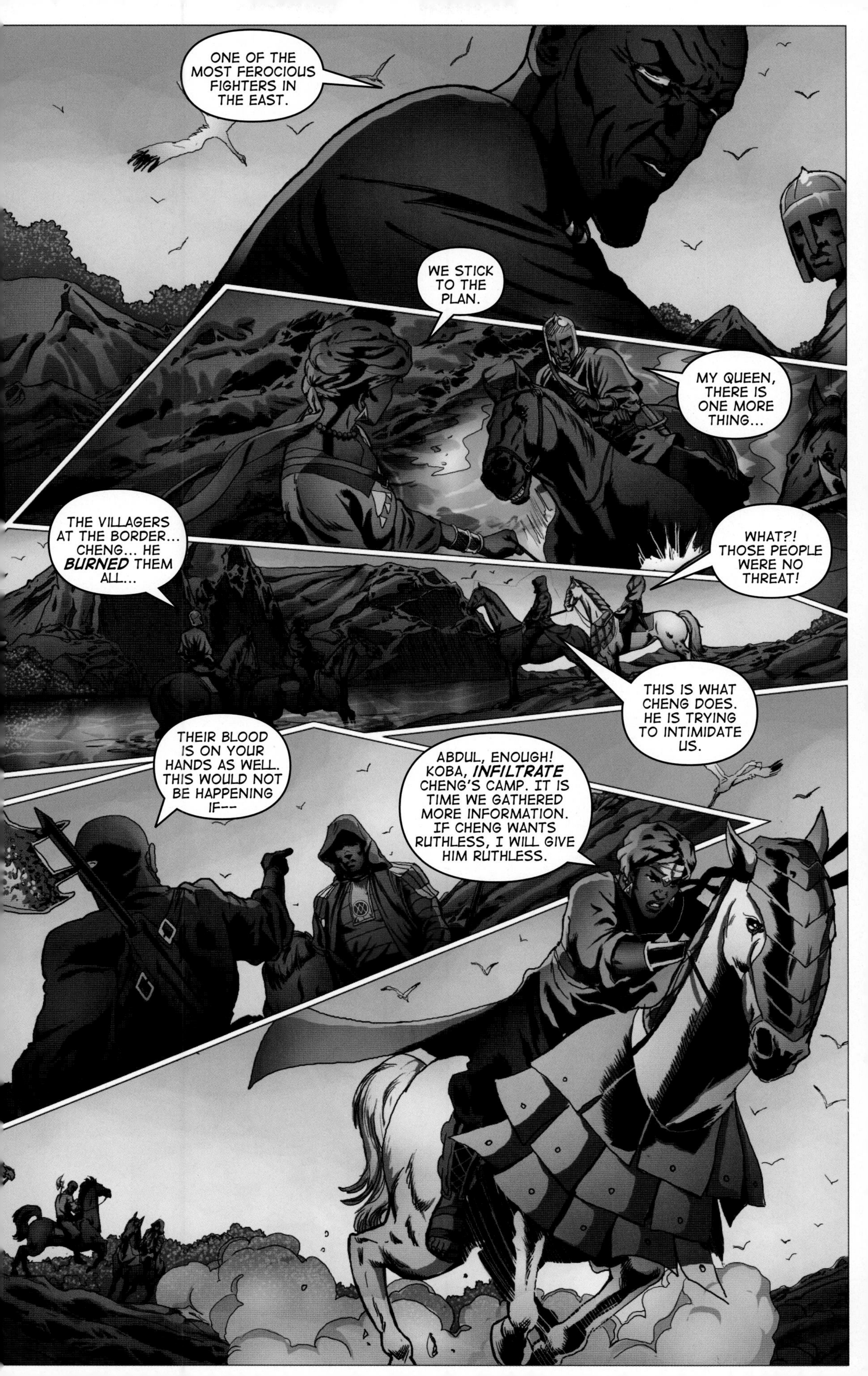
ONE OF THE MOST FEROCIOUS FIGHTERS IN THE EAST.
WE STICK TO THE PLAN.
MY QUEEN, THERE IS ONE MORE THING...
THE VILLAGERS AT THE BORDER... CHENG... HE *BURNED* THEM ALL...
WHAT?! THOSE PEOPLE WERE NO THREAT!
THIS IS WHAT CHENG DOES. HE IS TRYING TO INTIMIDATE US.
THEIR BLOOD IS ON YOUR HANDS AS WELL. THIS WOULD NOT BE HAPPENING IF--
ABDUL, ENOUGH! KOBA, *INFILTRATE* CHENG'S CAMP. IT IS TIME WE GATHERED MORE INFORMATION. IF CHENG WANTS RUTHLESS, I WILL GIVE HIM RUTHLESS.

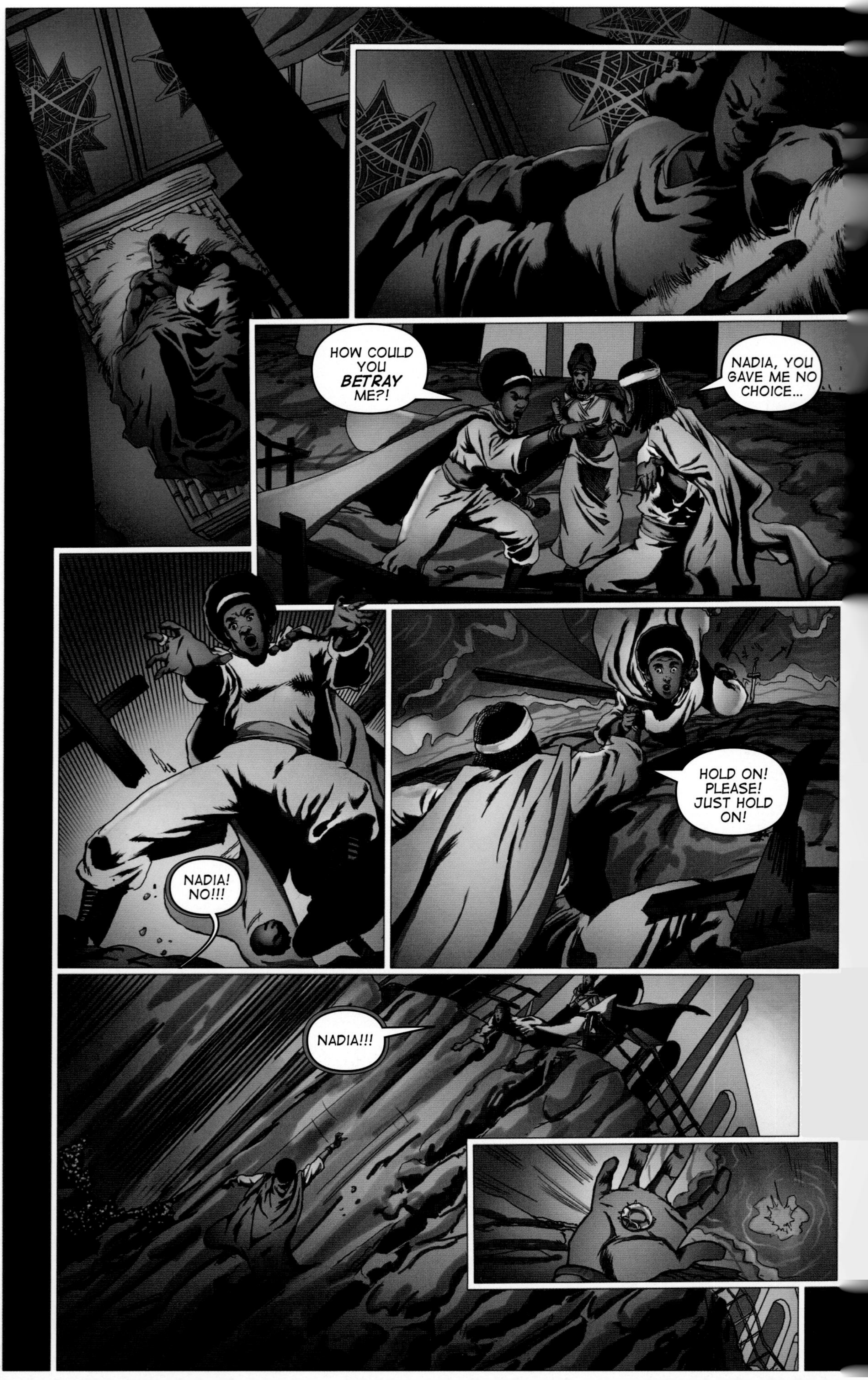
HOW COULD YOU BETRAY ME?!
NADIA, YOU GAVE ME NO CHOICE...
NADIA! NO!!!
HOLD ON! PLEASE! JUST HOLD ON!
NADIA!!!

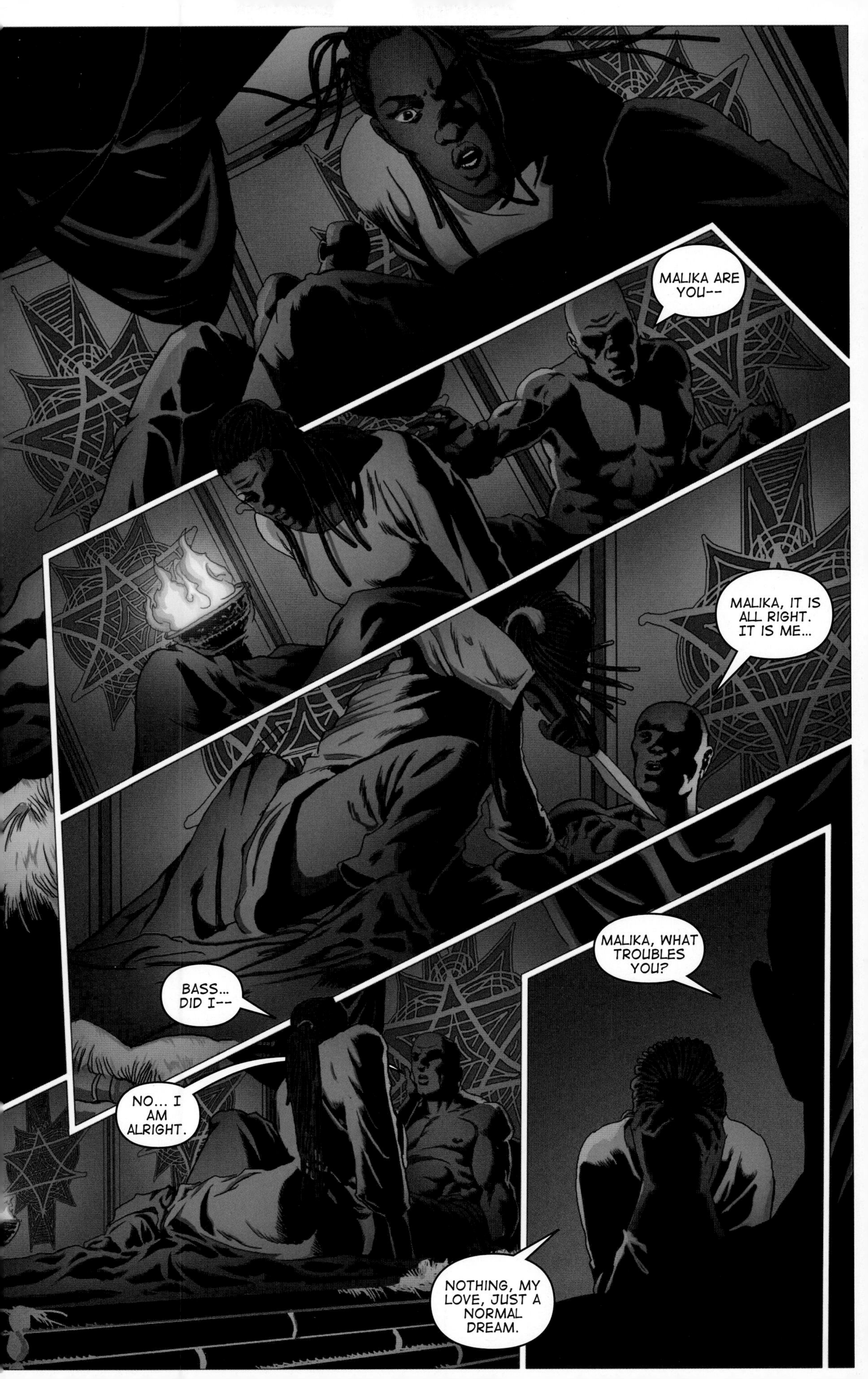
MALIKA ARE YOU--
MALIKA, IT IS ALL RIGHT. IT IS ME...
BASS... DID I--
NO... I AM ALRIGHT.
MALIKA, WHAT TROUBLES YOU?
NOTHING, MY LOVE, JUST A NORMAL DREAM.

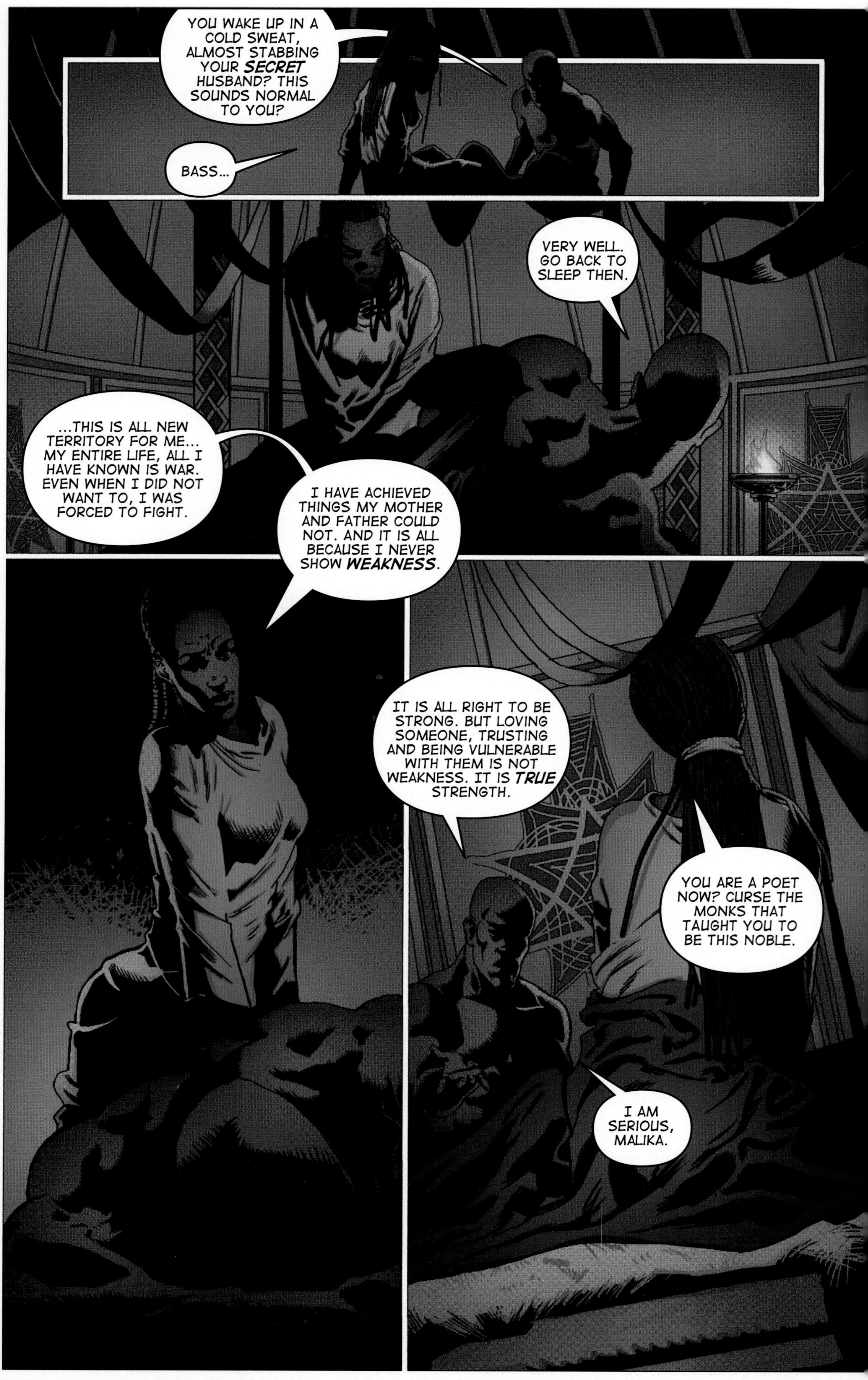
YOU WAKE UP IN A COLD SWEAT, ALMOST STABBING YOUR SECRET HUSBAND? THIS SOUNDS NORMAL TO YOU?
BASS...
VERY WELL. GO BACK TO SLEEP THEN.
...THIS IS ALL NEW TERRITORY FOR ME... MY ENTIRE LIFE, ALL I HAVE KNOWN IS WAR. EVEN WHEN I DID NOT WANT TO, I WAS FORCED TO FIGHT.
I HAVE ACHIEVED THINGS MY MOTHER AND FATHER COULD NOT. AND IT IS ALL BECAUSE I NEVER SHOW WEAKNESS.
IT IS ALL RIGHT TO BE STRONG. BUT LOVING SOMEONE, TRUSTING AND BEING VULNERABLE WITH THEM IS NOT WEAKNESS. IT IS TRUE STRENGTH.
YOU ARE A POET NOW? CURSE THE MONKS THAT TAUGHT YOU TO BE THIS NOBLE.
I AM SERIOUS, MALIKA.

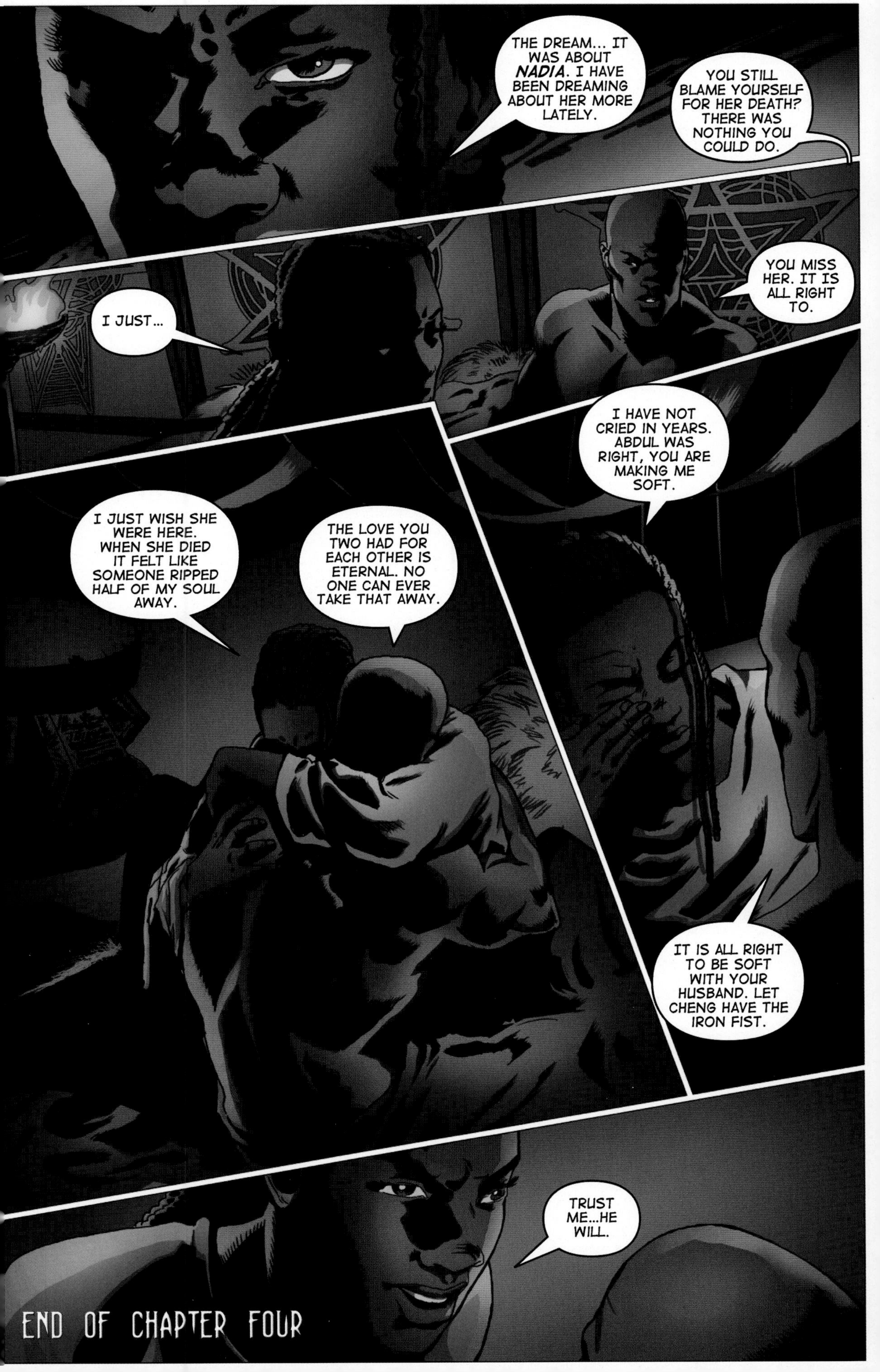
THE DREAM... IT WAS ABOUT **NADIA**. I HAVE BEEN DREAMING ABOUT HER MORE LATELY.
YOU STILL BLAME YOURSELF FOR HER DEATH? THERE WAS NOTHING YOU COULD DO.
I JUST...
YOU MISS HER. IT IS ALL RIGHT TO.
I HAVE NOT CRIED IN YEARS. ABDUL WAS RIGHT, YOU ARE MAKING ME SOFT.
I JUST WISH SHE WERE HERE. WHEN SHE DIED IT FELT LIKE SOMEONE RIPPED HALF OF MY SOUL AWAY.
THE LOVE YOU TWO HAD FOR EACH OTHER IS ETERNAL. NO ONE CAN EVER TAKE THAT AWAY.
IT IS ALL RIGHT TO BE SOFT WITH YOUR HUSBAND. LET CHENG HAVE THE IRON FIST.
TRUST ME...HE WILL.
END OF CHAPTER FOUR

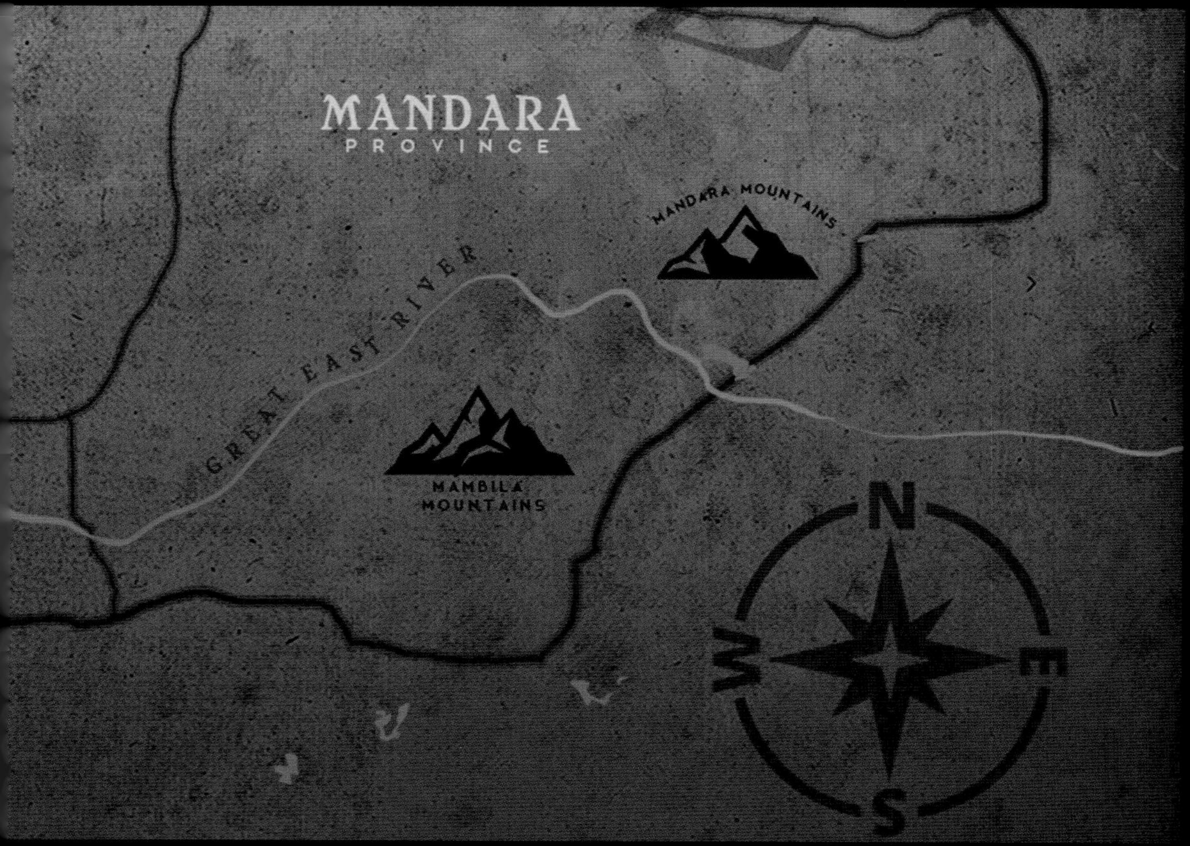
MANDARA
PROVINCE
MANDARA MOUNTAINS
GREAT EAST RIVER
MAMBILA
MOUNTAINS
N
E
S
W

THE MANDARA PROVINCE

The Mandara Province is located to the east of the City of Azzaz. The towering Manbila and Mandara mountains combined with the rough terrain at the border, provide a perfect deterrent to would-be attackers from the east. Chief Nchare currently governs the Mandara Province.

Fun Fact: The creation of the Mandara Province takes inspiration from the real life Mandara Mountains. A volcanic range along the northern part of the Cameroon-Nigeria border.

CHAPTER FIVE

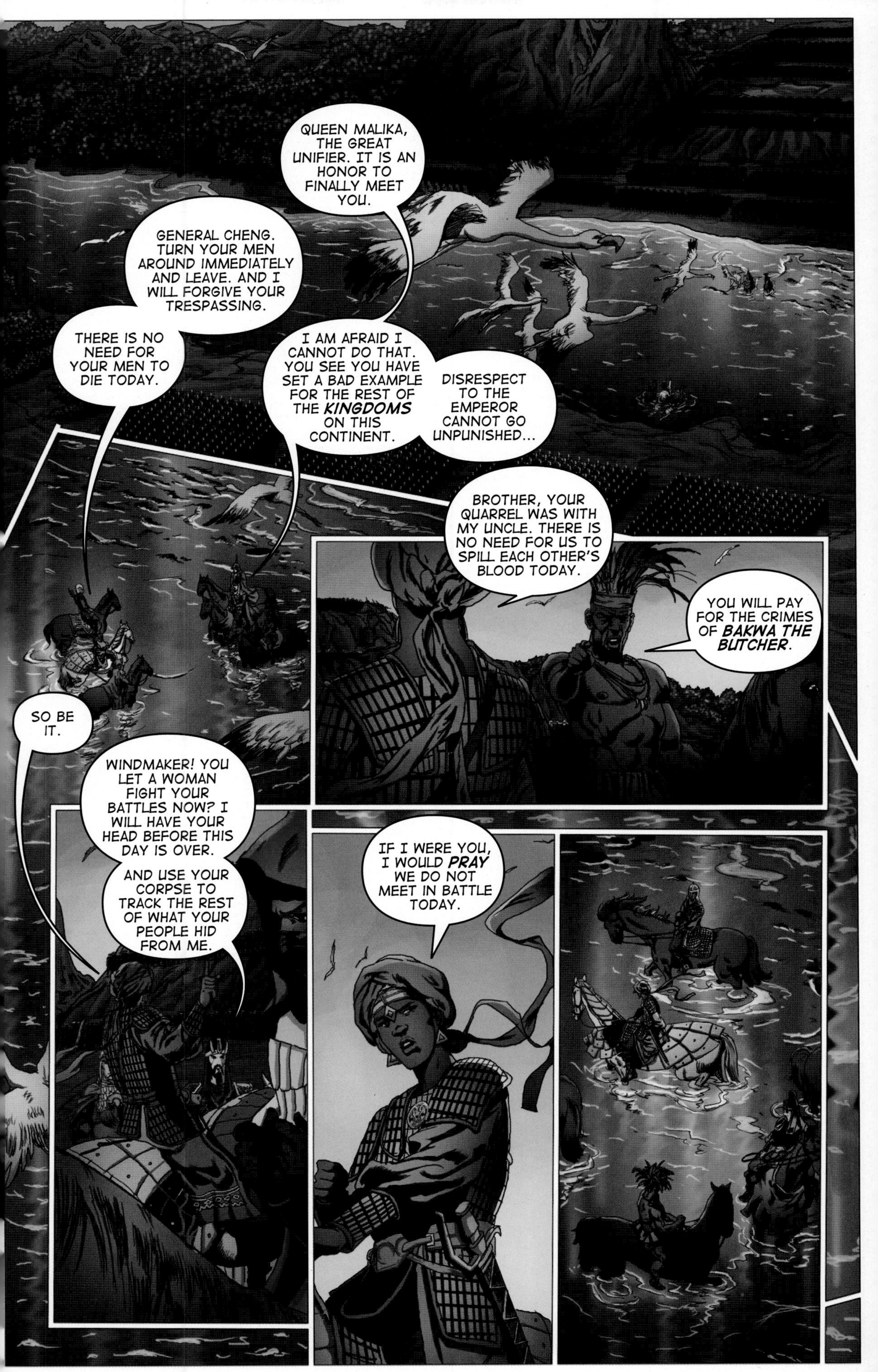
QUEEN MALIKA, THE GREAT UNIFIER. IT IS AN HONOR TO FINALLY MEET YOU.
GENERAL CHENG. TURN YOUR MEN AROUND IMMEDIATELY AND LEAVE. AND I WILL FORGIVE YOUR TRESPASSING.
THERE IS NO NEED FOR YOUR MEN TO DIE TODAY.
I AM AFRAID I CANNOT DO THAT. YOU SEE YOU HAVE SET A BAD EXAMPLE FOR THE REST OF THE KINGDOMS ON THIS CONTINENT.
DISRESPECT TO THE EMPEROR CANNOT GO UNPUNISHED...
BROTHER, YOUR QUARREL WAS WITH MY UNCLE. THERE IS NO NEED FOR US TO SPILL EACH OTHER'S BLOOD TODAY.
YOU WILL PAY FOR THE CRIMES OF BAKWA THE BUTCHER.
SO BE IT.
WINDMAKER! YOU LET A WOMAN FIGHT YOUR BATTLES NOW? I WILL HAVE YOUR HEAD BEFORE THIS DAY IS OVER.
AND USE YOUR CORPSE TO TRACK THE REST OF WHAT YOUR PEOPLE HID FROM ME.
IF I WERE YOU, I WOULD PRAY WE DO NOT MEET IN BATTLE TODAY.

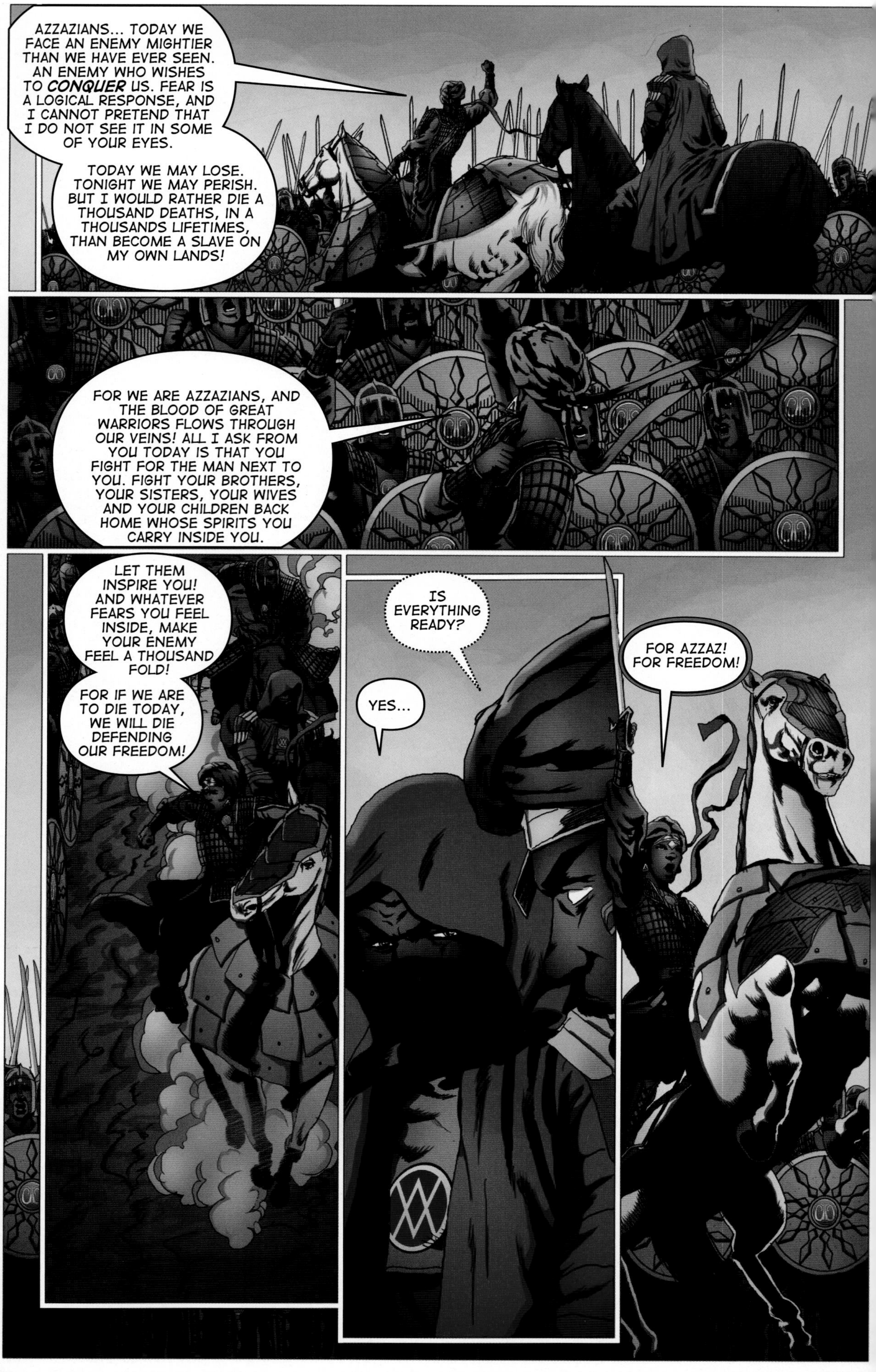
AZZAZIANS... TODAY WE FACE AN ENEMY MIGHTIER THAN WE HAVE EVER SEEN. AN ENEMY WHO WISHES TO *CONQUER* US. FEAR IS A LOGICAL RESPONSE, AND I CANNOT PRETEND THAT I DO NOT SEE IT IN SOME OF YOUR EYES.
TODAY WE MAY LOSE. TONIGHT WE MAY PERISH. BUT I WOULD RATHER DIE A THOUSAND DEATHS, IN A THOUSANDS LIFETIMES, THAN BECOME A SLAVE ON MY OWN LANDS!
FOR WE ARE AZZAZIANS, AND THE BLOOD OF GREAT WARRIORS FLOWS THROUGH OUR VEINS! ALL I ASK FROM YOU TODAY IS THAT YOU FIGHT FOR THE MAN NEXT TO YOU. FIGHT YOUR BROTHERS, YOUR SISTERS, YOUR WIVES AND YOUR CHILDREN BACK HOME WHOSE SPIRITS YOU CARRY INSIDE YOU.
LET THEM INSPIRE YOU! AND WHATEVER FEARS YOU FEEL INSIDE, MAKE YOUR ENEMY FEEL A THOUSAND FOLD!
FOR IF WE ARE TO DIE TODAY, WE WILL DIE DEFENDING OUR FREEDOM!
IS EVERYTHING READY?
YES...
FOR AZZAZ! FOR FREEDOM!

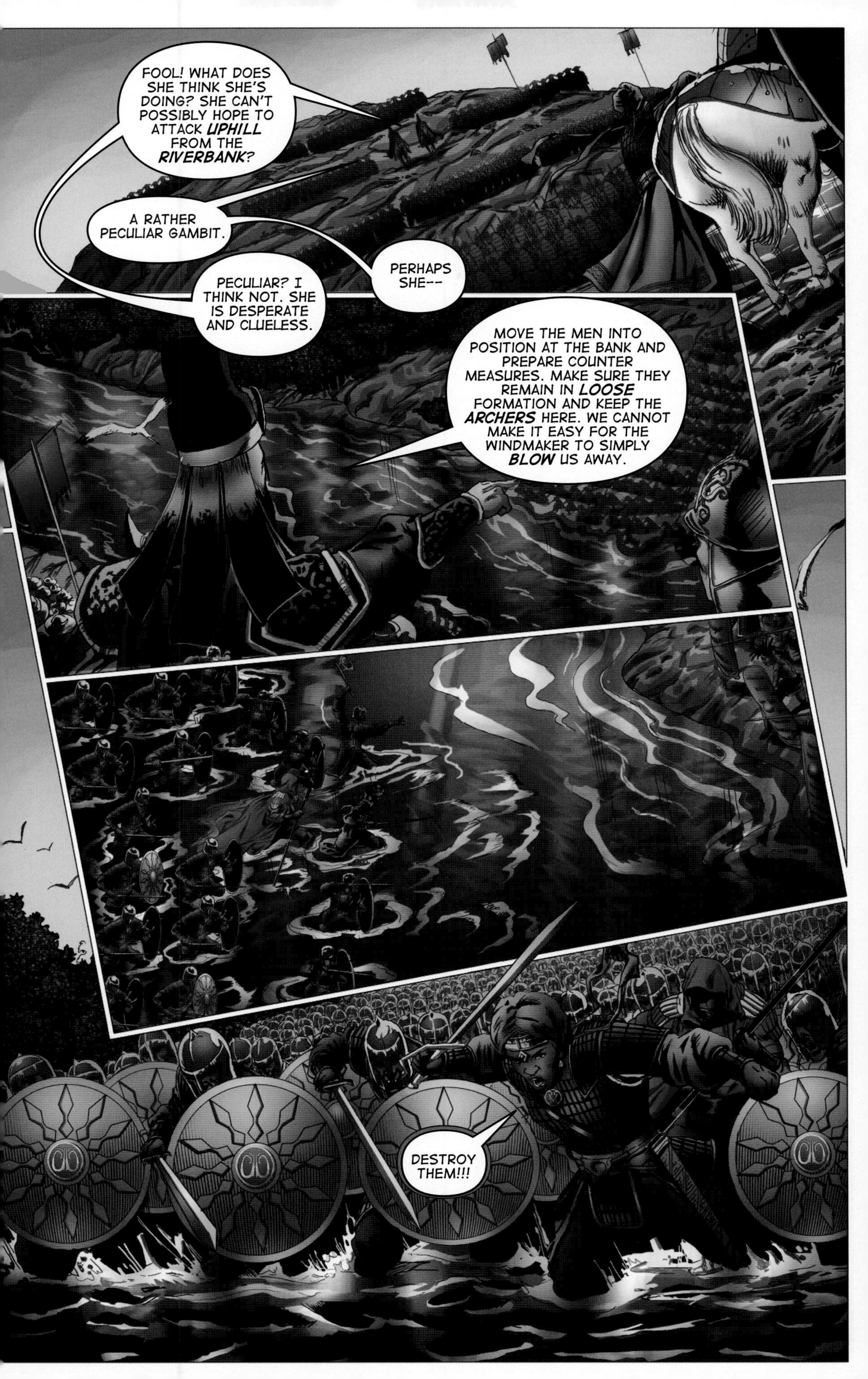
FOOL! WHAT DOES SHE THINK SHE'S DOING? SHE CAN'T POSSIBLY HOPE TO ATTACK UPHILL FROM THE RIVERBANK?
A RATHER PECULIAR GAMBIT.
PERHAPS SHE--
PECULIAR? I THINK NOT. SHE IS DESPERATE AND CLUELESS.
MOVE THE MEN INTO POSITION AT THE BANK AND PREPARE COUNTER MEASURES. MAKE SURE THEY REMAIN IN LOOSE FORMATION AND KEEP THE ARCHERS HERE. WE CANNOT MAKE IT EASY FOR THE WINDMAKER TO SIMPLY BLOW US AWAY.
DESTROY THEM!!!

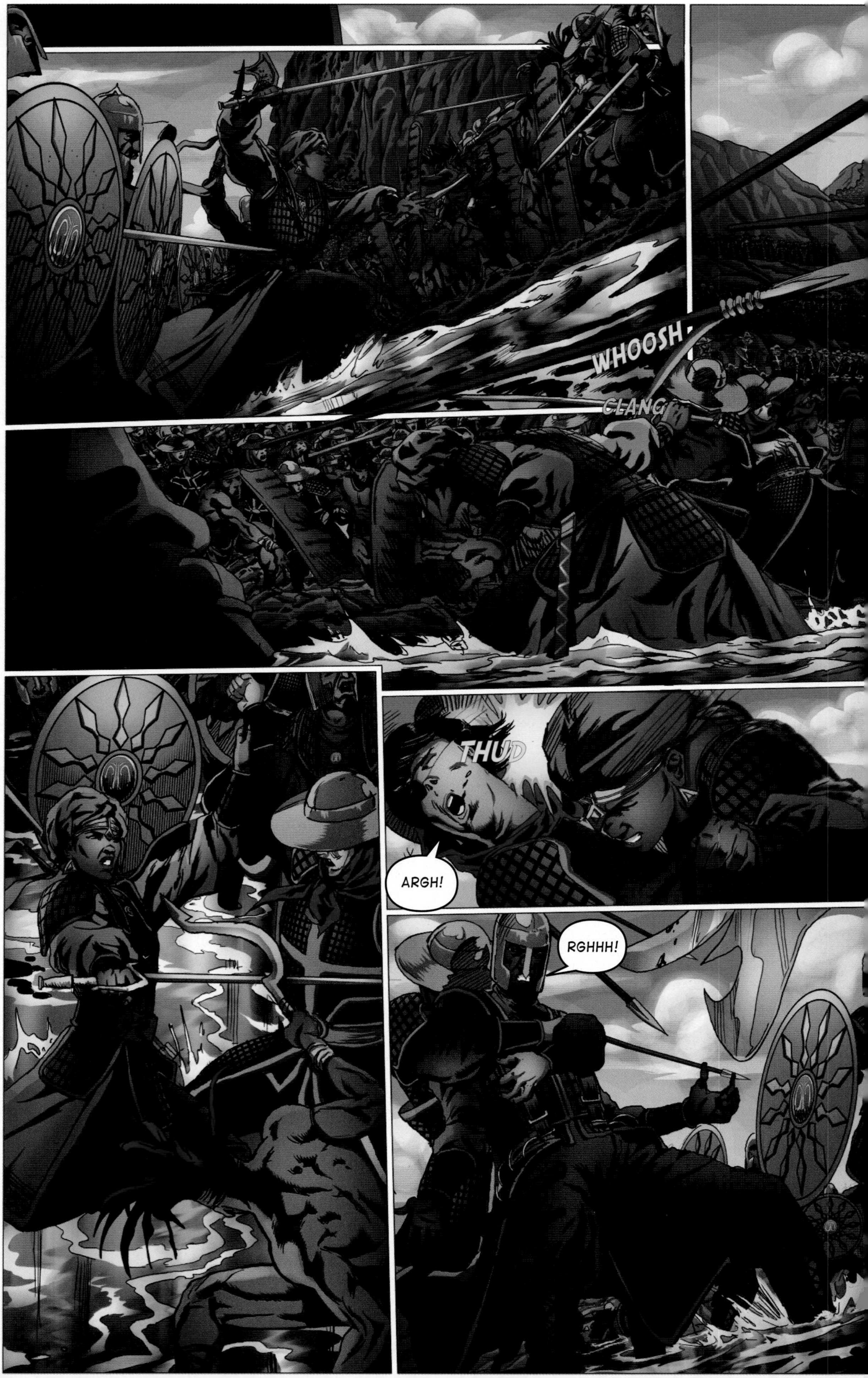
WHOOSH
CLANG
THUD
ARGH!
RGHHH!

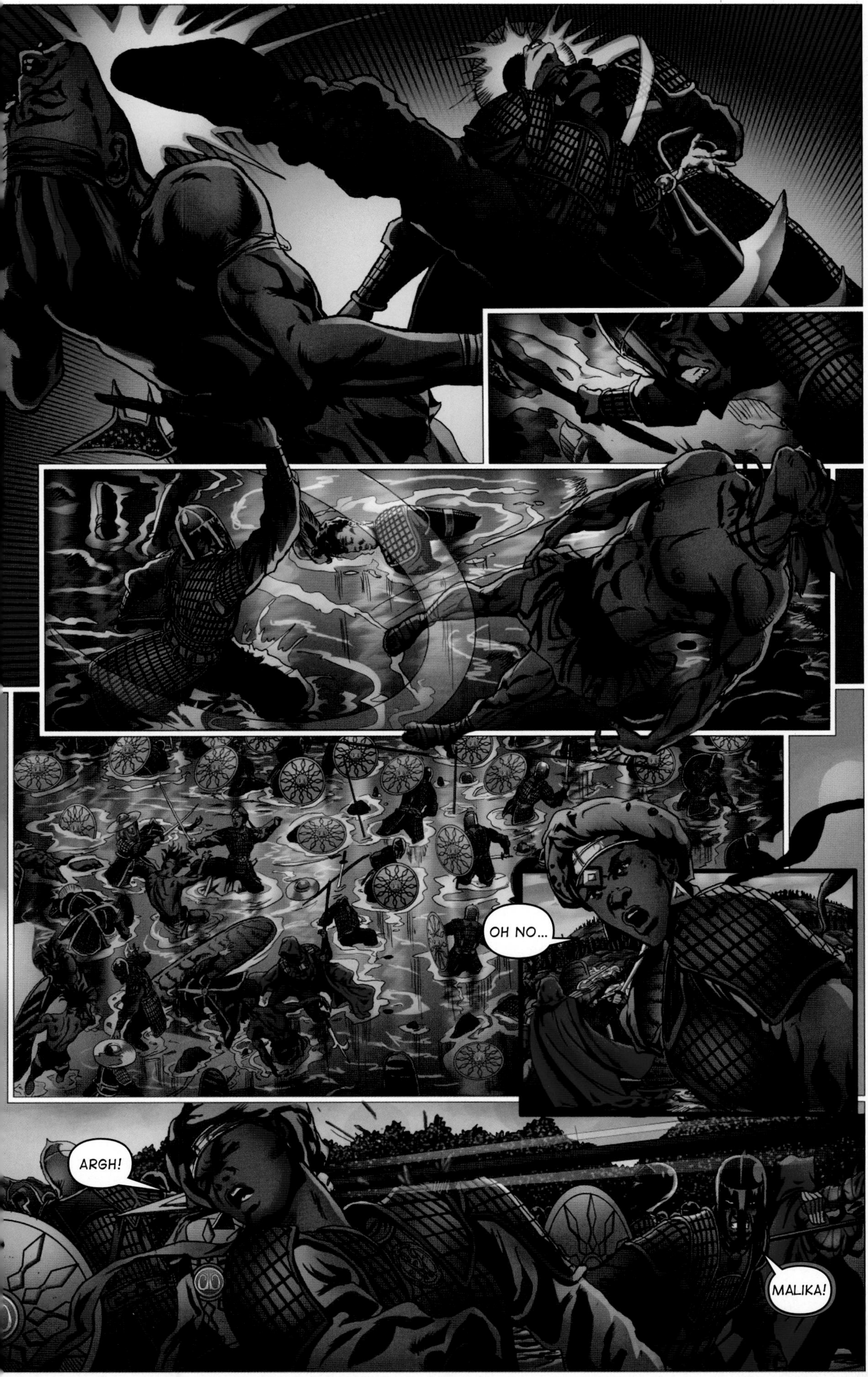
OH NO...
ARGH!
MALIKA!

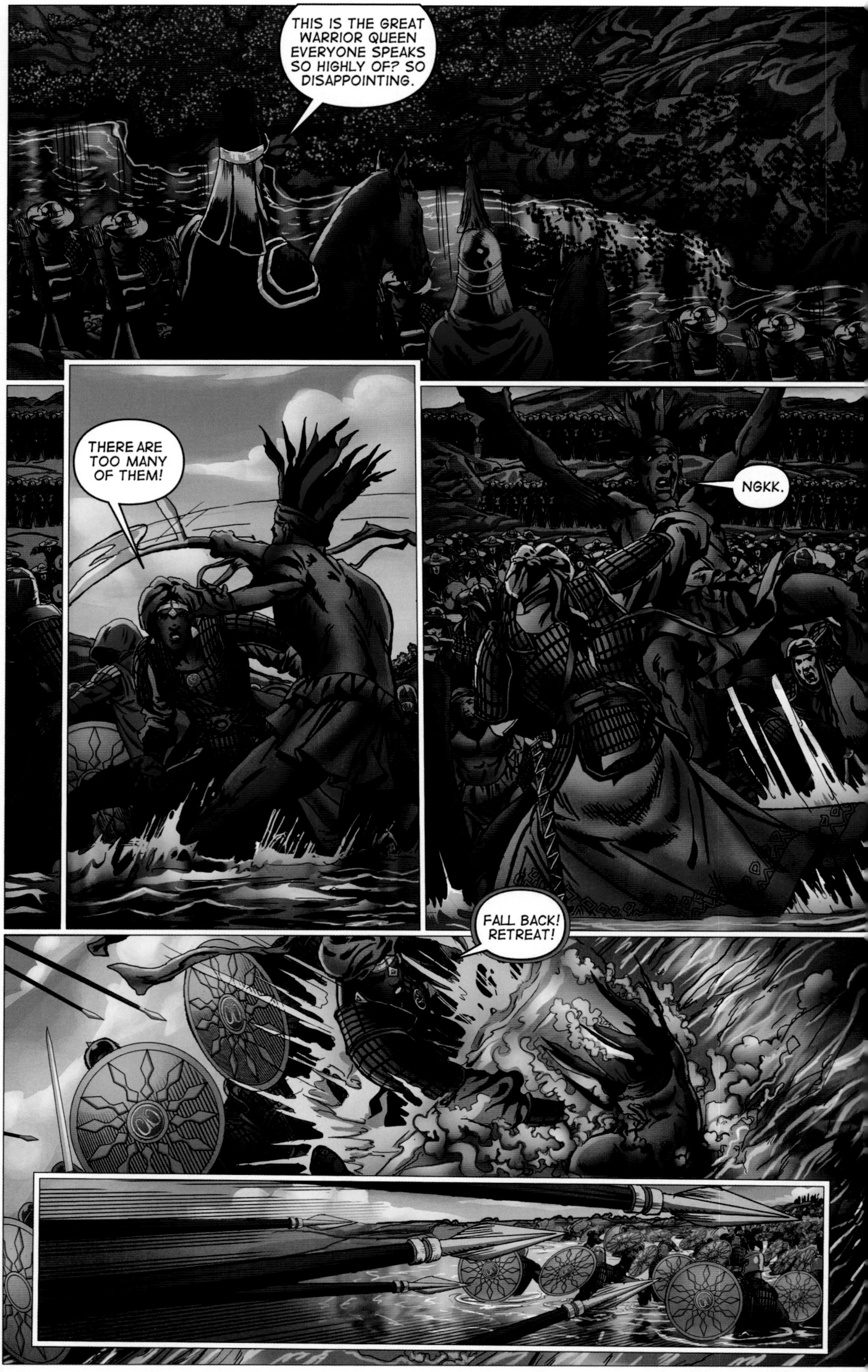
THIS IS THE GREAT WARRIOR QUEEN EVERYONE SPEAKS SO HIGHLY OF? SO DISAPPOINTING.
THERE ARE TOO MANY OF THEM!
NGKK.
FALL BACK! RETREAT!

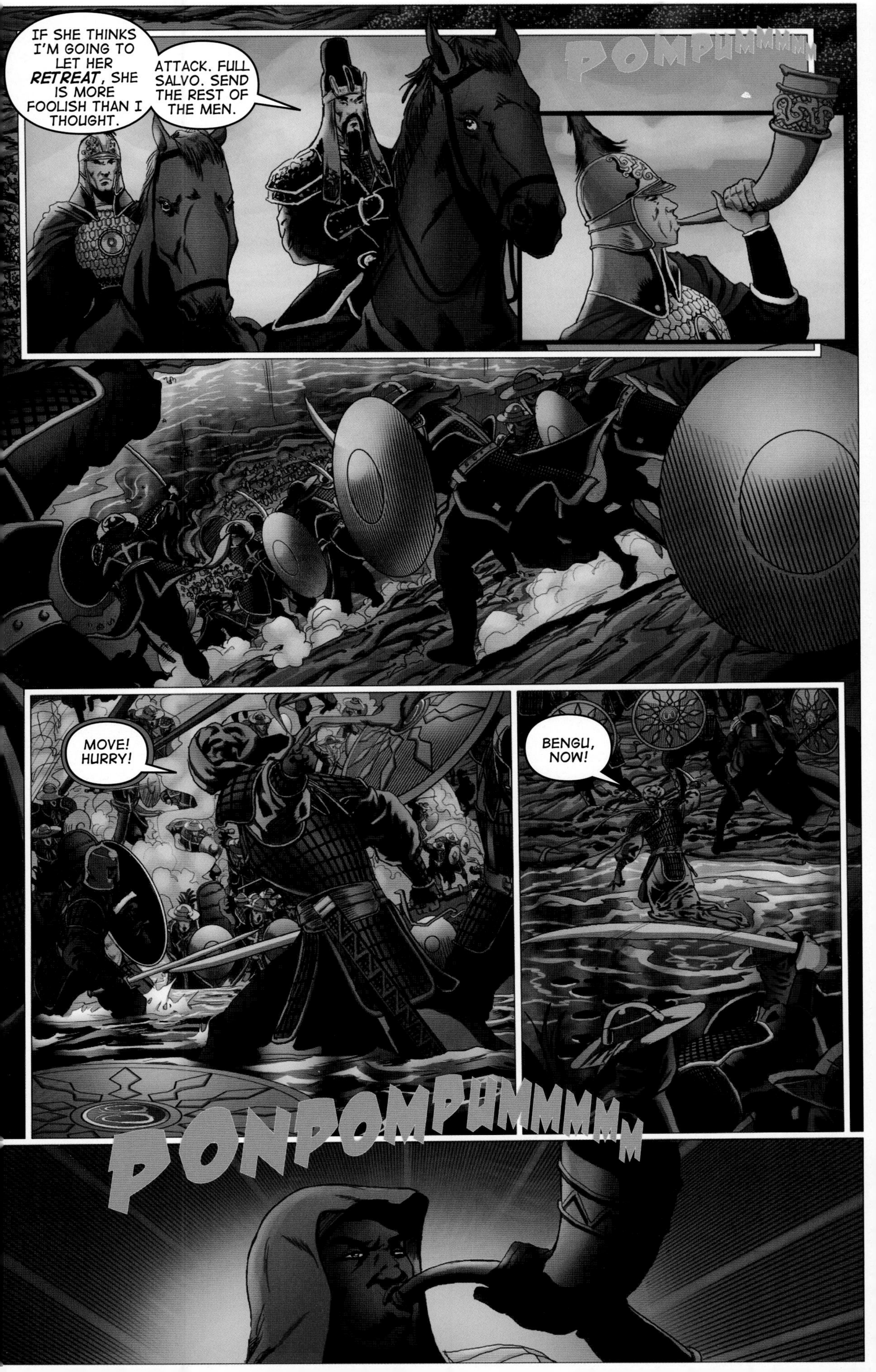
IF SHE THINKS I'M GOING TO LET HER RETREAT, SHE IS MORE FOOLISH THAN I THOUGHT.
ATTACK. FULL SALVO. SEND THE REST OF THE MEN.
POMPUMMMMM
MOVE! HURRY!
BENGU, NOW!
PONPOMPUMMMMM

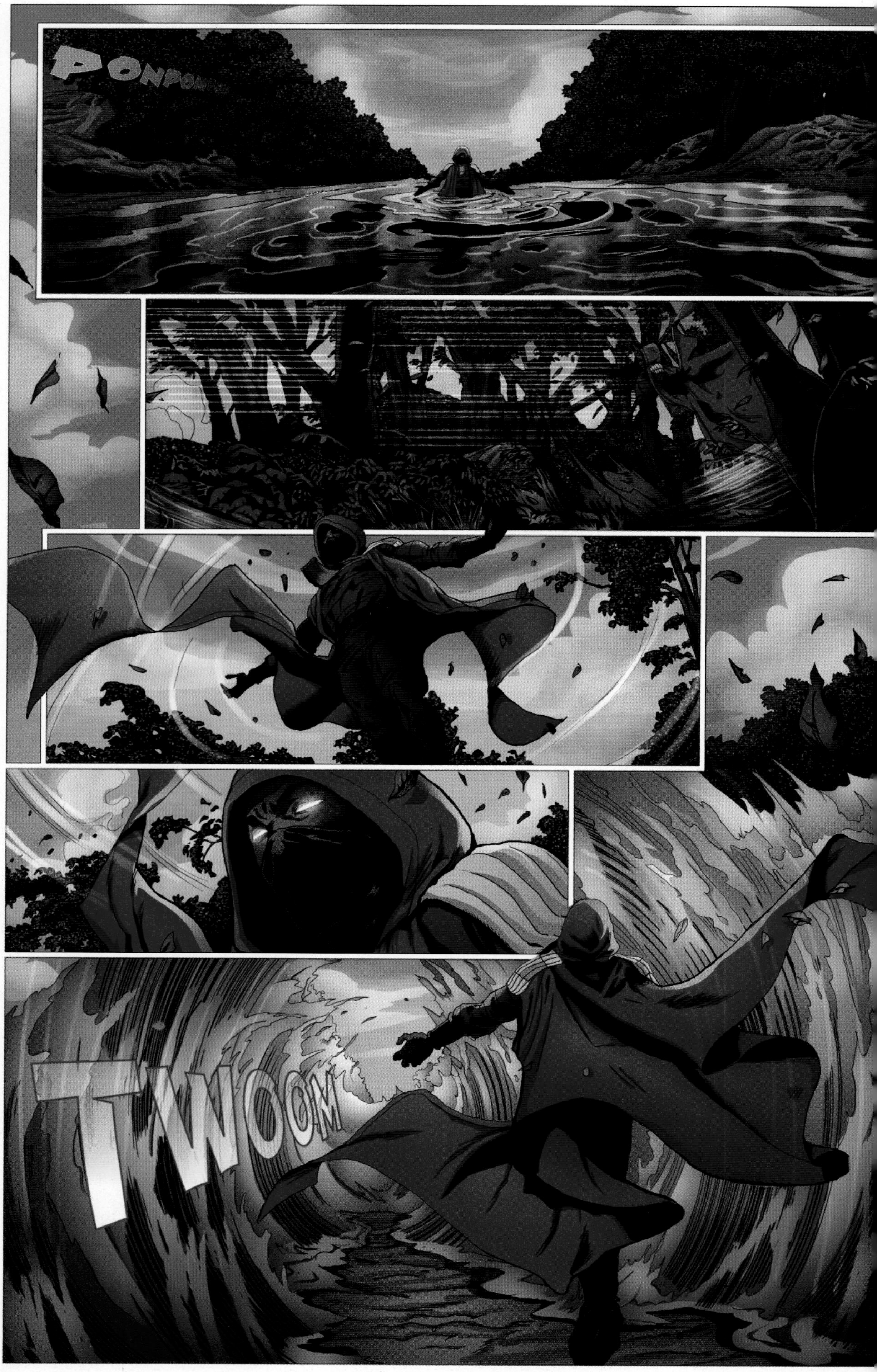
PONPON
TWOOM

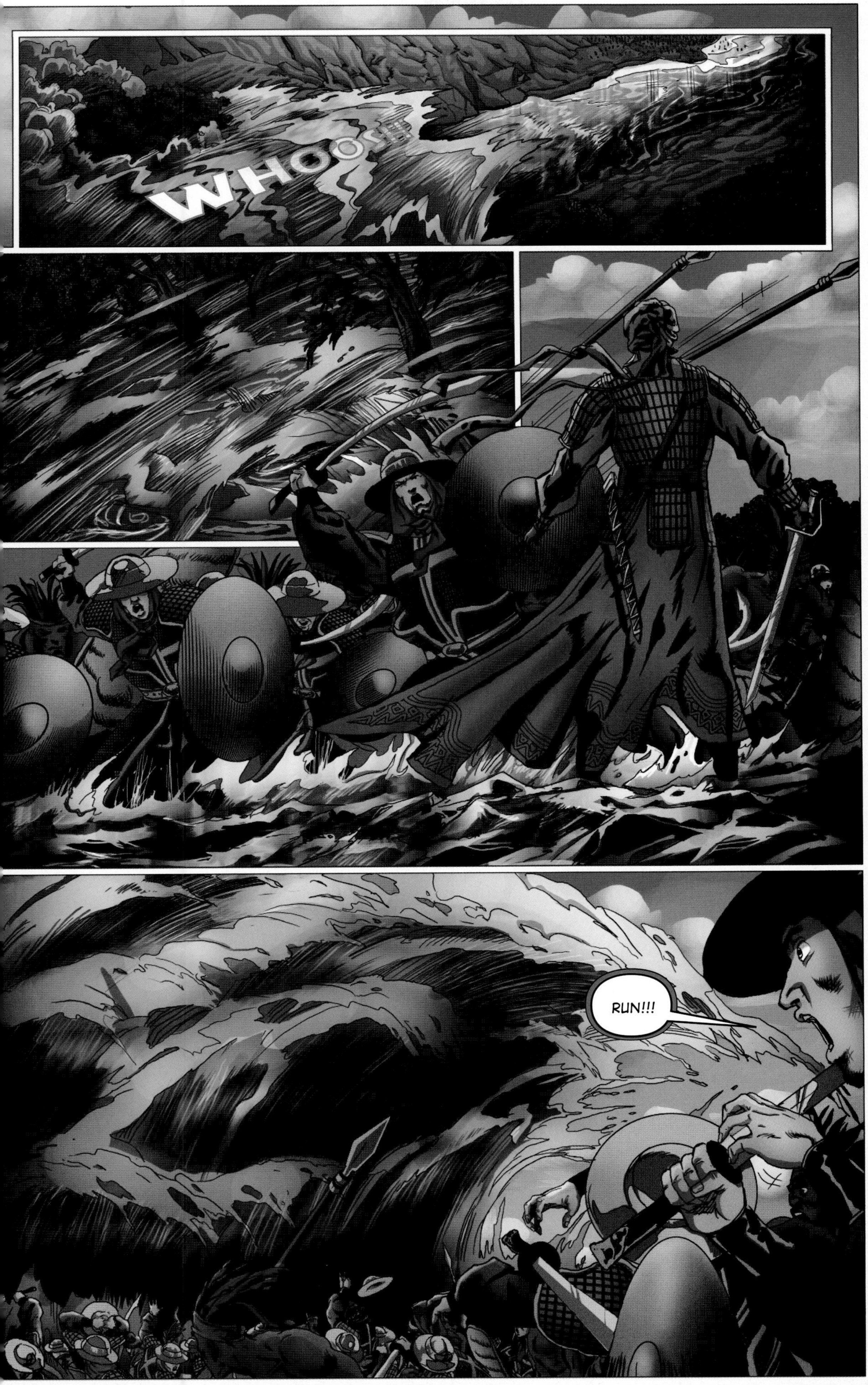
WHOOSH!
RUN!!!

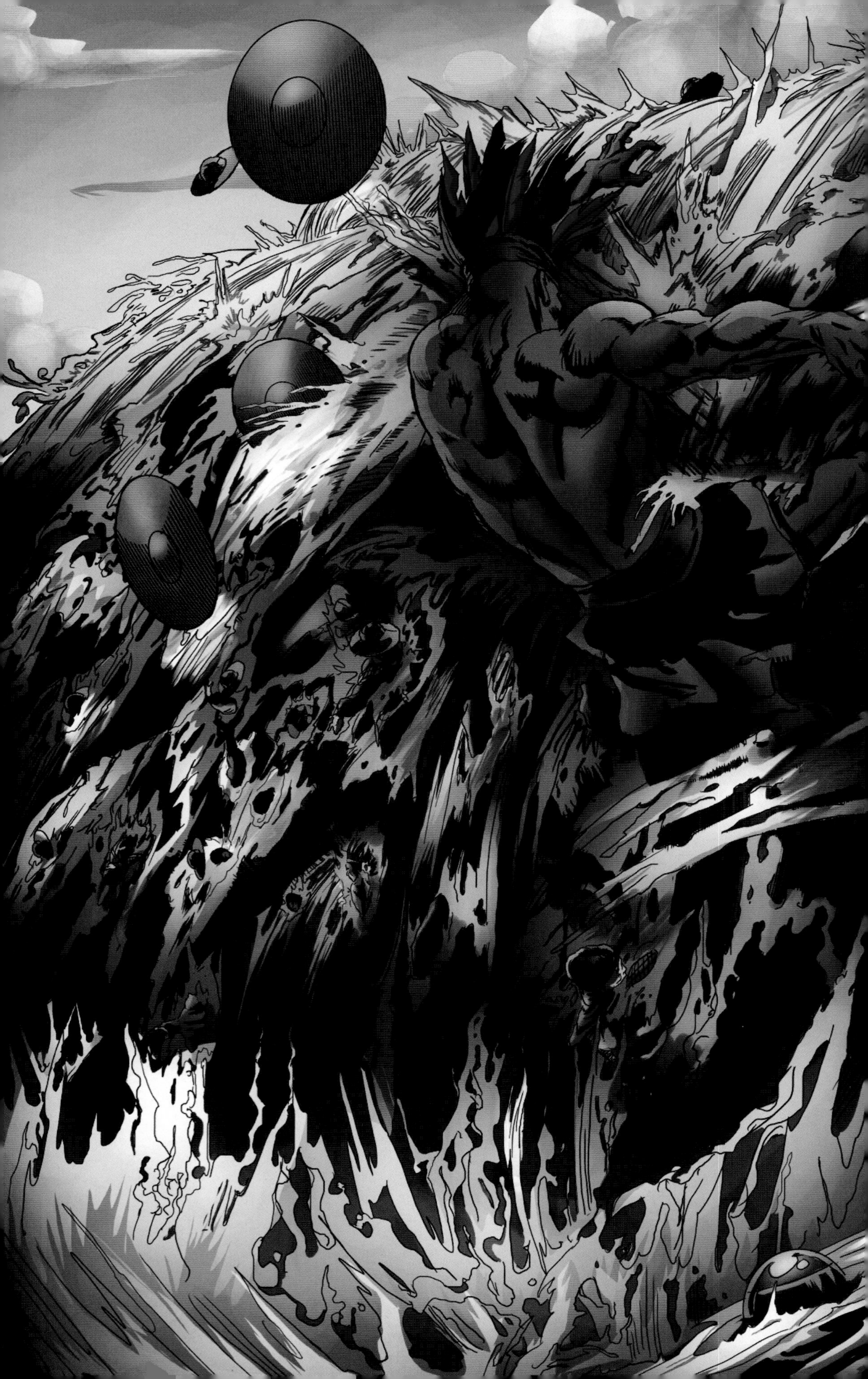

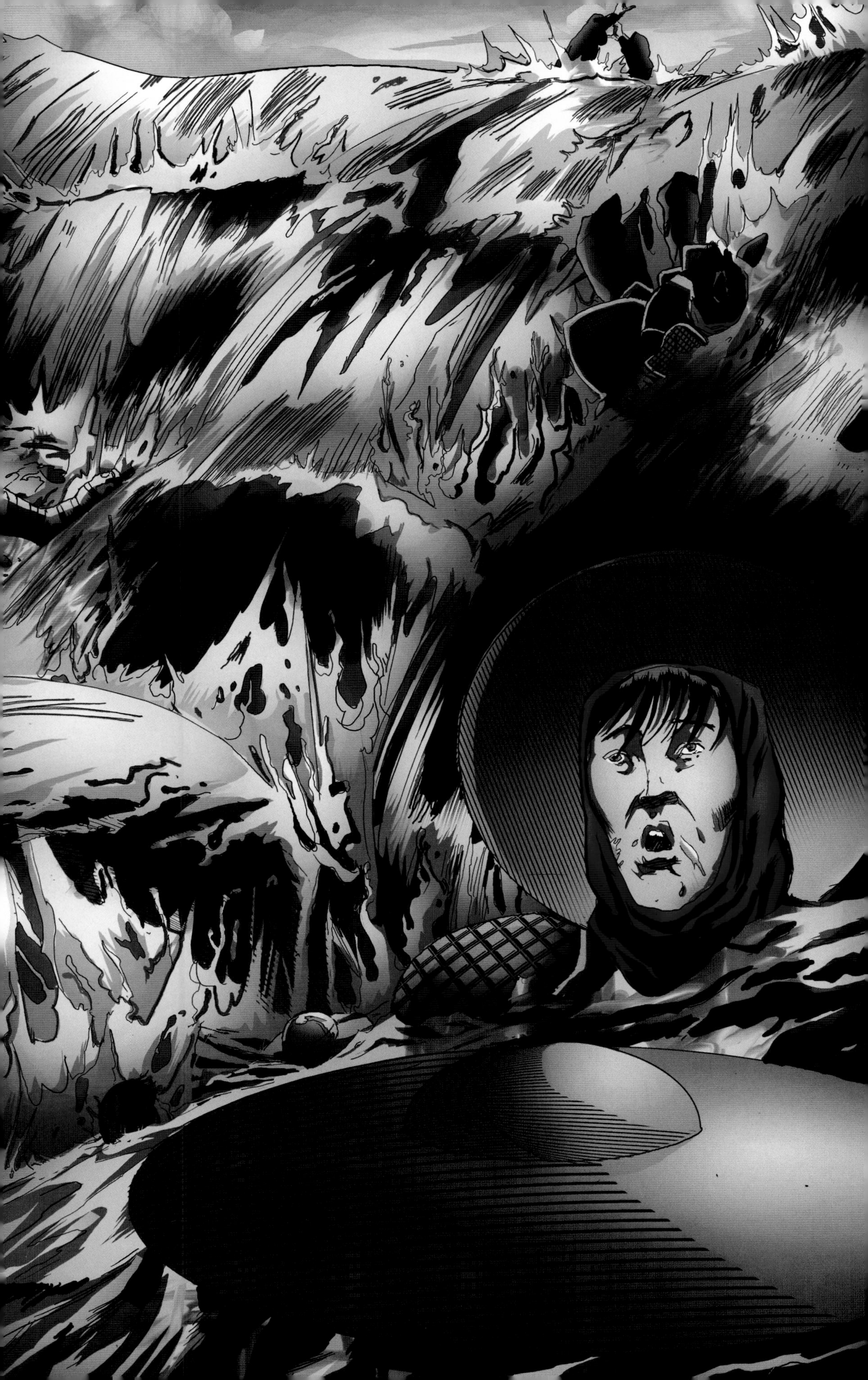

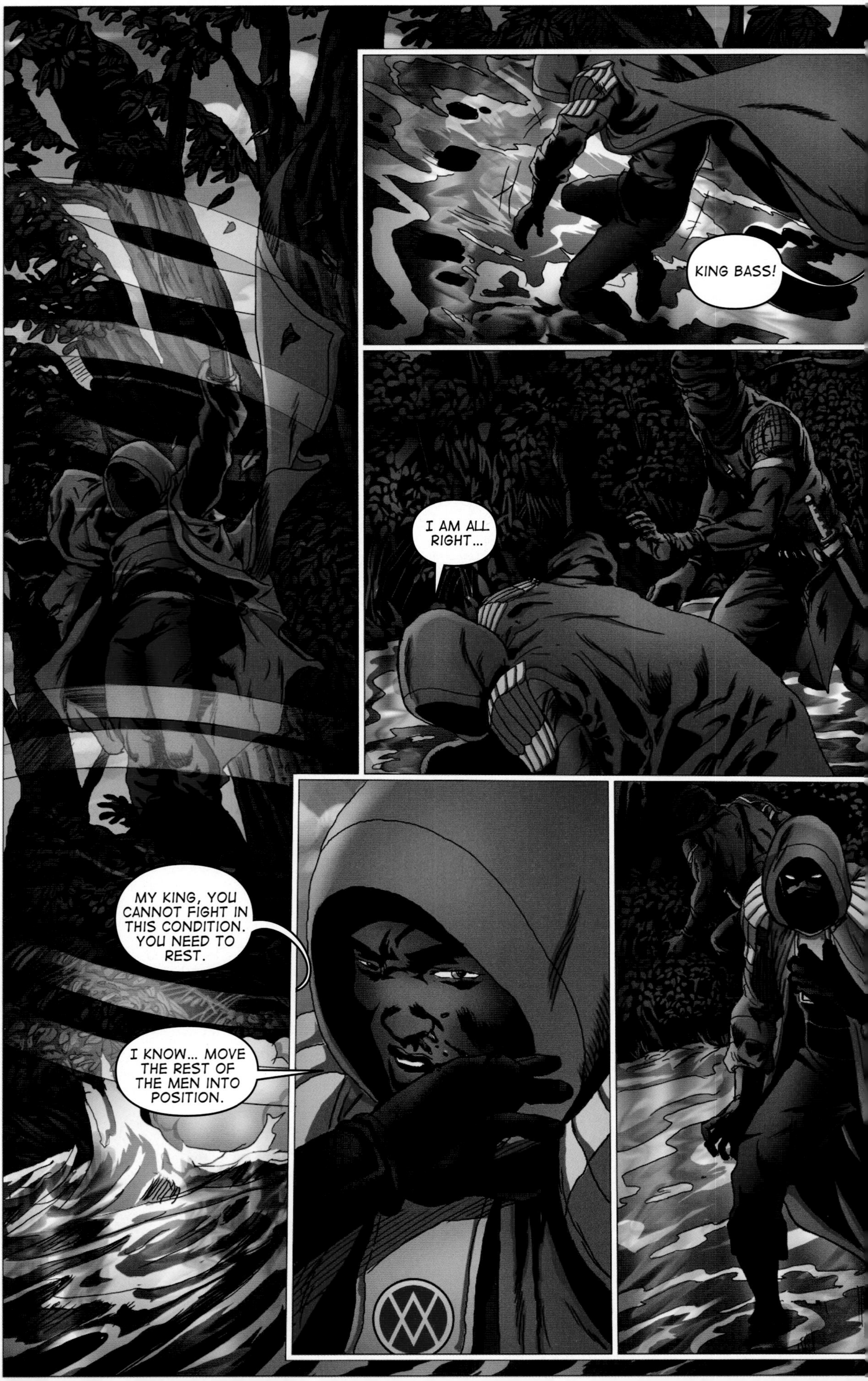
KING BASS!
I AM ALL RIGHT...
MY KING, YOU CANNOT FIGHT IN THIS CONDITION. YOU NEED TO REST.
I KNOW... MOVE THE REST OF THE MEN INTO POSITION.

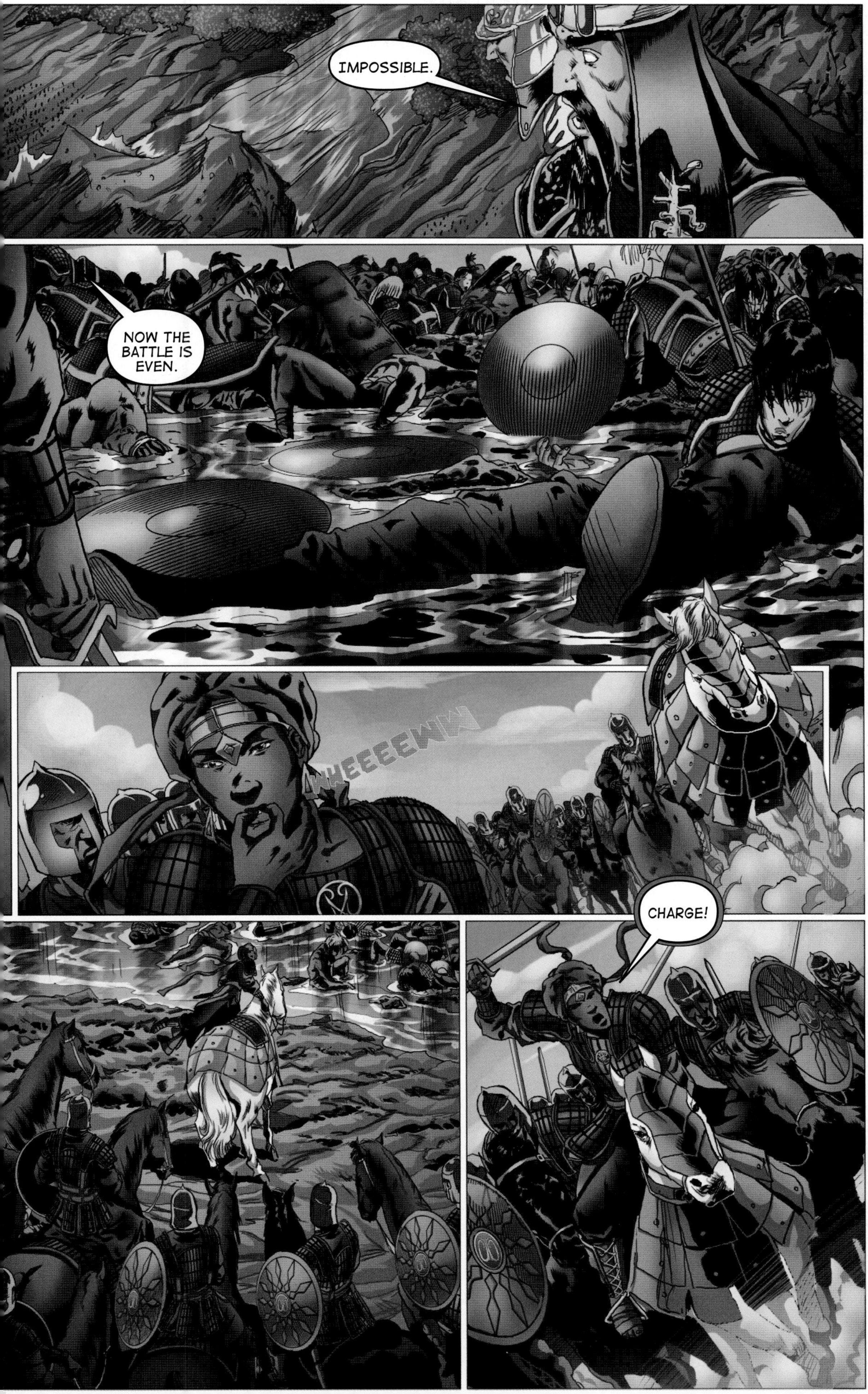
IMPOSSIBLE.
NOW THE BATTLE IS EVEN.
WHEEEEENN
CHARGE!

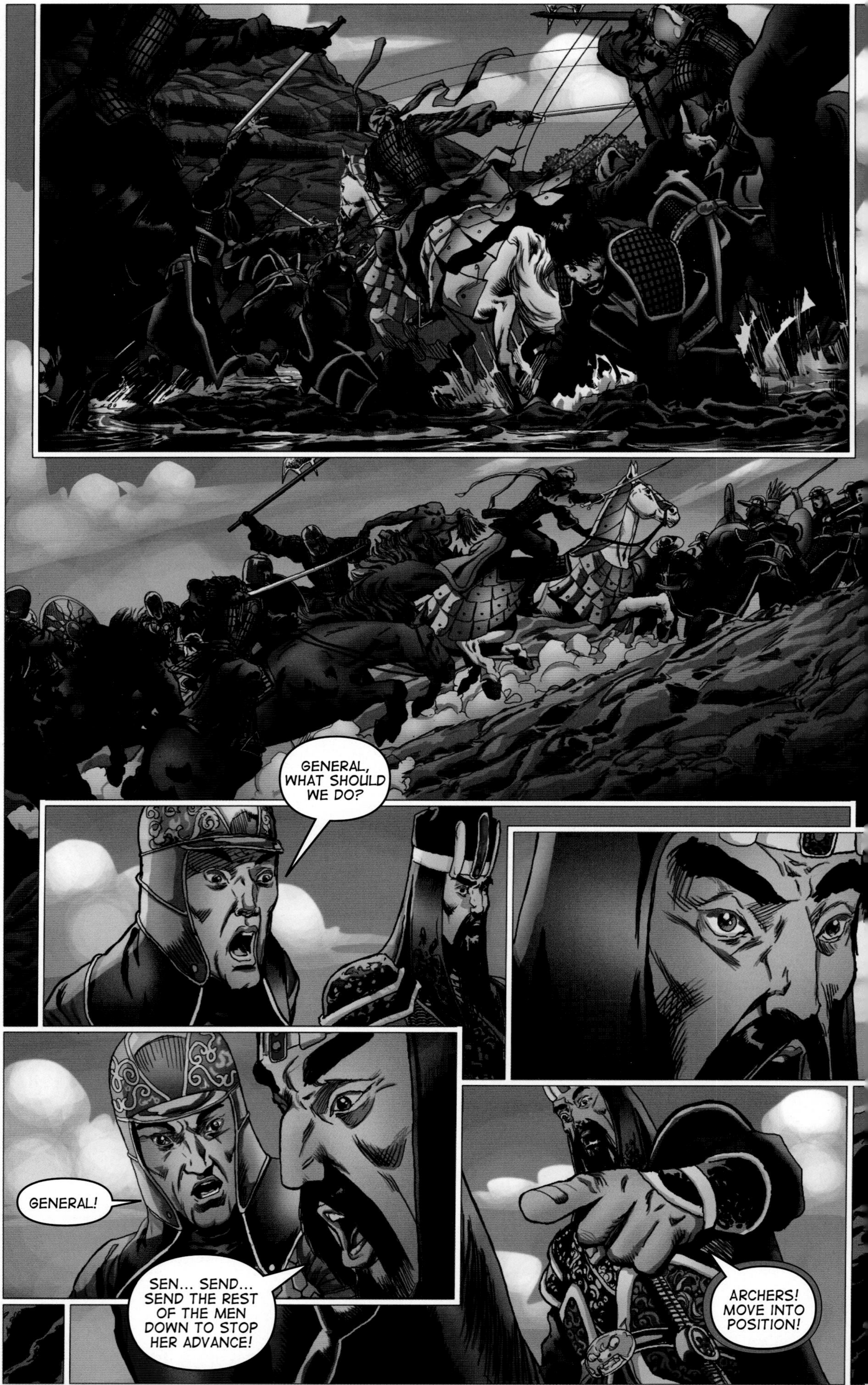
GENERAL, WHAT SHOULD WE DO?
GENERAL!
SEN... SEND... SEND THE REST OF THE MEN DOWN TO STOP HER ADVANCE!
ARCHERS! MOVE INTO POSITION!

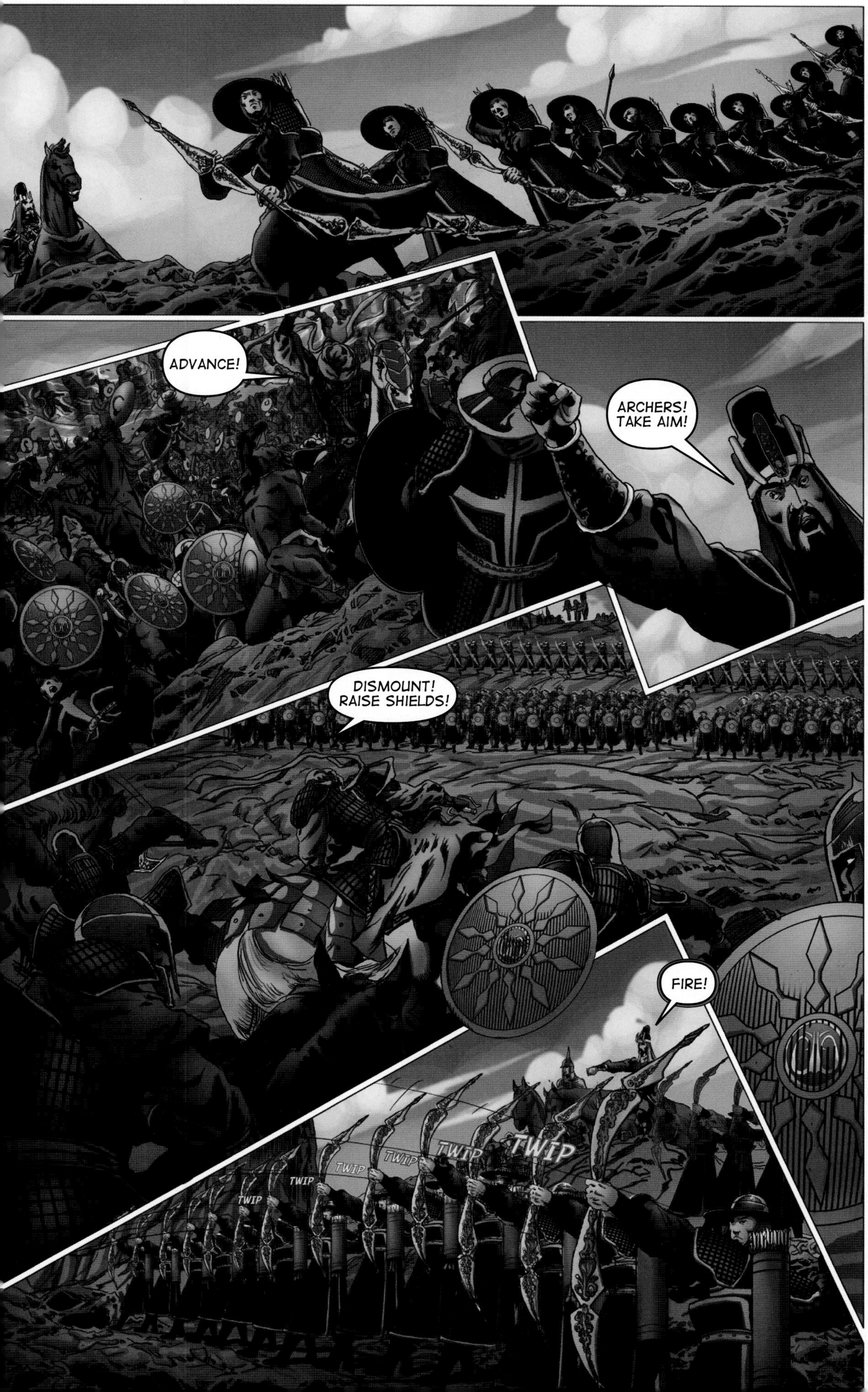
ADVANCE!
ARCHERS! TAKE AIM!
DISMOUNT! RAISE SHIELDS!
FIRE!
TWIP
TWIP
TWIP
TWIP
TWIP
TWIP

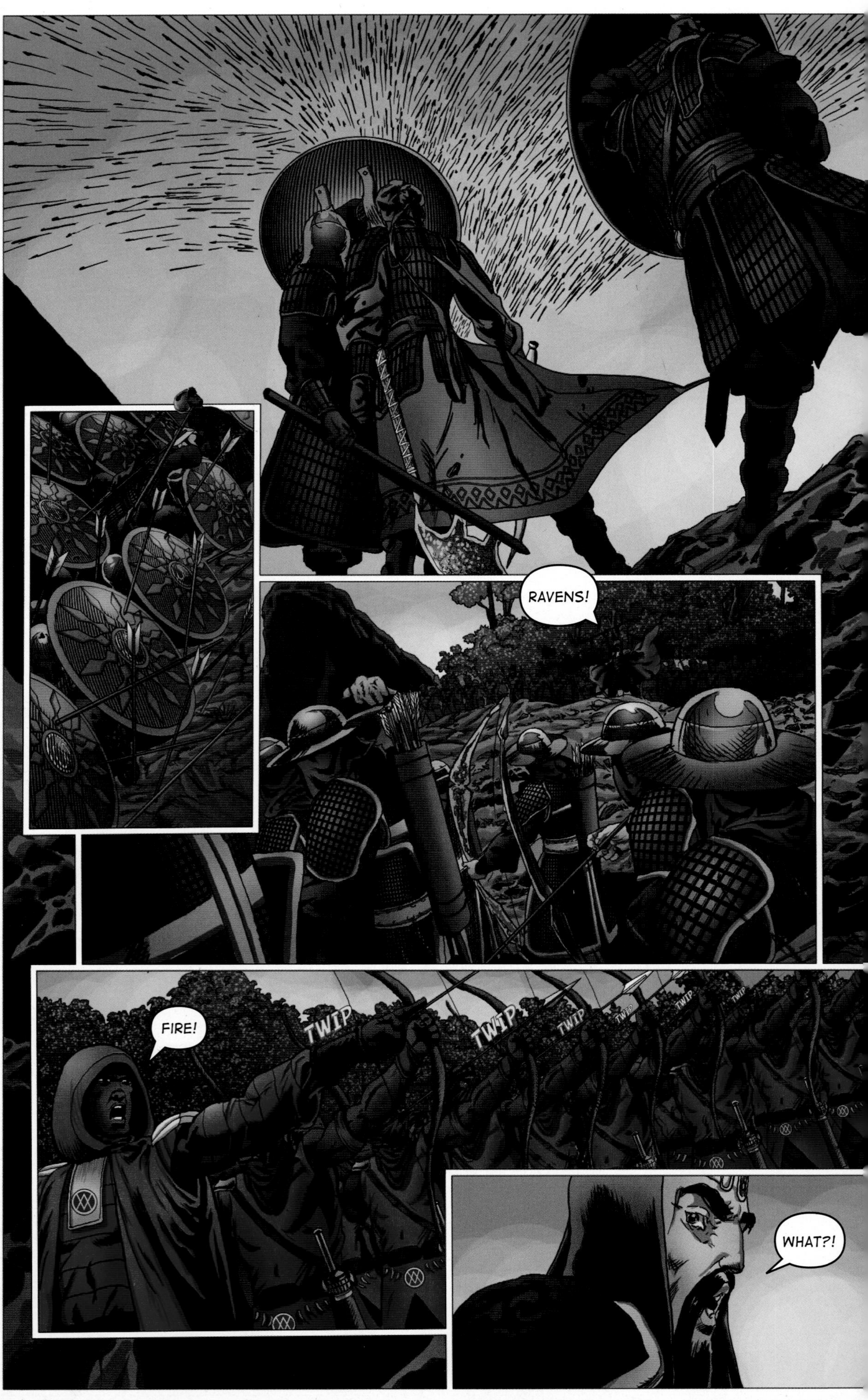
RAVENS!
FIRE!
TWIP
TWIP
TWIP
TWIP
TWIP
TWIP
WHAT?!

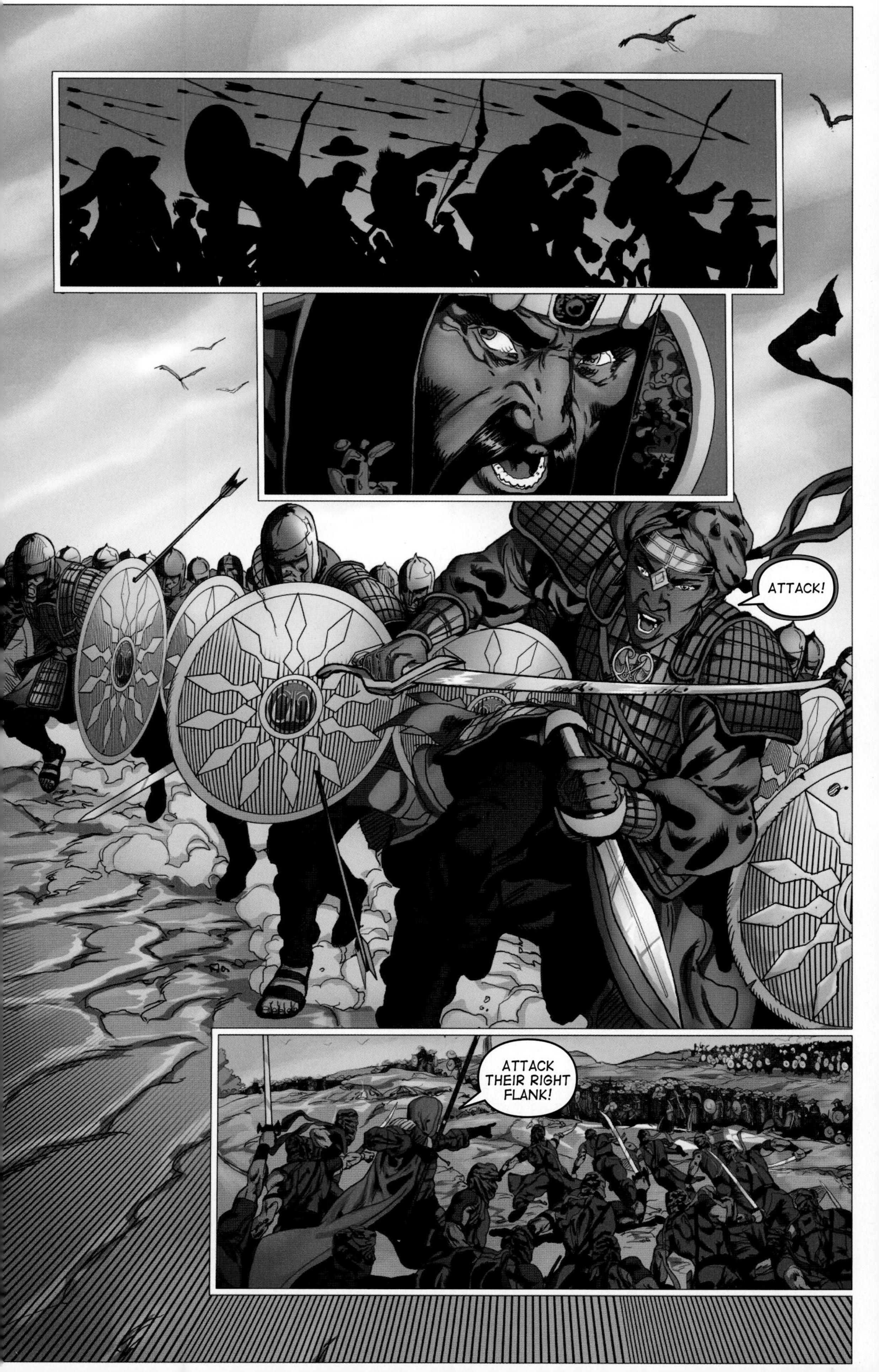
ATTACK!
ATTACK THEIR RIGHT FLANK!

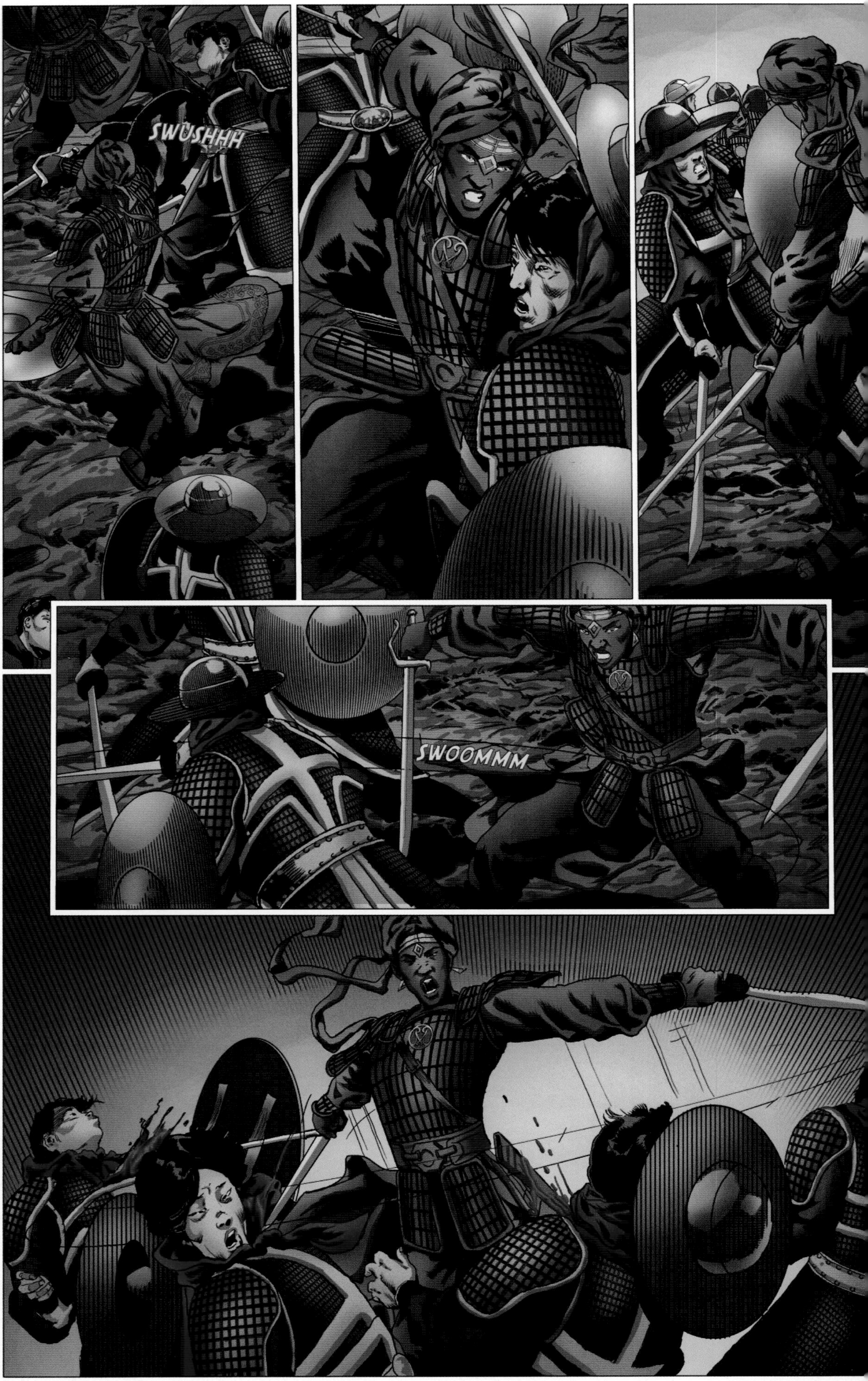
SWUSHHH
SWOOMMM

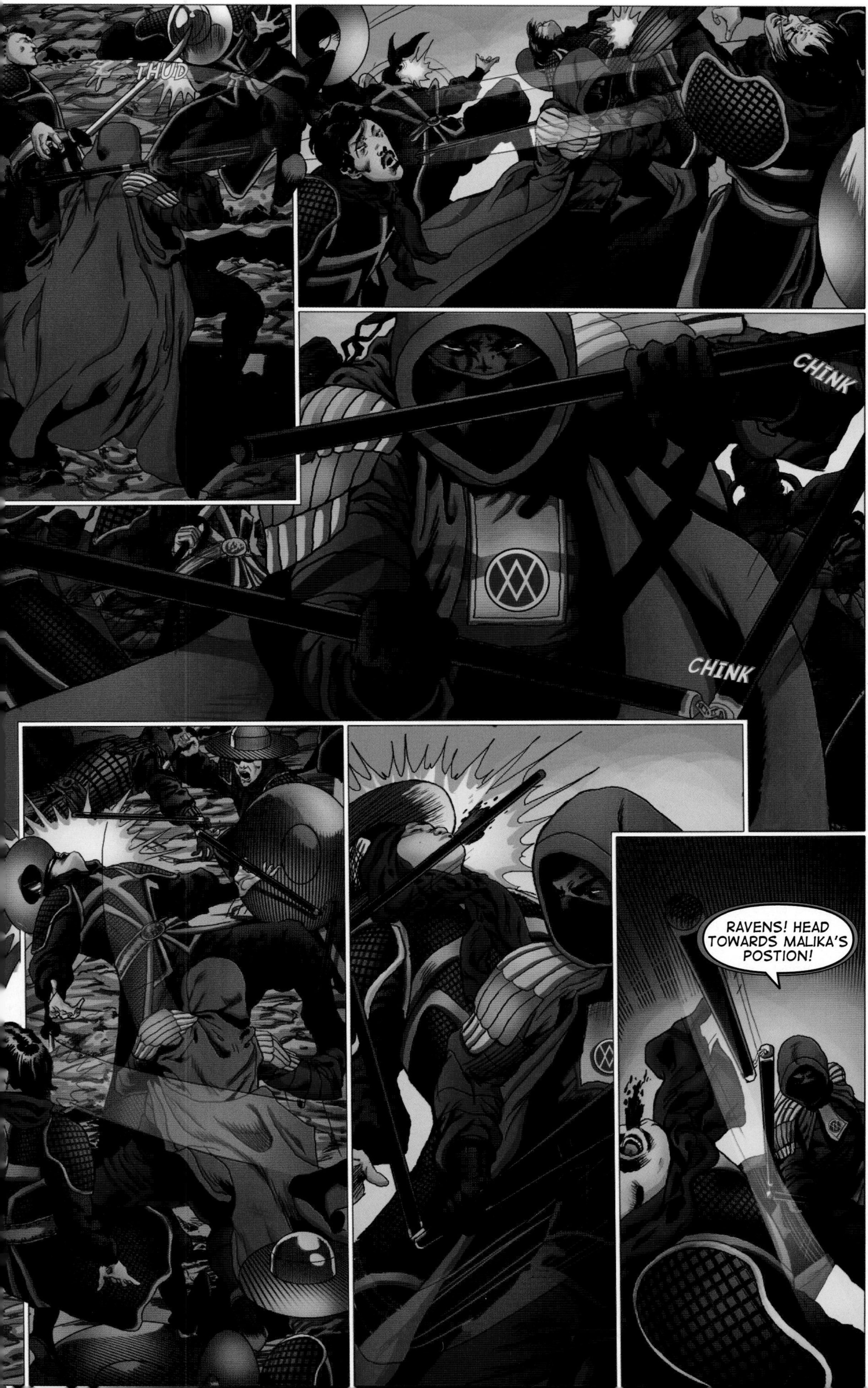
THUD
CHINK
CHINK
RAVENS! HEAD TOWARDS MALIKA'S POSTION!

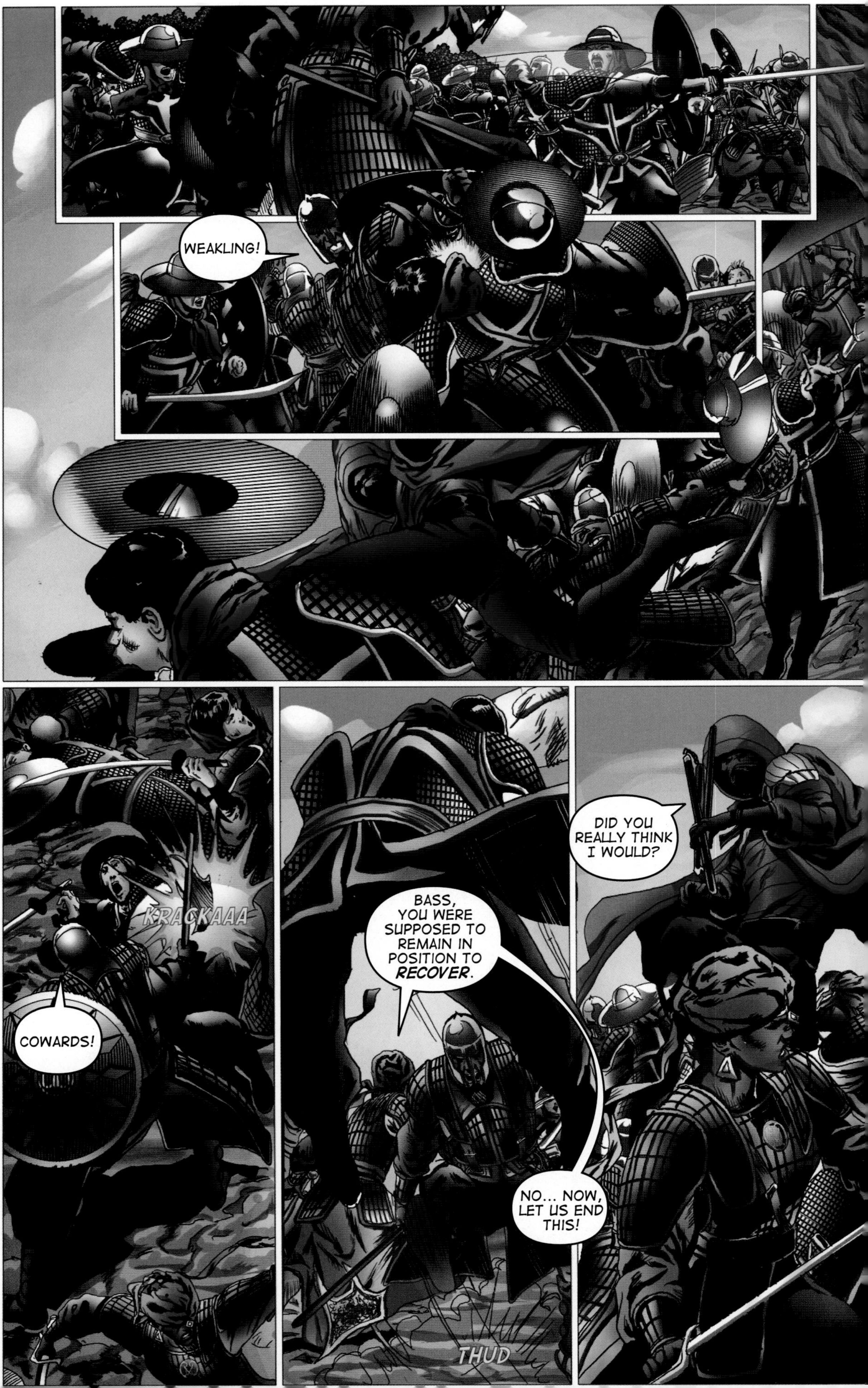
WEAKLING!
KRACKAAA
COWARDS!
BASS, YOU WERE SUPPOSED TO REMAIN IN POSITION TO RECOVER.
NO... NOW, LET US END THIS!
THUD
DID YOU REALLY THINK I WOULD?

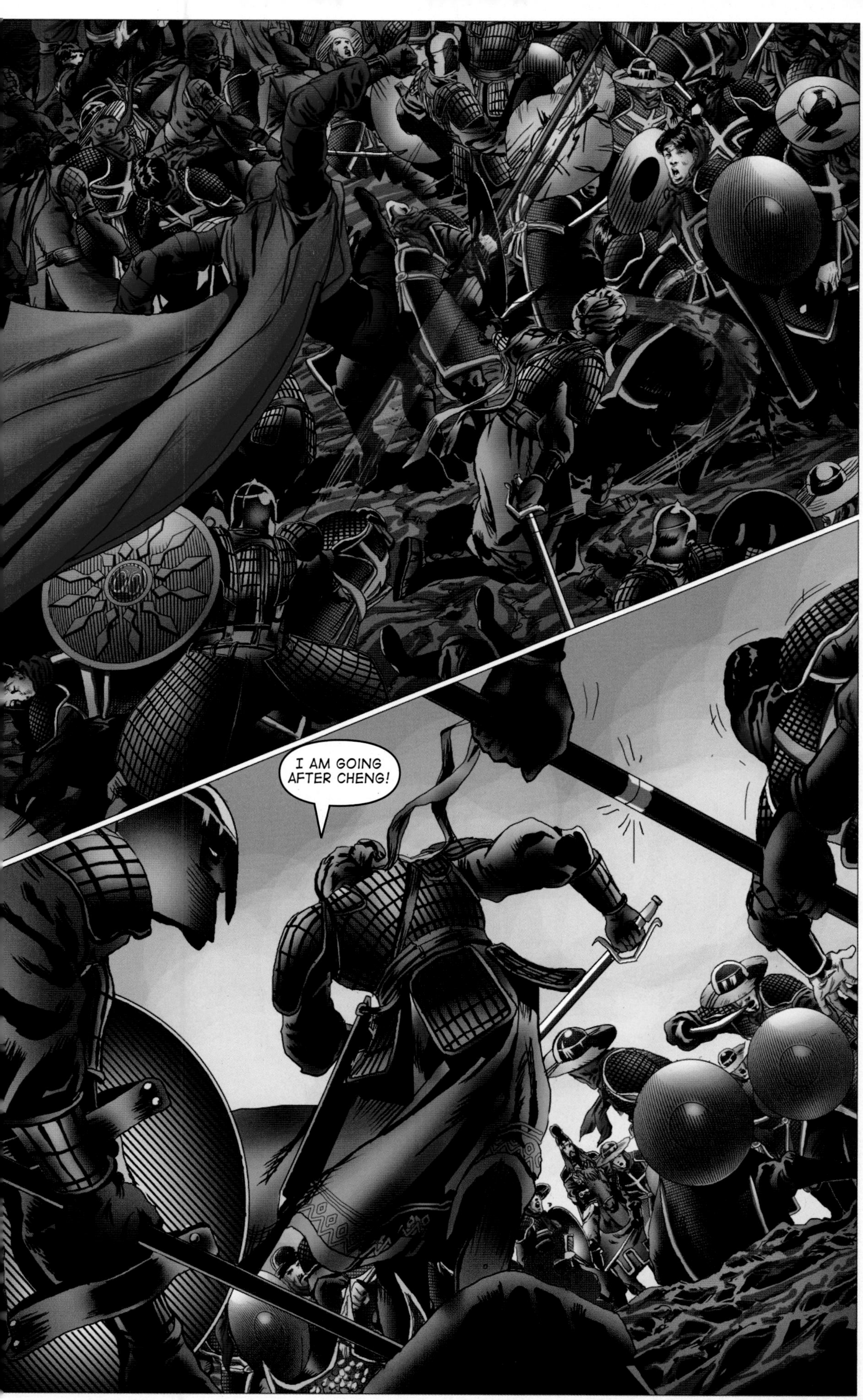
I AM GOING AFTER CHENG!

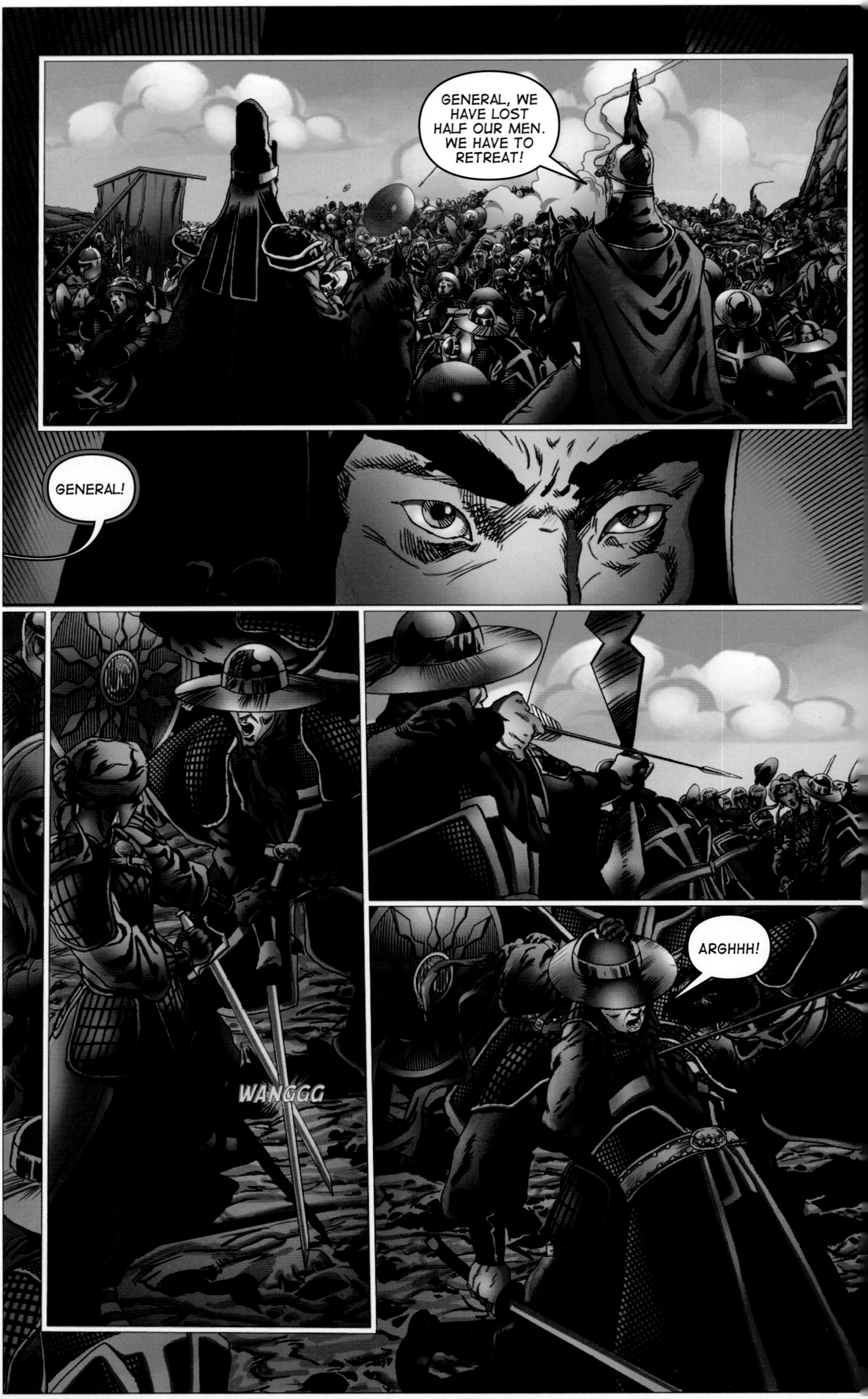
GENERAL, WE HAVE LOST HALF OUR MEN. WE HAVE TO RETREAT!
GENERAL!
WANGGG
ARGHHH!

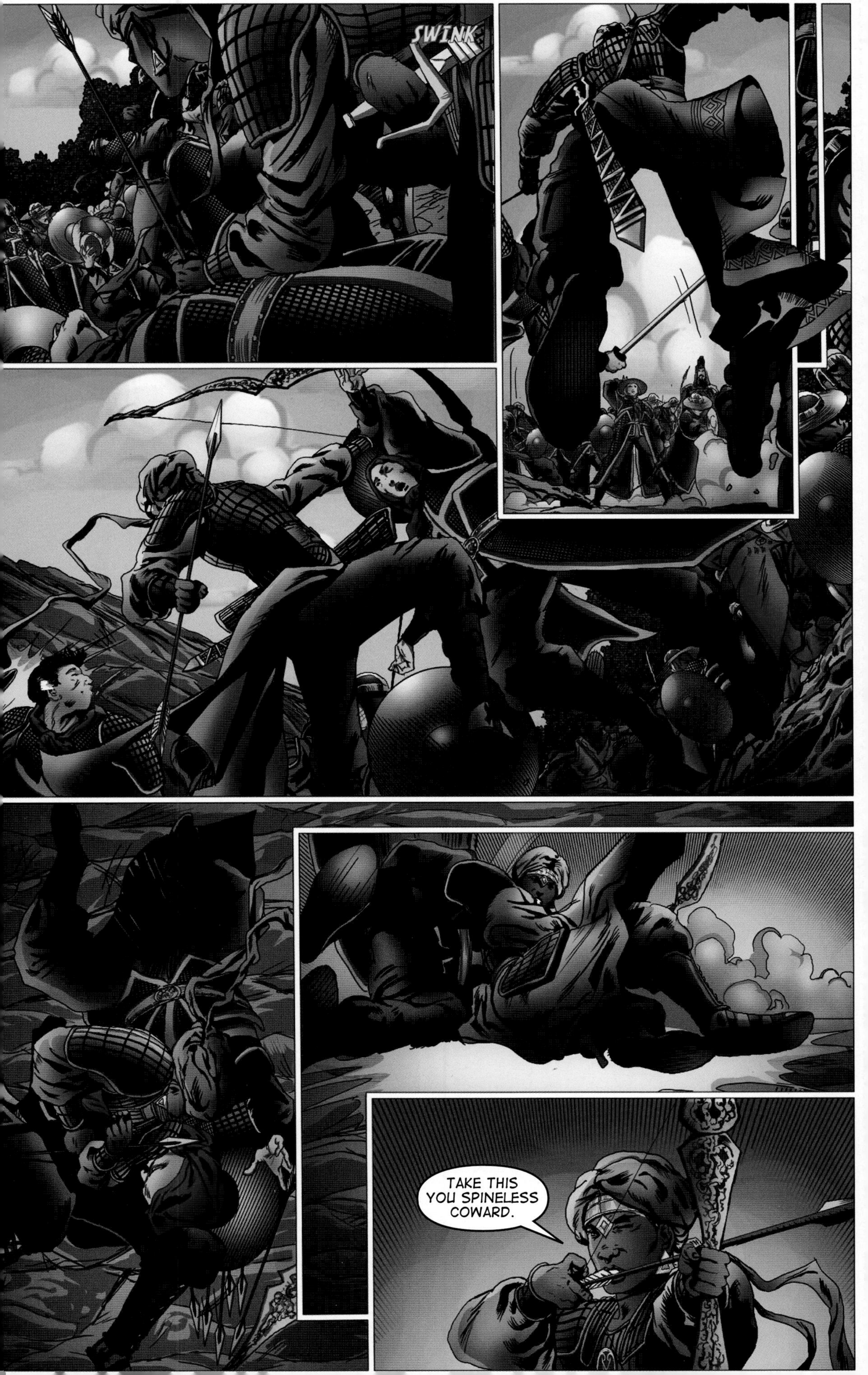
SWINK
TAKE THIS YOU SPINELESS COWARD.

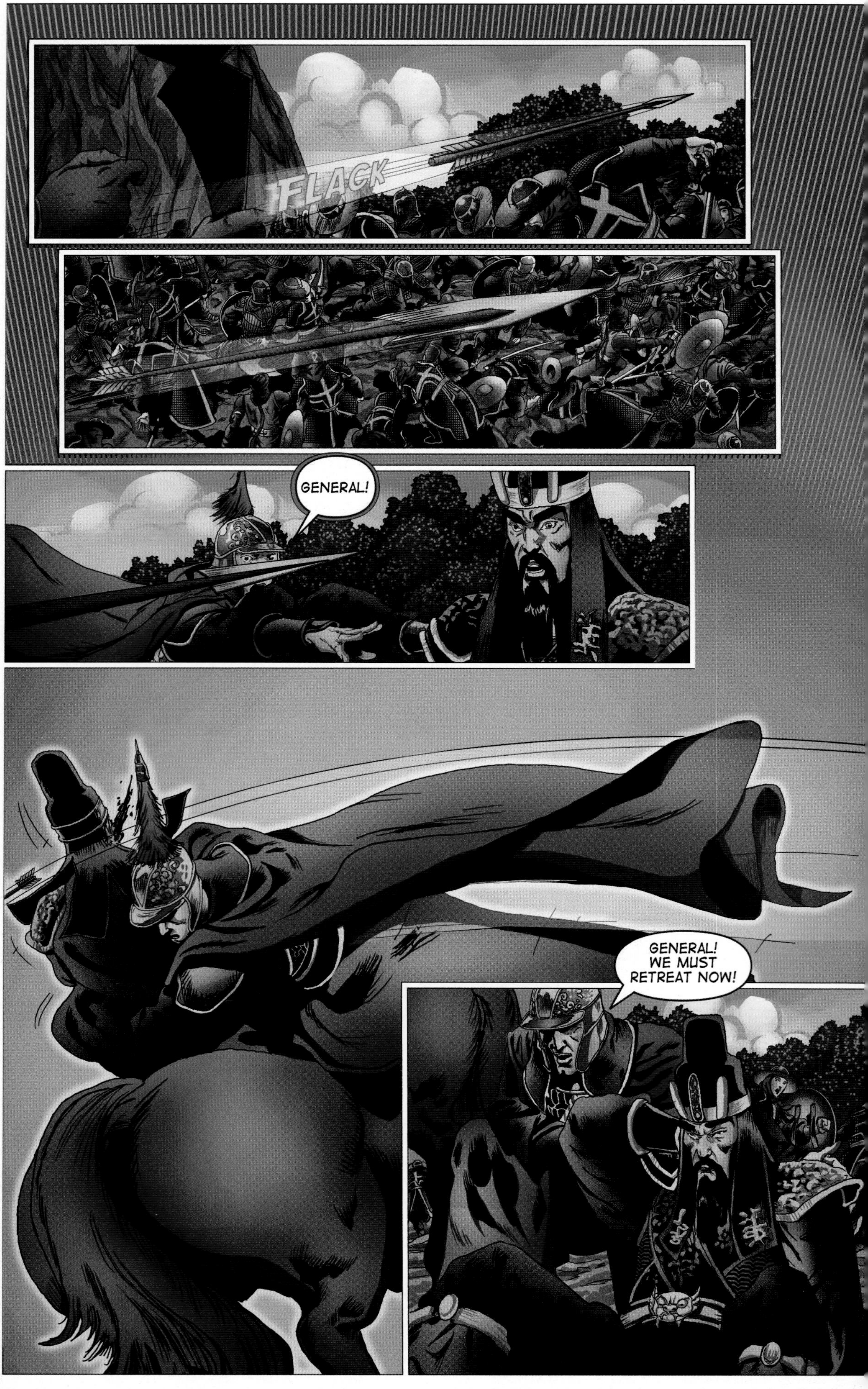
FLACK
GENERAL!
GENERAL! WE MUST RETREAT NOW!

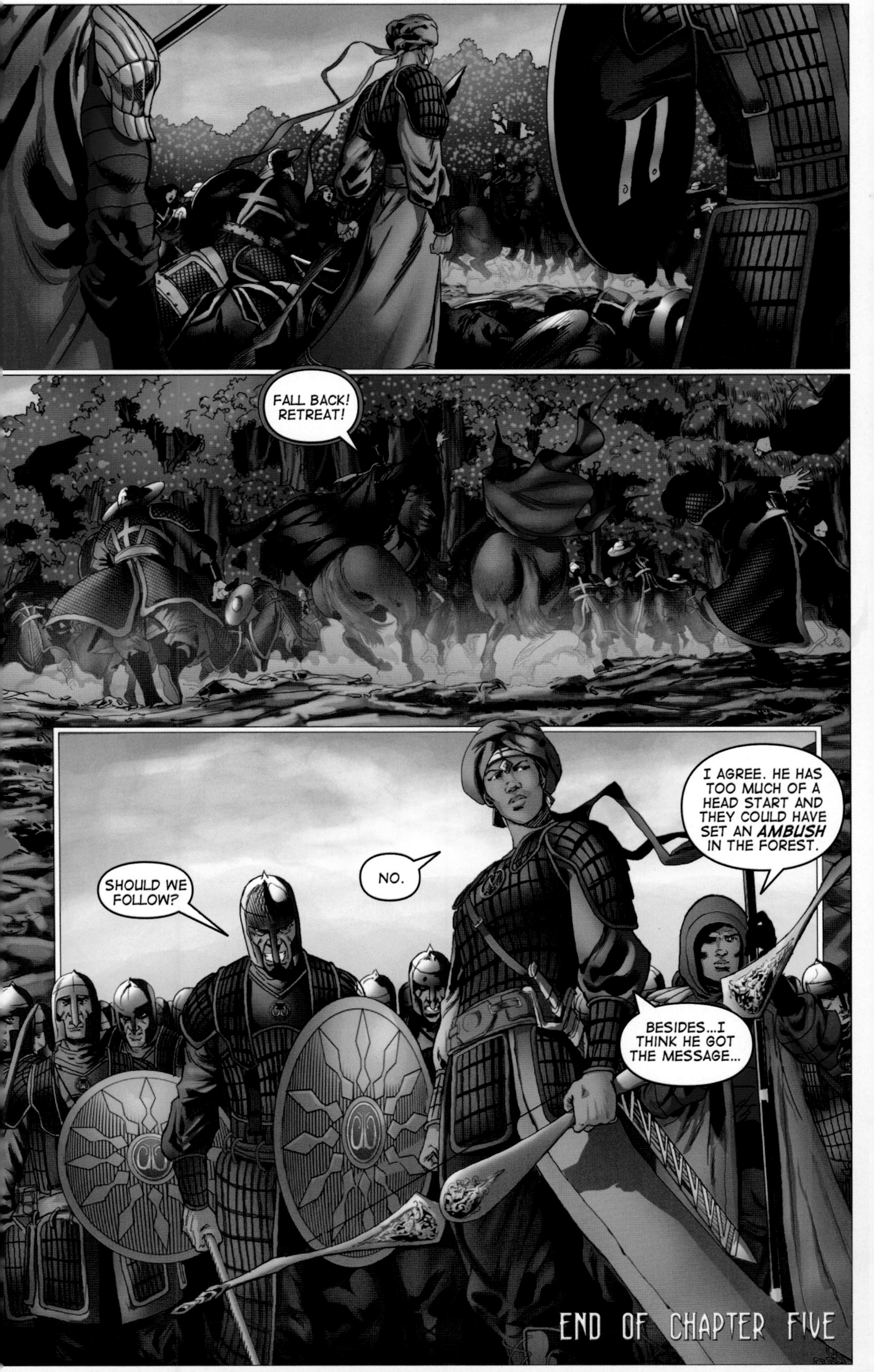
FALL BACK! RETREAT!
SHOULD WE FOLLOW?
NO.
I AGREE. HE HAS TOO MUCH OF A HEAD START AND THEY COULD HAVE SET AN ***AMBUSH*** IN THE FOREST.
BESIDES...I THINK HE GOT THE MESSAGE...
END OF CHAPTER FIVE

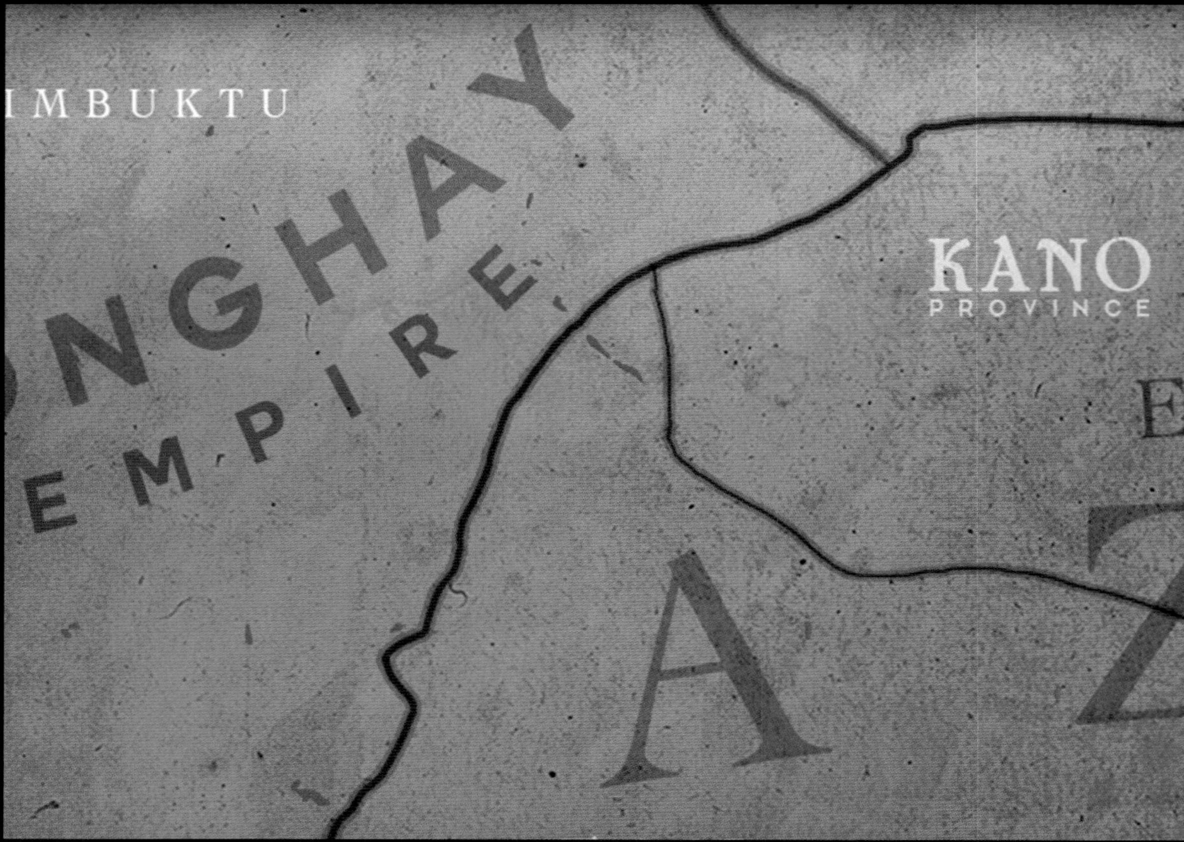
IMBUKTU
NGHAY
EMPIRE
KANO
PROVINCE

THE KANO PROVINCE

The Kano Province, located to the north of the Azzazian empire, is famous for its Nomadic cattle rearers. The Azzazian empire depends on the Kano Province for its supply of livestock. Chief Ramfa currently governs the Kano Province.

Fun Fact: The creation of the Kano Province takes inspiration from the real life Kingdom of Kano. Now located in what is currently Northern Nigeria, the Kingdom of Kano's existence dates back to 1000 AD.

CHAPTER SIX

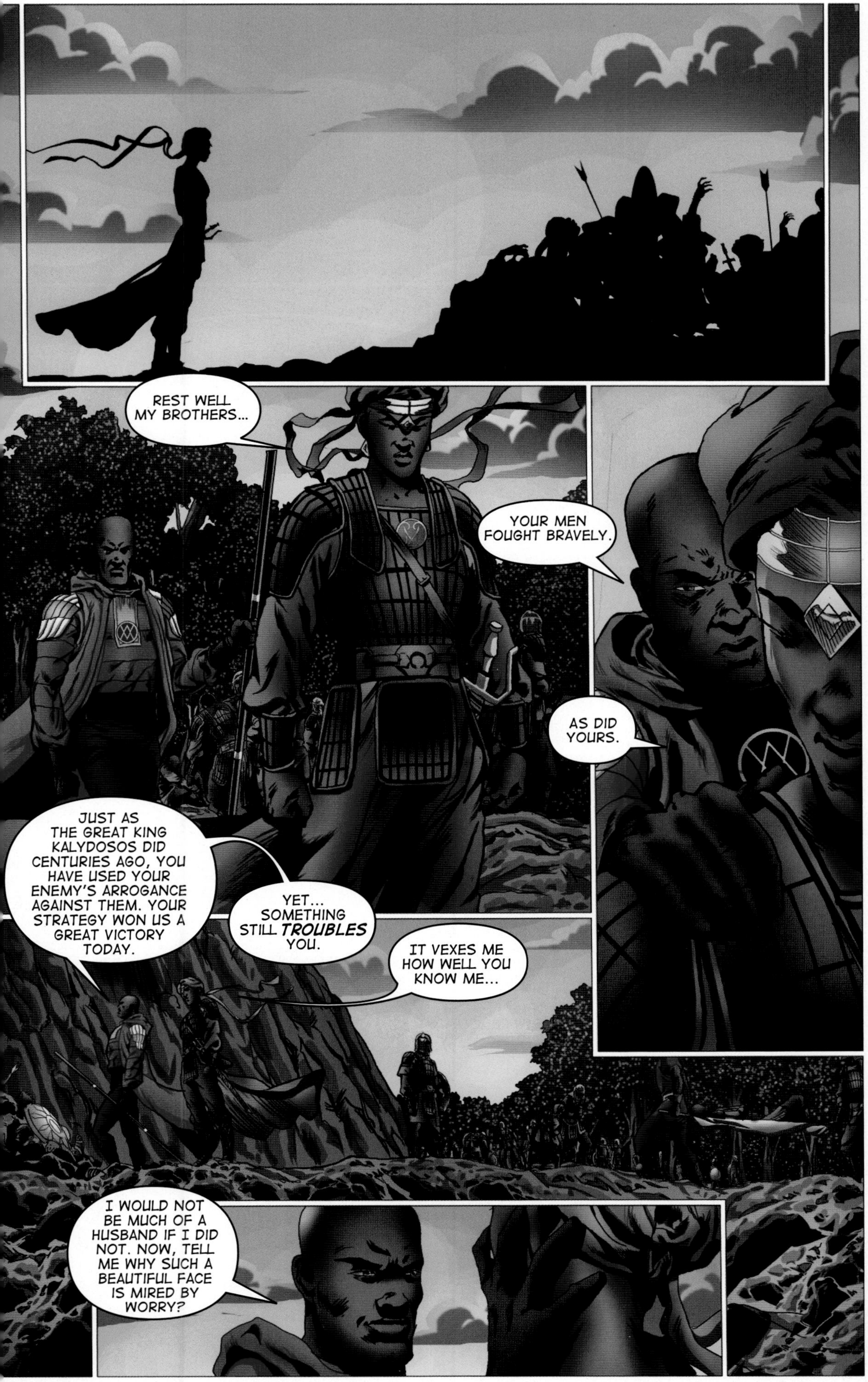
REST WELL MY BROTHERS...
YOUR MEN FOUGHT BRAVELY.
AS DID YOURS.
JUST AS THE GREAT KING KALYDOSOS DID CENTURIES AGO, YOU HAVE USED YOUR ENEMY'S ARROGANCE AGAINST THEM. YOUR STRATEGY WON US A GREAT VICTORY TODAY.
YET... SOMETHING STILL TROUBLES YOU.
IT VEXES ME HOW WELL YOU KNOW ME...
I WOULD NOT BE MUCH OF A HUSBAND IF I DID NOT. NOW, TELL ME WHY SUCH A BEAUTIFUL FACE IS MIRED BY WORRY?

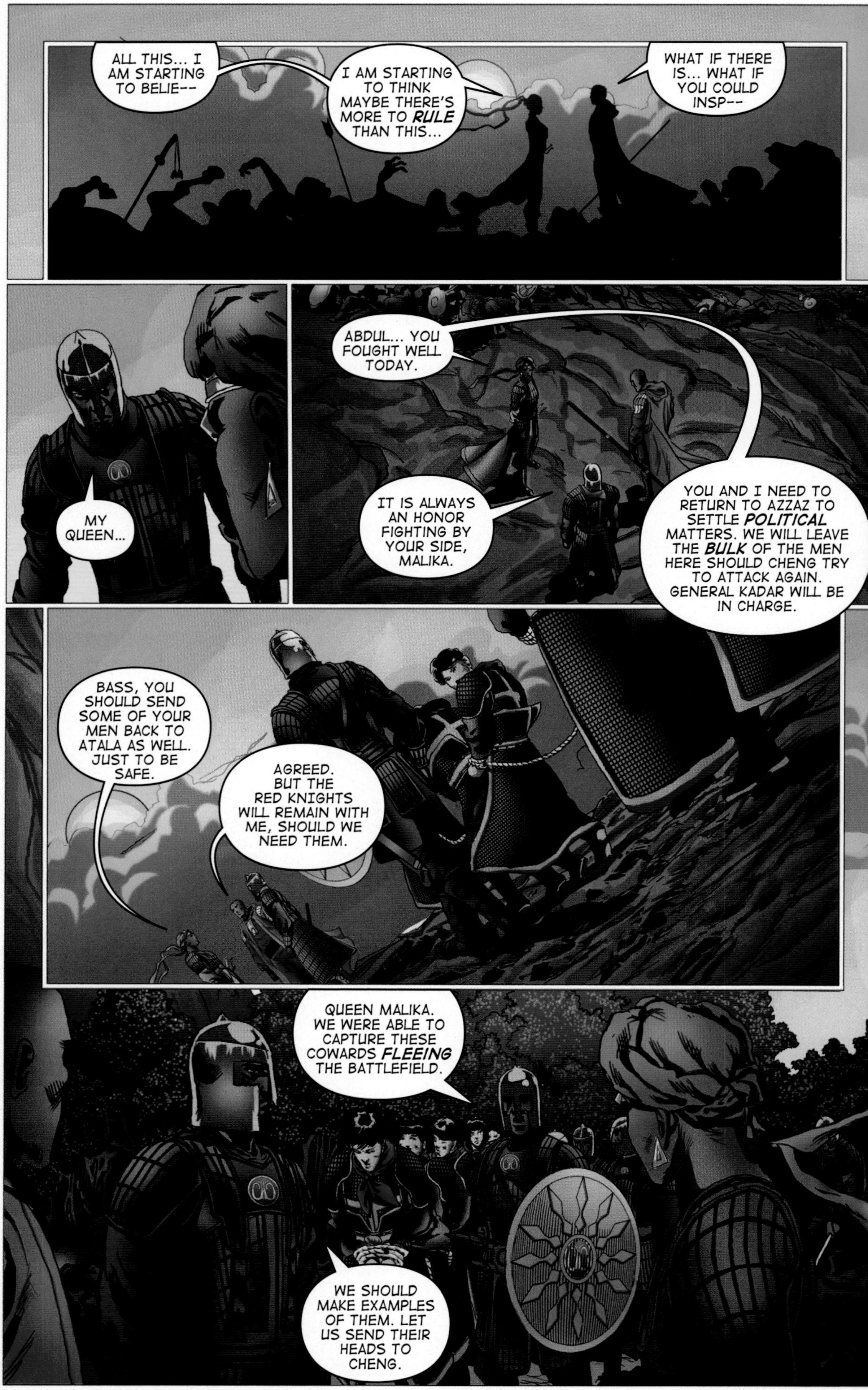
ALL THIS... I AM STARTING TO BELIE--
I AM STARTING TO THINK MAYBE THERE'S MORE TO RULE THAN THIS...
WHAT IF THERE IS... WHAT IF YOU COULD INSP--
MY QUEEN...
ABDUL... YOU FOUGHT WELL TODAY.
IT IS ALWAYS AN HONOR FIGHTING BY YOUR SIDE, MALIKA.
YOU AND I NEED TO RETURN TO AZZAZ TO SETTLE POLITICAL MATTERS. WE WILL LEAVE THE BULK OF THE MEN HERE SHOULD CHENG TRY TO ATTACK AGAIN. GENERAL KADAR WILL BE IN CHARGE.
BASS, YOU SHOULD SEND SOME OF YOUR MEN BACK TO ATALA AS WELL. JUST TO BE SAFE.
AGREED. BUT THE RED KNIGHTS WILL REMAIN WITH ME, SHOULD WE NEED THEM.
QUEEN MALIKA. WE WERE ABLE TO CAPTURE THESE COWARDS FLEEING THE BATTLEFIELD.
WE SHOULD MAKE EXAMPLES OF THEM. LET US SEND THEIR HEADS TO CHENG.

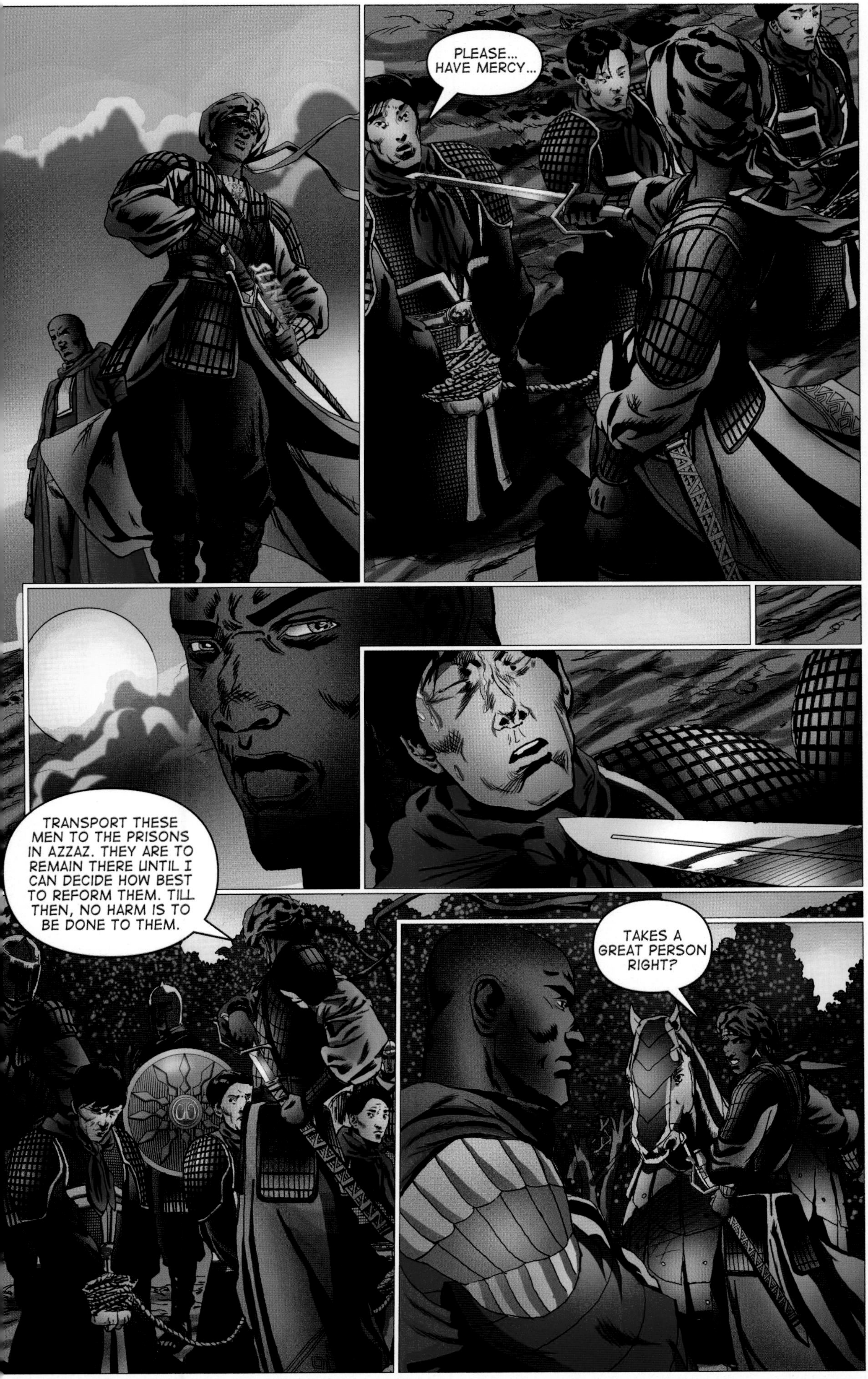
PLEASE... HAVE MERCY...
TRANSPORT THESE MEN TO THE PRISONS IN AZZAZ. THEY ARE TO REMAIN THERE UNTIL I CAN DECIDE HOW BEST TO REFORM THEM. TILL THEN, NO HARM IS TO BE DONE TO THEM.
TAKES A GREAT PERSON RIGHT?

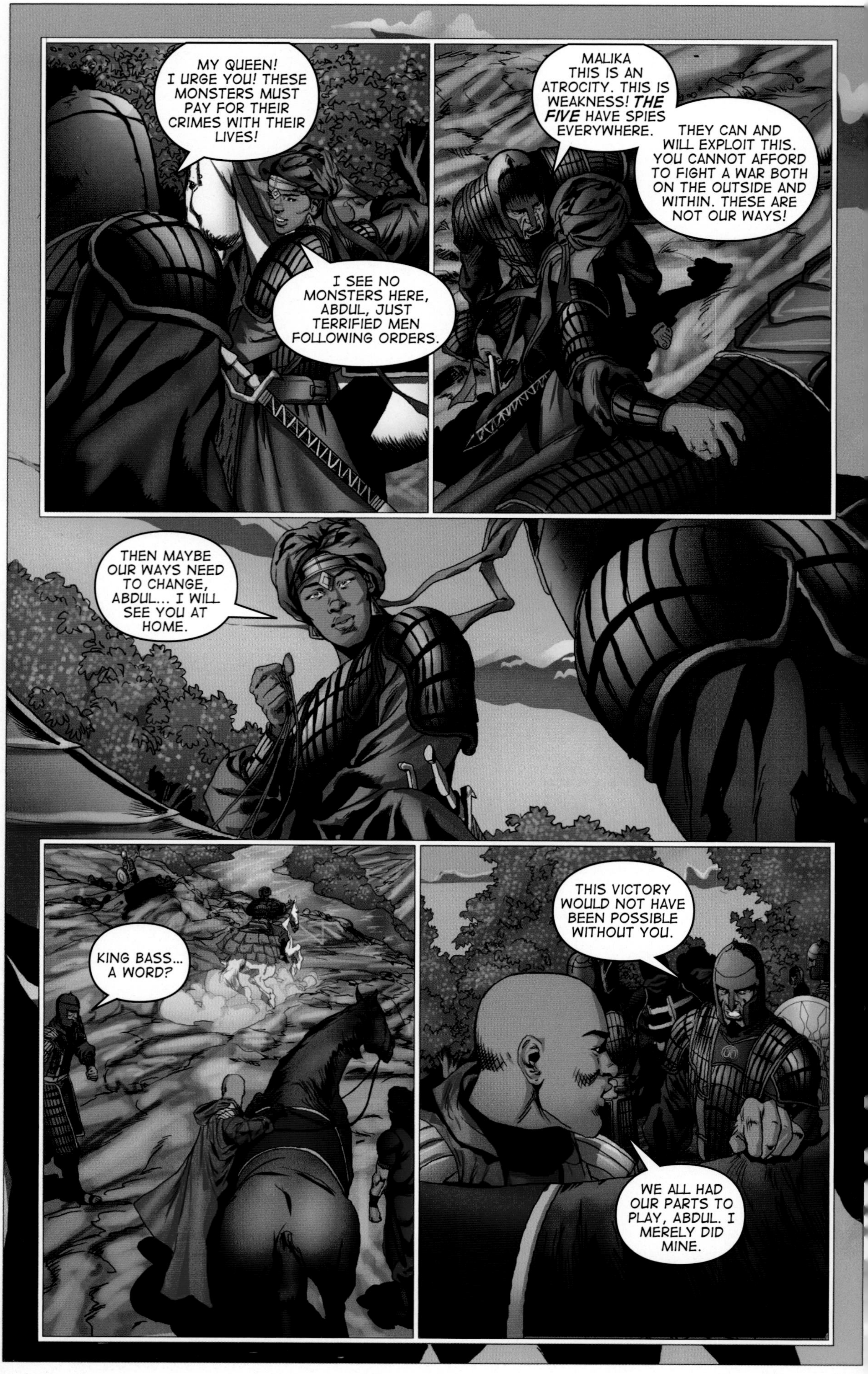
MY QUEEN! I URGE YOU! THESE MONSTERS MUST PAY FOR THEIR CRIMES WITH THEIR LIVES!
I SEE NO MONSTERS HERE, ABDUL, JUST TERRIFIED MEN FOLLOWING ORDERS.
MALIKA THIS IS AN ATROCITY. THIS IS WEAKNESS! ***THE FIVE*** HAVE SPIES EVERYWHERE.
THEY CAN AND WILL EXPLOIT THIS. YOU CANNOT AFFORD TO FIGHT A WAR BOTH ON THE OUTSIDE AND WITHIN. THESE ARE NOT OUR WAYS!
THEN MAYBE OUR WAYS NEED TO CHANGE, ABDUL... I WILL SEE YOU AT HOME.
KING BASS... A WORD?
THIS VICTORY WOULD NOT HAVE BEEN POSSIBLE WITHOUT YOU.
WE ALL HAD OUR PARTS TO PLAY, ABDUL. I MERELY DID MINE.

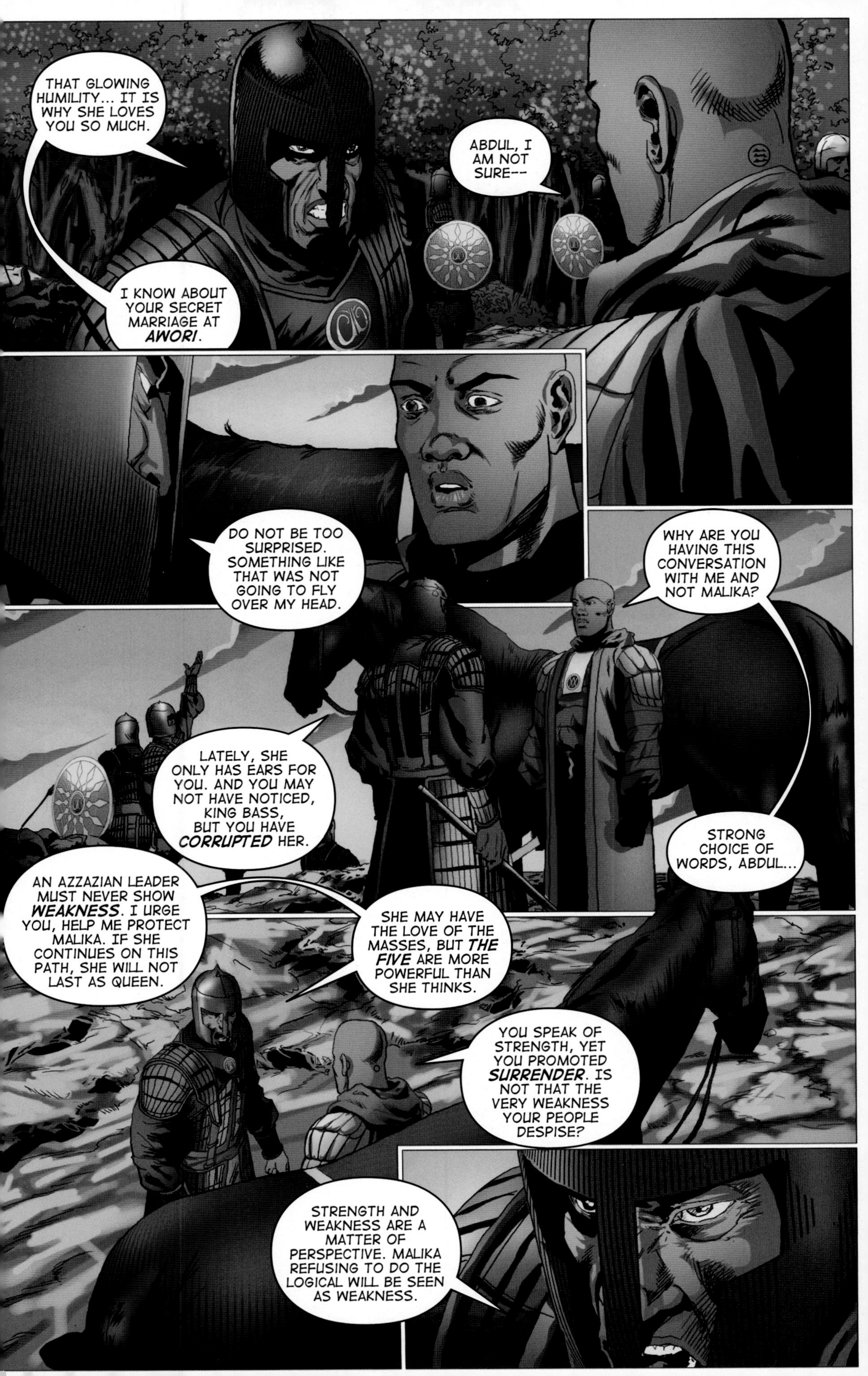
THAT GLOWING HUMILITY... IT IS WHY SHE LOVES YOU SO MUCH.
ABDUL, I AM NOT SURE--
I KNOW ABOUT YOUR SECRET MARRIAGE AT AWORI.
DO NOT BE TOO SURPRISED. SOMETHING LIKE THAT WAS NOT GOING TO FLY OVER MY HEAD.
WHY ARE YOU HAVING THIS CONVERSATION WITH ME AND NOT MALIKA?
LATELY, SHE ONLY HAS EARS FOR YOU. AND YOU MAY NOT HAVE NOTICED, KING BASS, BUT YOU HAVE CORRUPTED HER.
STRONG CHOICE OF WORDS, ABDUL...
AN AZZAZIAN LEADER MUST NEVER SHOW WEAKNESS. I URGE YOU, HELP ME PROTECT MALIKA. IF SHE CONTINUES ON THIS PATH, SHE WILL NOT LAST AS QUEEN.
SHE MAY HAVE THE LOVE OF THE MASSES, BUT THE FIVE ARE MORE POWERFUL THAN SHE THINKS.
YOU SPEAK OF STRENGTH, YET YOU PROMOTED SURRENDER. IS NOT THAT THE VERY WEAKNESS YOUR PEOPLE DESPISE?
STRENGTH AND WEAKNESS ARE A MATTER OF PERSPECTIVE. MALIKA REFUSING TO DO THE LOGICAL WILL BE SEEN AS WEAKNESS.

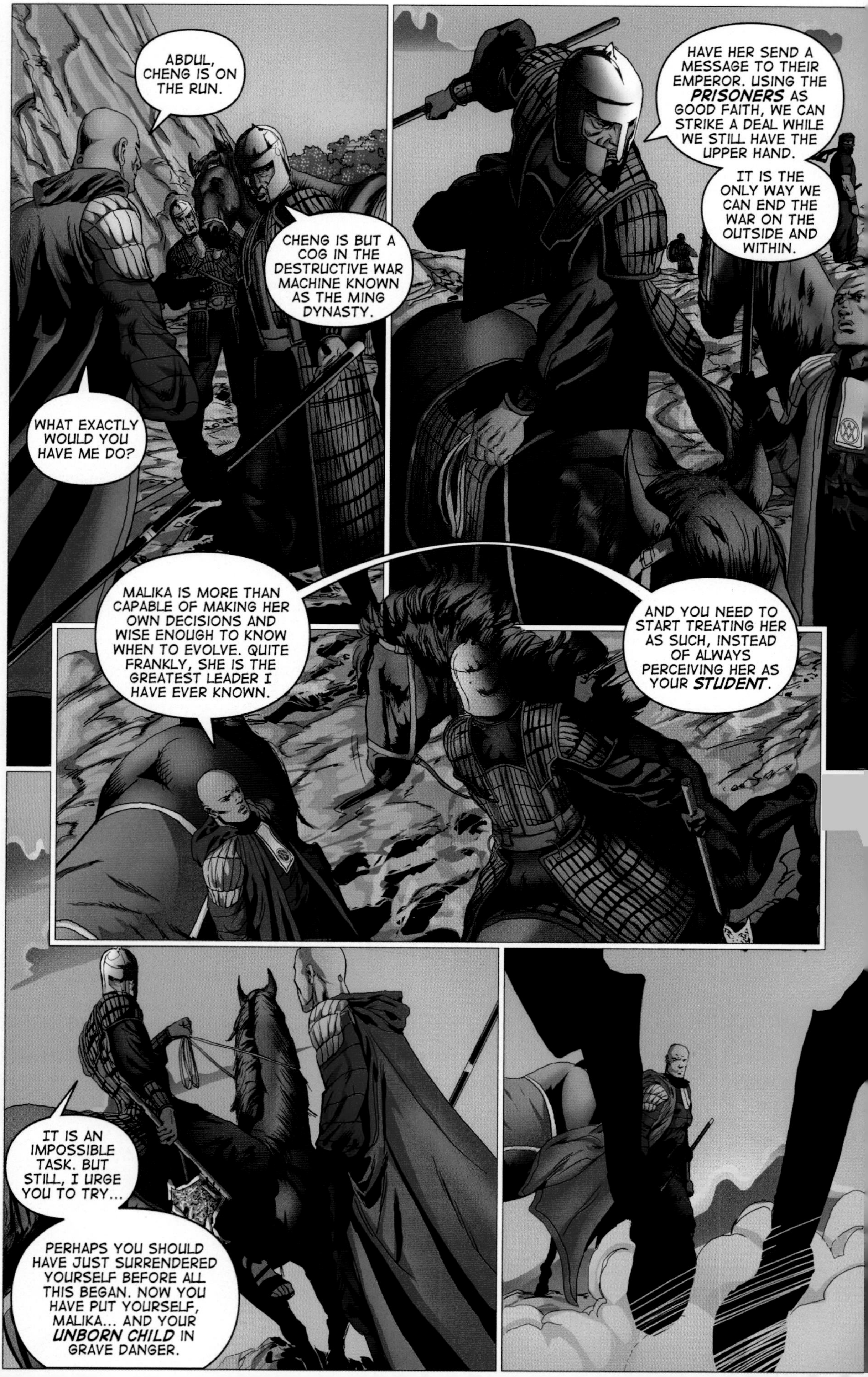
ABDUL, CHENG IS ON THE RUN.
CHENG IS BUT A COG IN THE DESTRUCTIVE WAR MACHINE KNOWN AS THE MING DYNASTY.
WHAT EXACTLY WOULD YOU HAVE ME DO?
HAVE HER SEND A MESSAGE TO THEIR EMPEROR. USING THE PRISONERS AS GOOD FAITH, WE CAN STRIKE A DEAL WHILE WE STILL HAVE THE UPPER HAND.
IT IS THE ONLY WAY WE CAN END THE WAR ON THE OUTSIDE AND WITHIN.
MALIKA IS MORE THAN CAPABLE OF MAKING HER OWN DECISIONS AND WISE ENOUGH TO KNOW WHEN TO EVOLVE. QUITE FRANKLY, SHE IS THE GREATEST LEADER I HAVE EVER KNOWN.
AND YOU NEED TO START TREATING HER AS SUCH, INSTEAD OF ALWAYS PERCEIVING HER AS YOUR STUDENT.
IT IS AN IMPOSSIBLE TASK. BUT STILL, I URGE YOU TO TRY...
PERHAPS YOU SHOULD HAVE JUST SURRENDERED YOURSELF BEFORE ALL THIS BEGAN. NOW YOU HAVE PUT YOURSELF, MALIKA... AND YOUR UNBORN CHILD IN GRAVE DANGER.

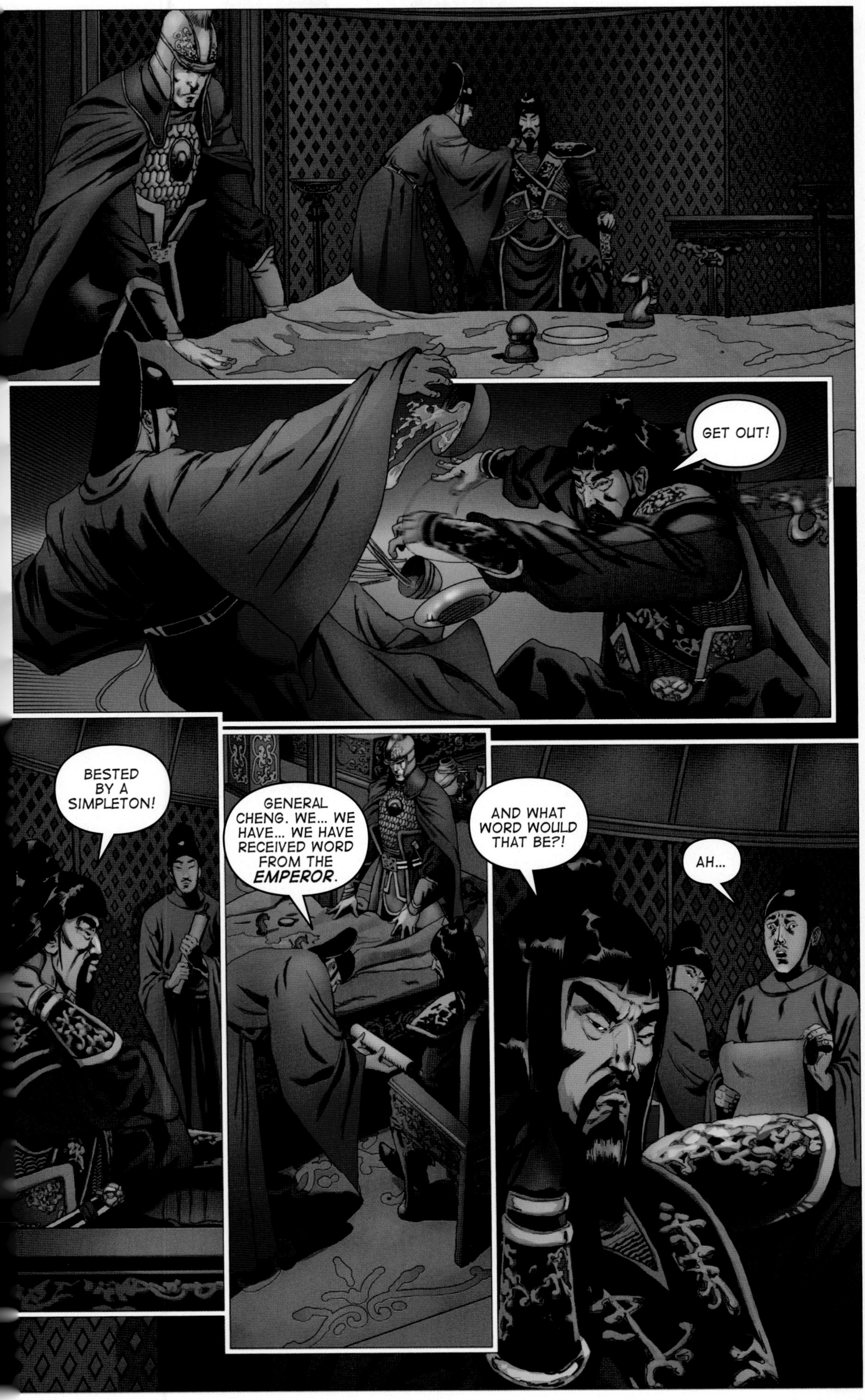
GET OUT!
BESTED BY A SIMPLETON!
GENERAL CHENG. WE... WE HAVE... WE HAVE RECEIVED WORD FROM THE *EMPEROR*.
AND WHAT WORD WOULD THAT BE?!
AH...

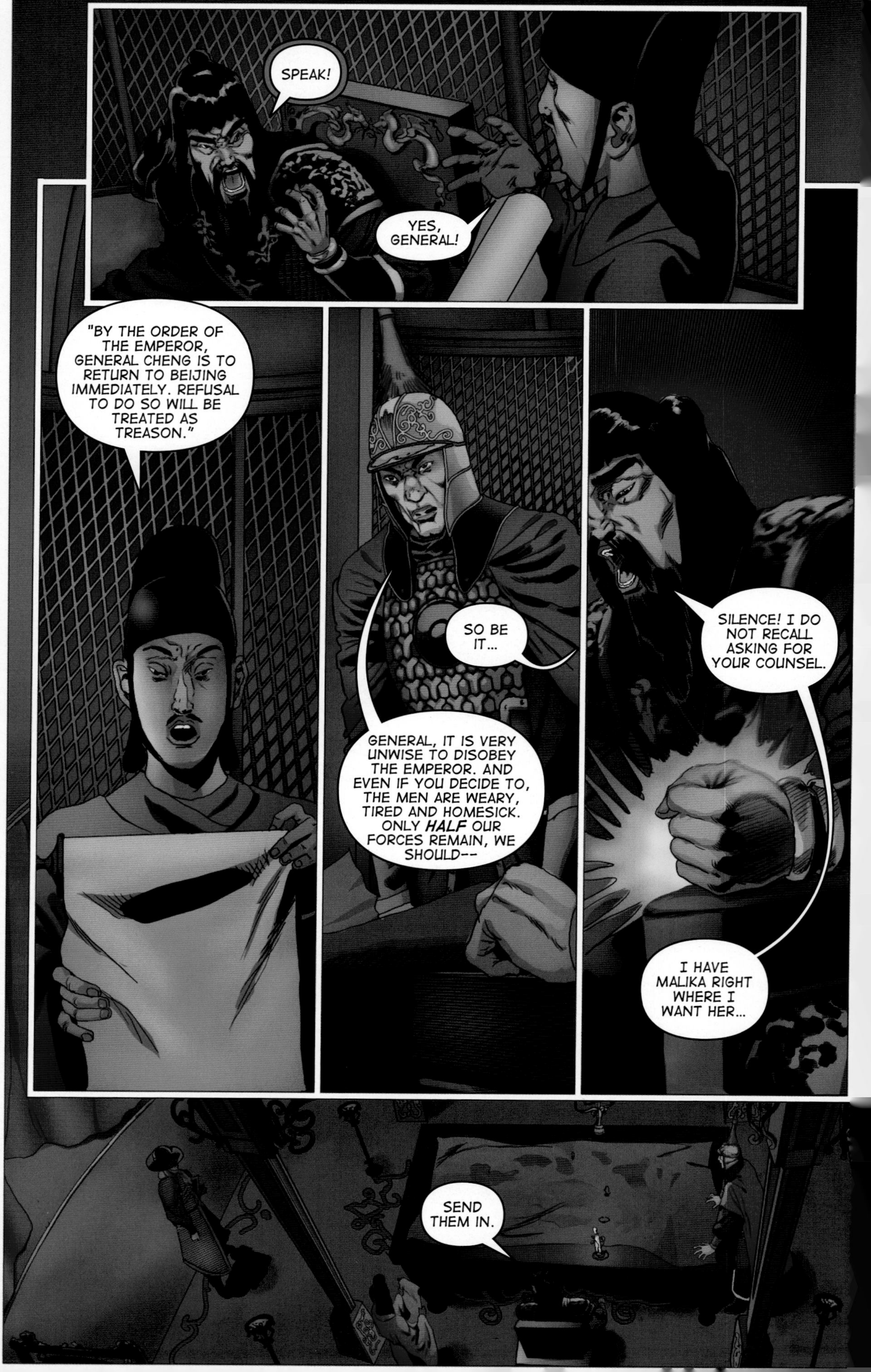
SPEAK!
YES, GENERAL!
"BY THE ORDER OF THE EMPEROR, GENERAL CHENG IS TO RETURN TO BEIJING IMMEDIATELY. REFUSAL TO DO SO WILL BE TREATED AS TREASON."
SO BE IT...
GENERAL, IT IS VERY UNWISE TO DISOBEY THE EMPEROR. AND EVEN IF YOU DECIDE TO, THE MEN ARE WEARY, TIRED AND HOMESICK. ONLY HALF OUR FORCES REMAIN, WE SHOULD--
SILENCE! I DO NOT RECALL ASKING FOR YOUR COUNSEL.
I HAVE MALIKA RIGHT WHERE I WANT HER...
SEND THEM IN.

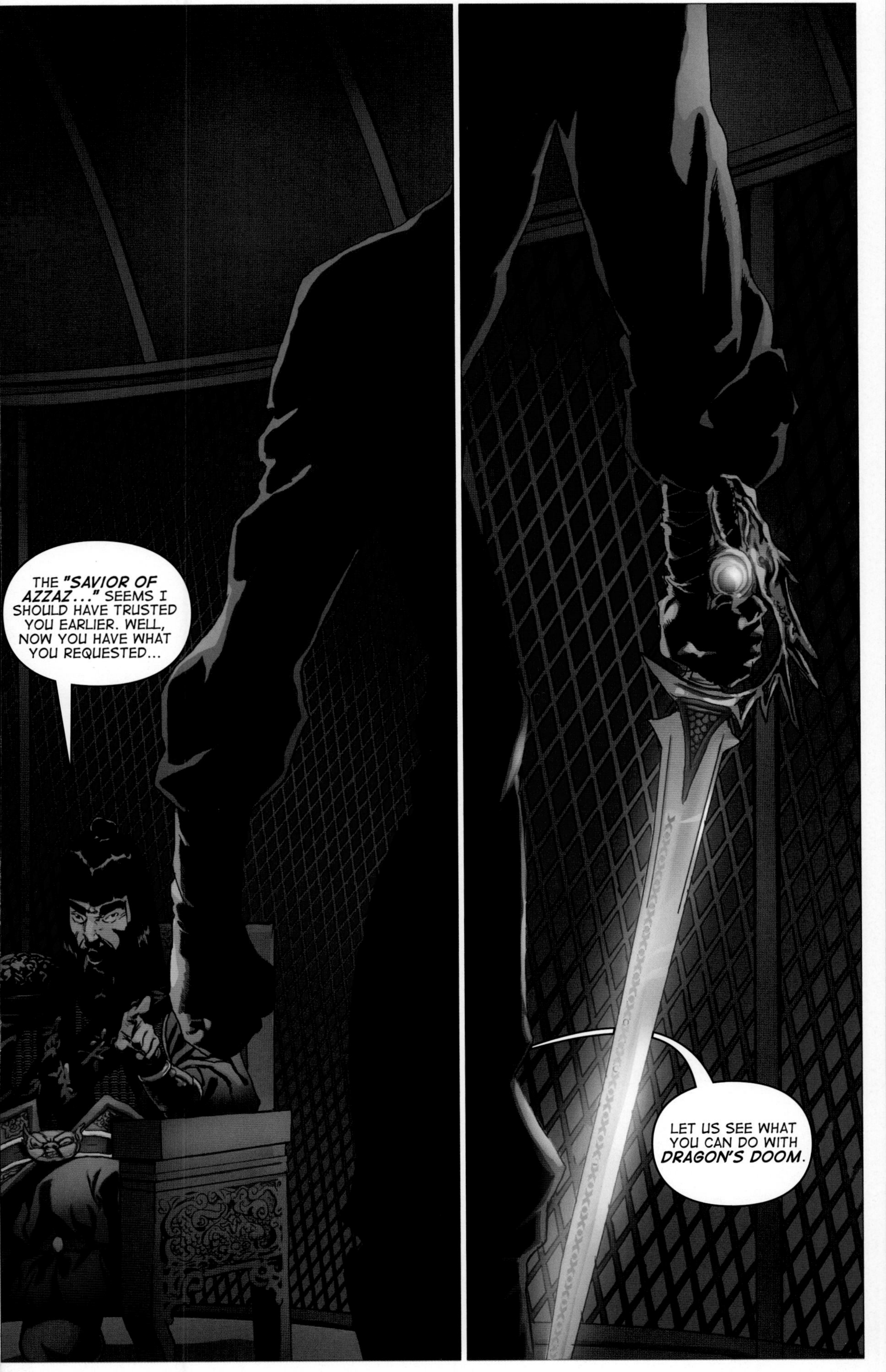
THE "SAVIOR OF AZZAZ..." SEEMS I SHOULD HAVE TRUSTED YOU EARLIER. WELL, NOW YOU HAVE WHAT YOU REQUESTED...
LET US SEE WHAT YOU CAN DO WITH DRAGON'S DOOM.

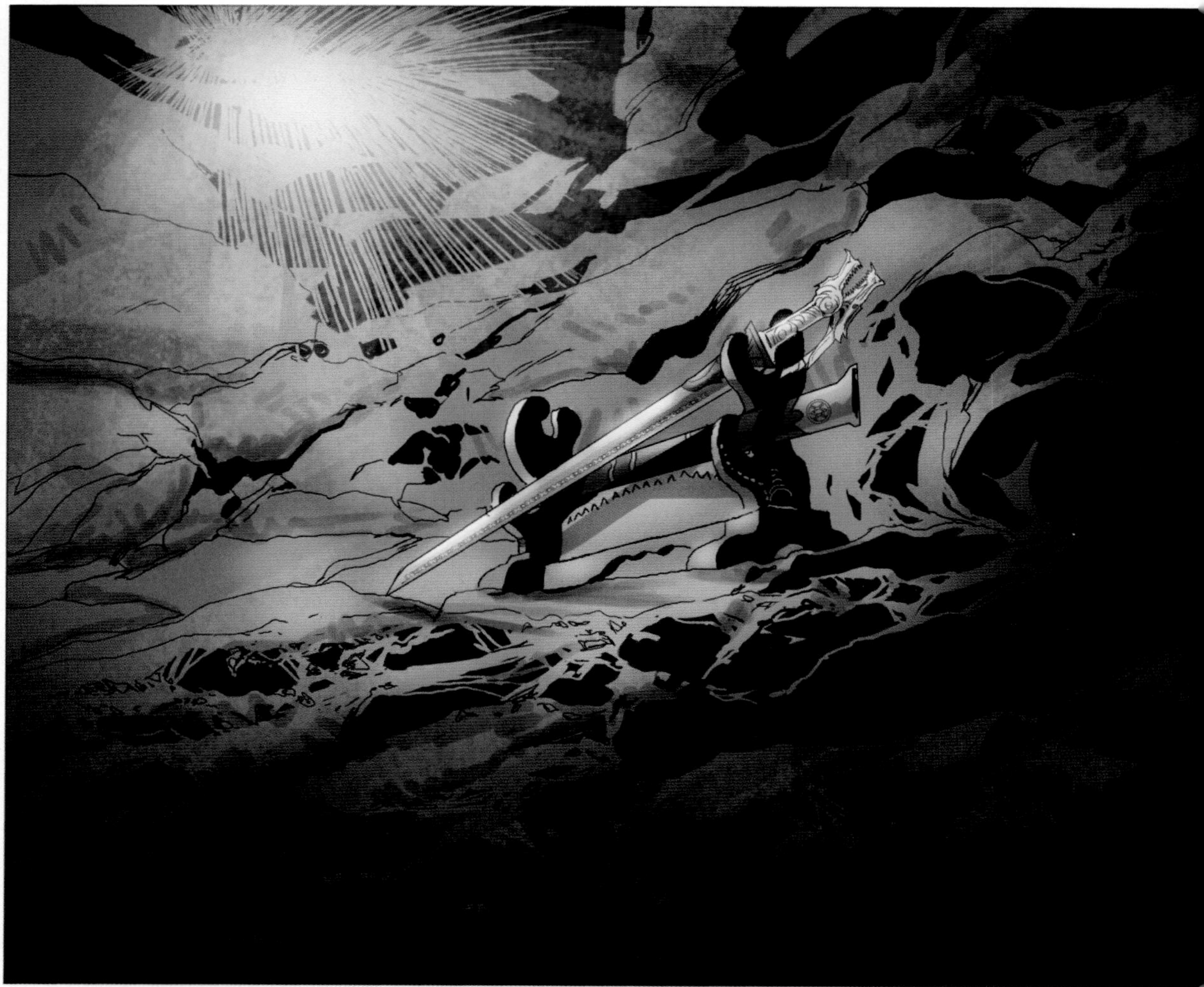

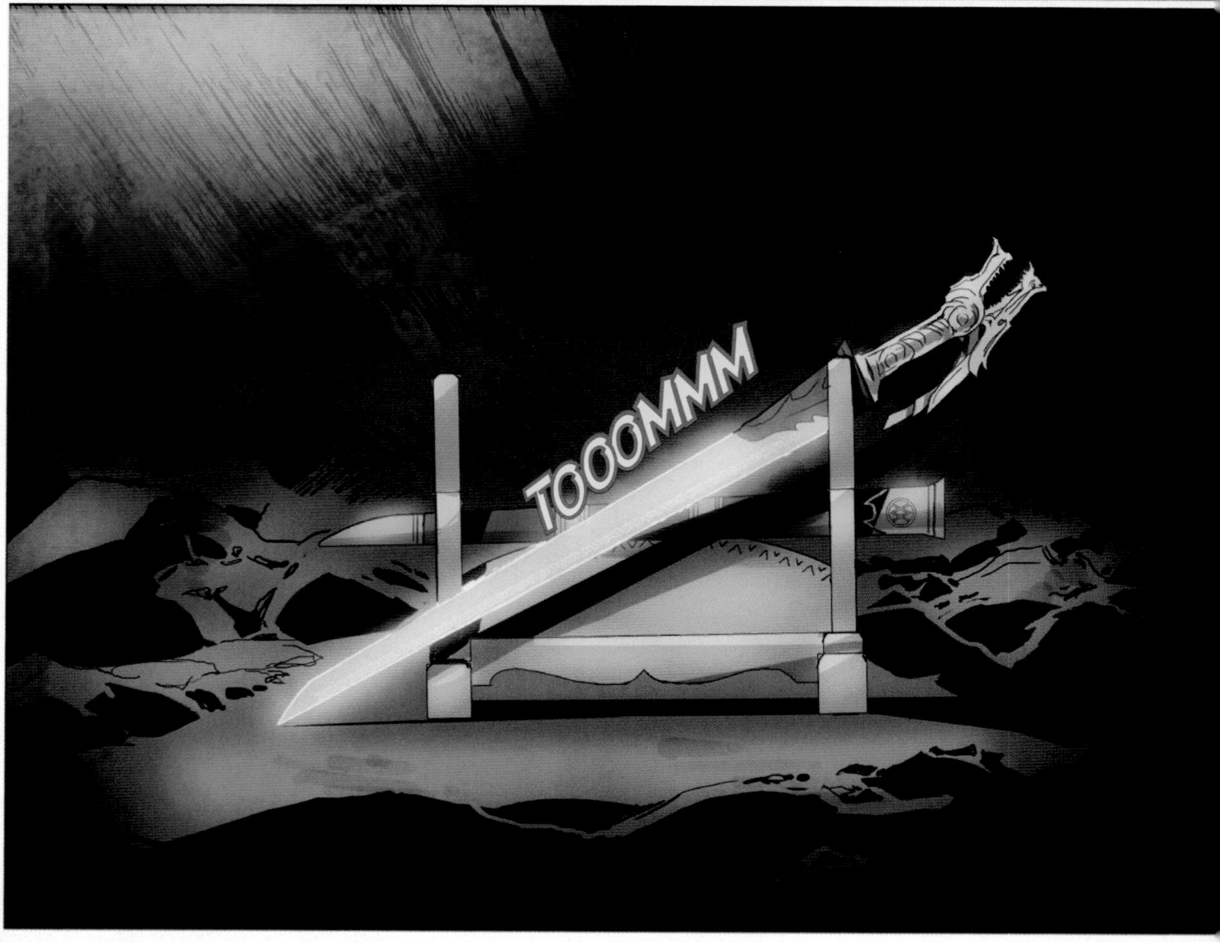
TOOOMMM

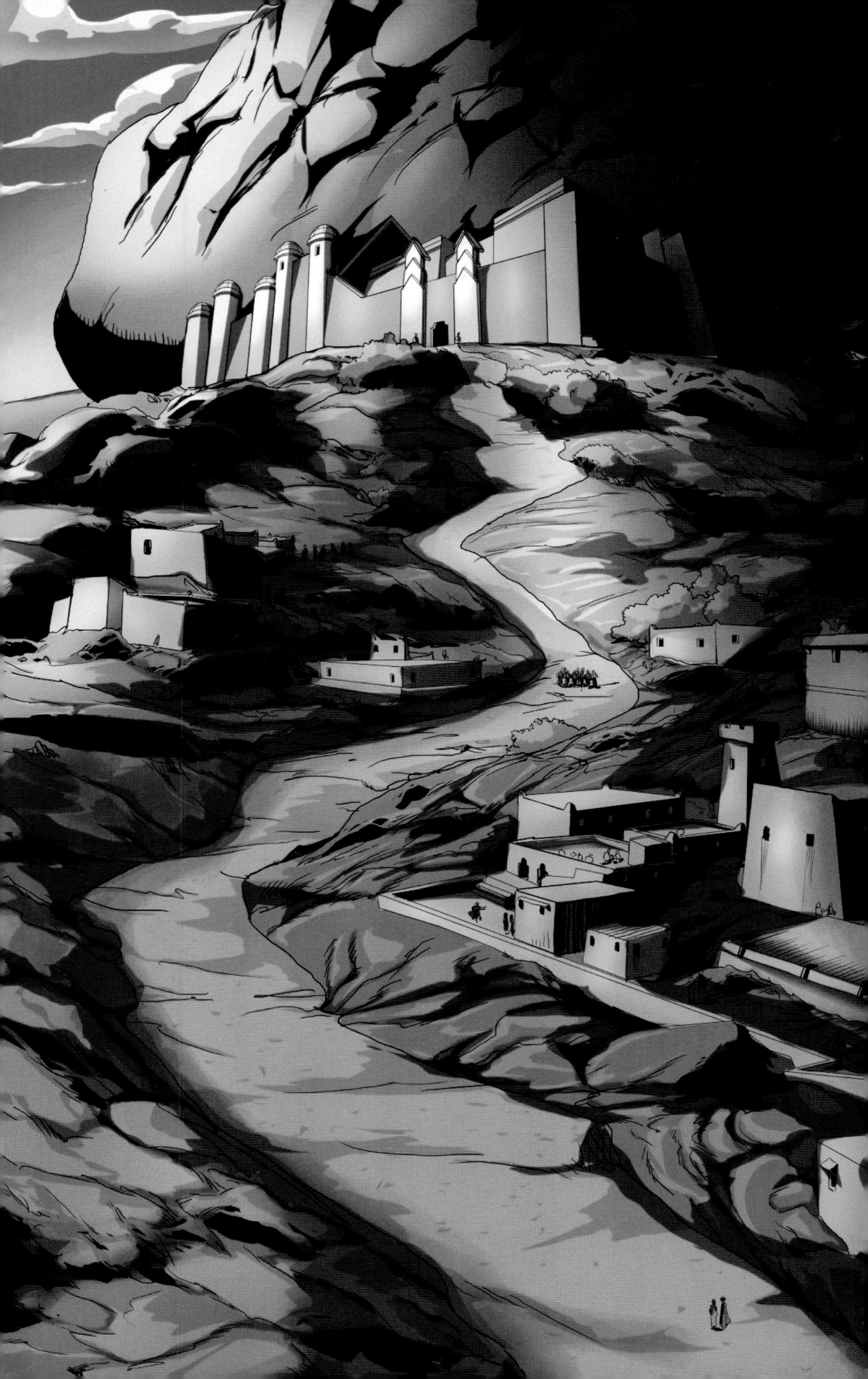

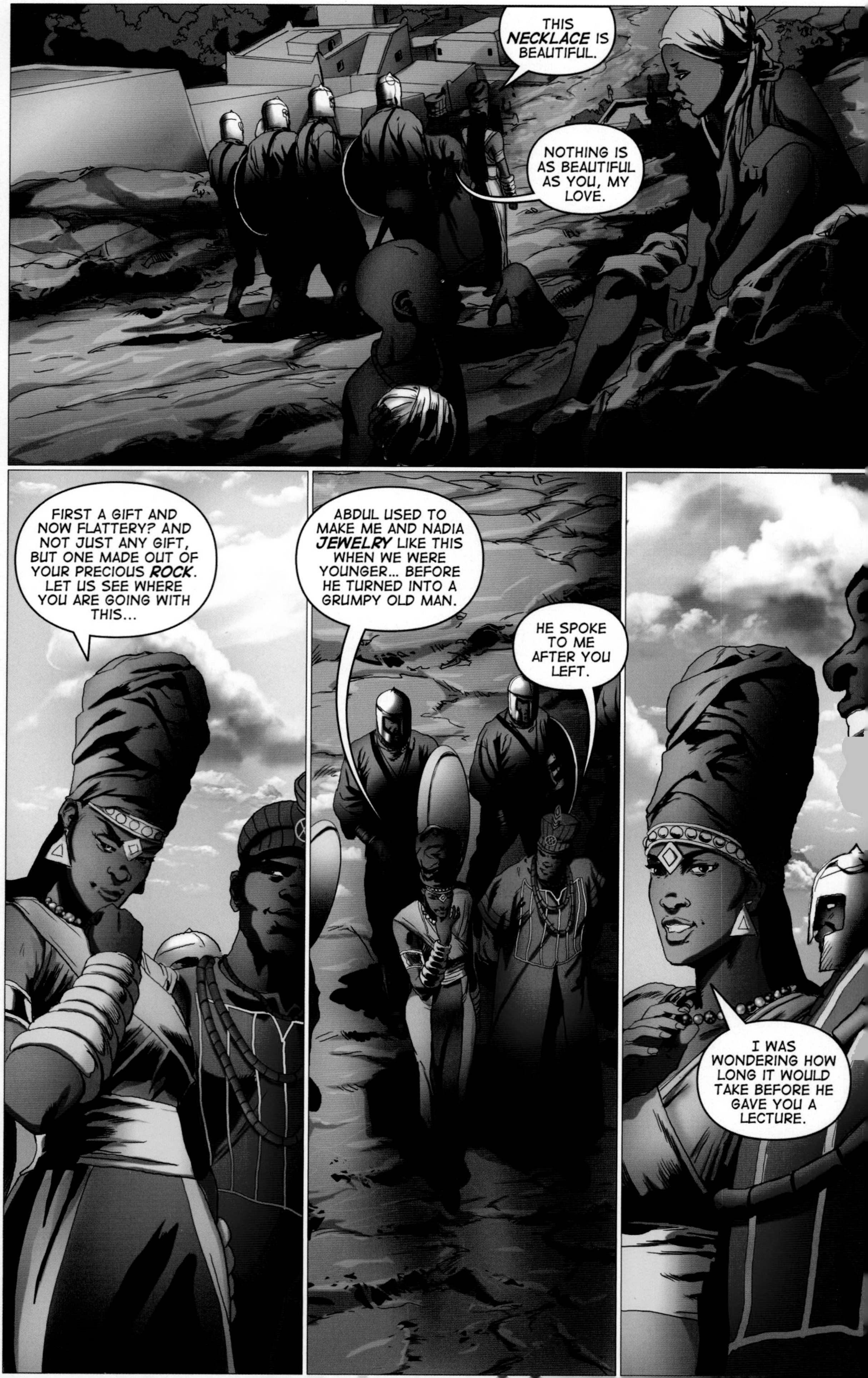
THIS NECKLACE IS BEAUTIFUL.
NOTHING IS AS BEAUTIFUL AS YOU, MY LOVE.
FIRST A GIFT AND NOW FLATTERY? AND NOT JUST ANY GIFT, BUT ONE MADE OUT OF YOUR PRECIOUS ROCK. LET US SEE WHERE YOU ARE GOING WITH THIS...
ABDUL USED TO MAKE ME AND NADIA JEWELRY LIKE THIS WHEN WE WERE YOUNGER... BEFORE HE TURNED INTO A GRUMPY OLD MAN.
HE SPOKE TO ME AFTER YOU LEFT.
I WAS WONDERING HOW LONG IT WOULD TAKE BEFORE HE GAVE YOU A LECTURE.

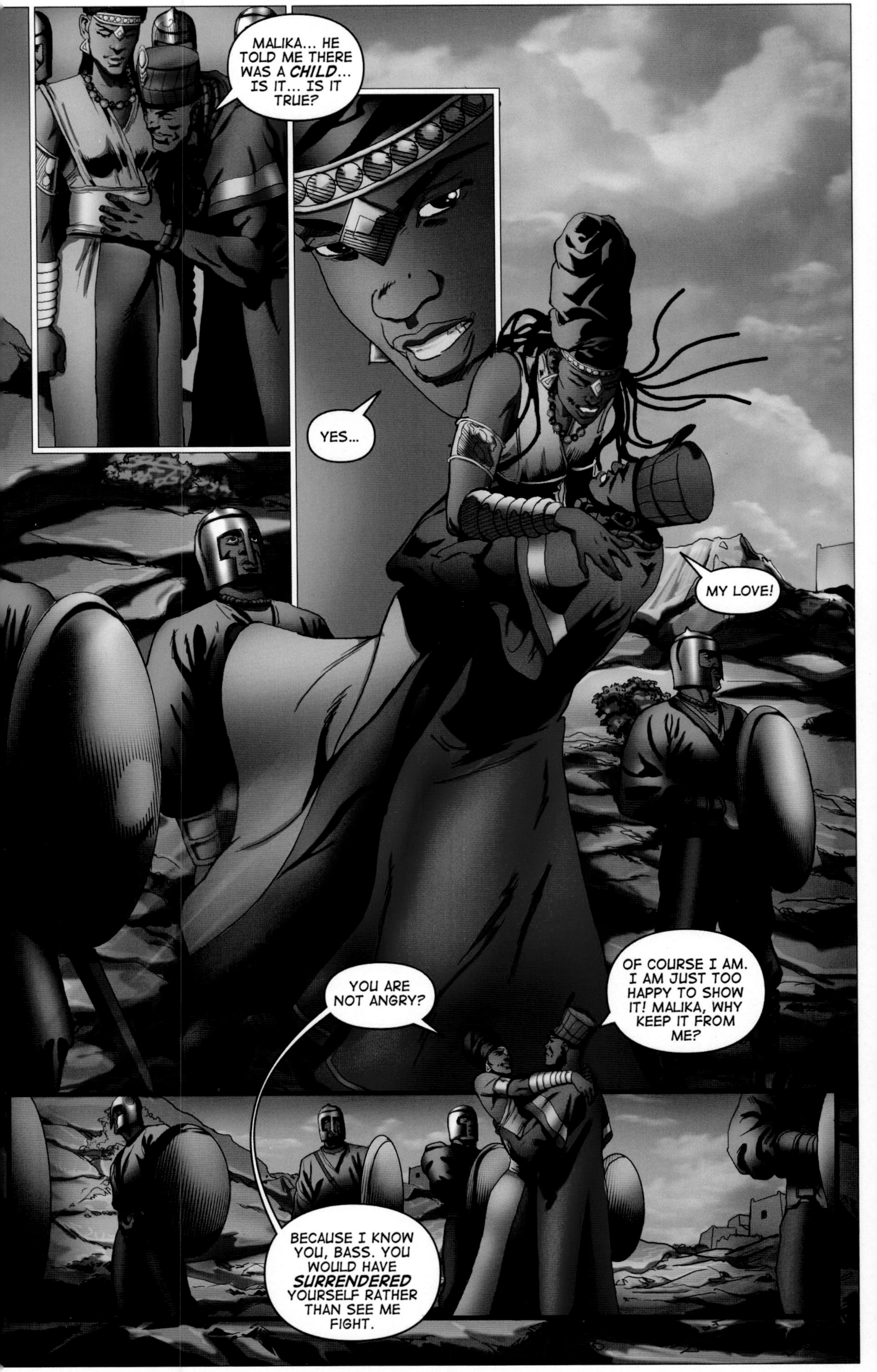
MALIKA... HE TOLD ME THERE WAS A CHILD... IS IT... IS IT TRUE?
YES...
MY LOVE!
YOU ARE NOT ANGRY?
OF COURSE I AM. I AM JUST TOO HAPPY TO SHOW IT! MALIKA, WHY KEEP IT FROM ME?
BECAUSE I KNOW YOU, BASS. YOU WOULD HAVE SURRENDERED YOURSELF RATHER THAN SEE ME FIGHT.

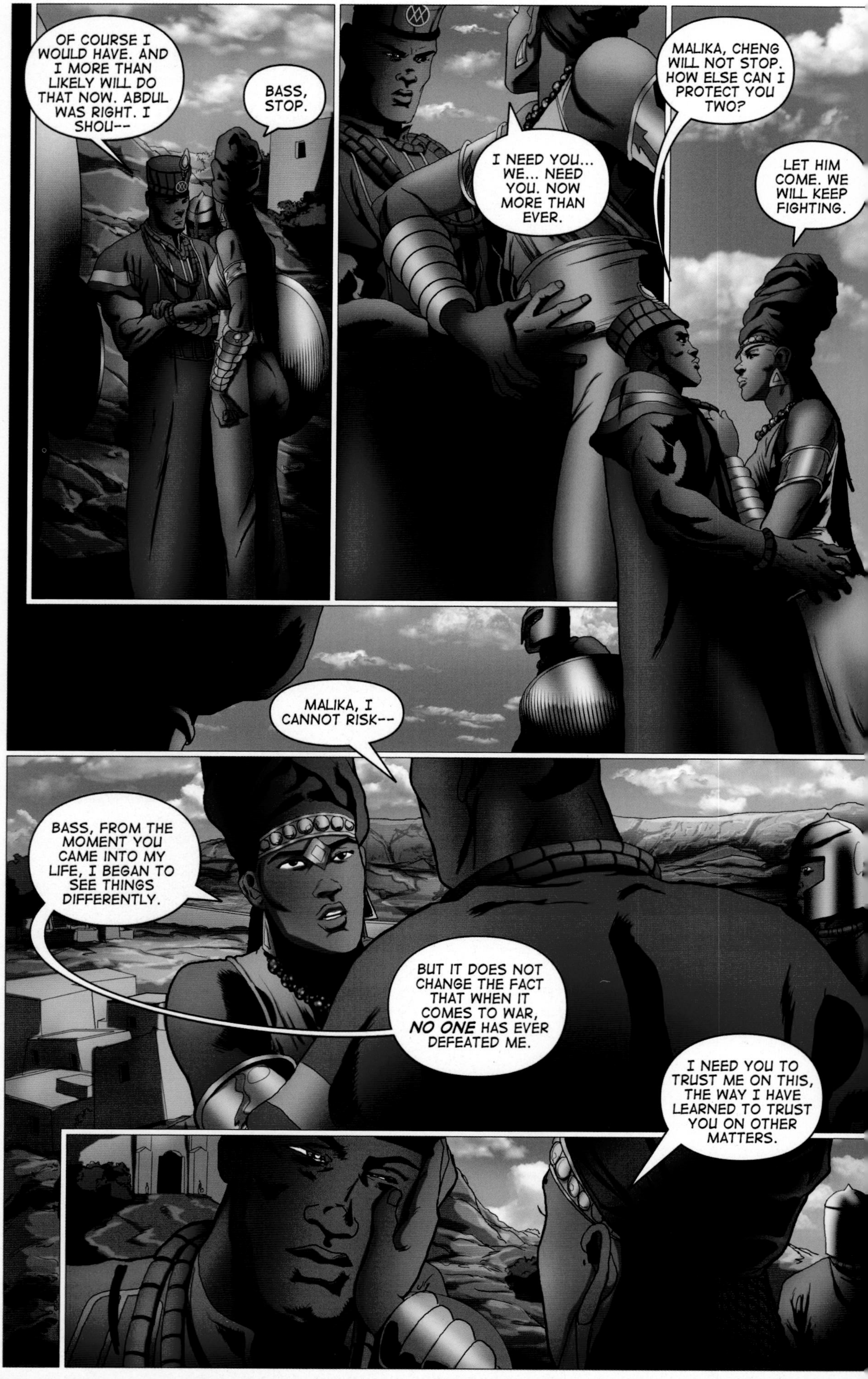
OF COURSE I WOULD HAVE. AND I MORE THAN LIKELY WILL DO THAT NOW. ABDUL WAS RIGHT. I SHOU--
BASS, STOP.
I NEED YOU... WE... NEED YOU. NOW MORE THAN EVER.
MALIKA, CHENG WILL NOT STOP. HOW ELSE CAN I PROTECT YOU TWO?
LET HIM COME. WE WILL KEEP FIGHTING.
MALIKA, I CANNOT RISK--
BASS, FROM THE MOMENT YOU CAME INTO MY LIFE, I BEGAN TO SEE THINGS DIFFERENTLY.
BUT IT DOES NOT CHANGE THE FACT THAT WHEN IT COMES TO WAR, NO ONE HAS EVER DEFEATED ME.
I NEED YOU TO TRUST ME ON THIS, THE WAY I HAVE LEARNED TO TRUST YOU ON OTHER MATTERS.

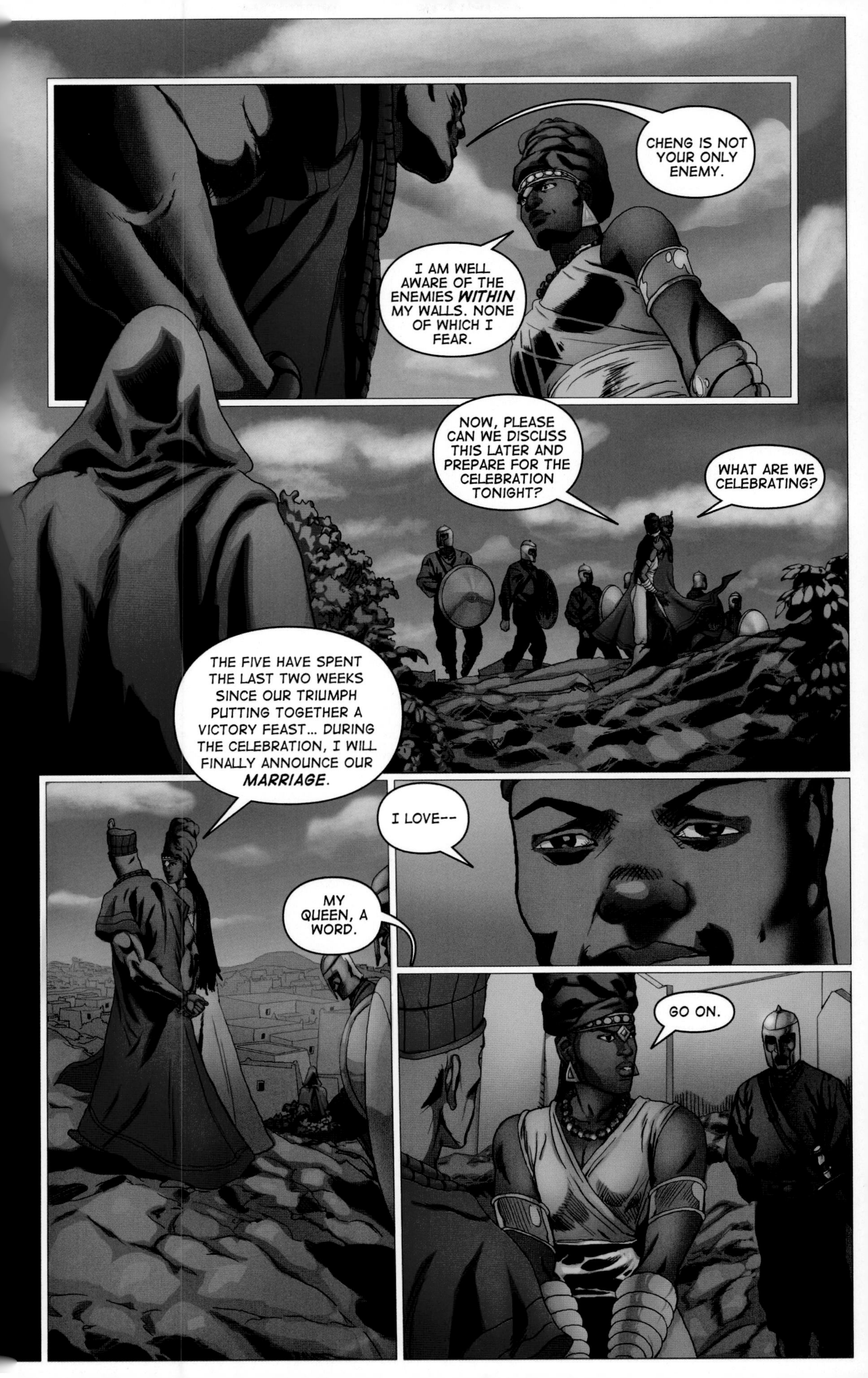
CHENG IS NOT YOUR ONLY ENEMY.
I AM WELL AWARE OF THE ENEMIES *WITHIN* MY WALLS. NONE OF WHICH I FEAR.
NOW, PLEASE CAN WE DISCUSS THIS LATER AND PREPARE FOR THE CELEBRATION TONIGHT?
WHAT ARE WE CELEBRATING?
THE FIVE HAVE SPENT THE LAST TWO WEEKS SINCE OUR TRIUMPH PUTTING TOGETHER A VICTORY FEAST... DURING THE CELEBRATION, I WILL FINALLY ANNOUNCE OUR *MARRIAGE*.
I LOVE--
MY QUEEN, A WORD.
GO ON.

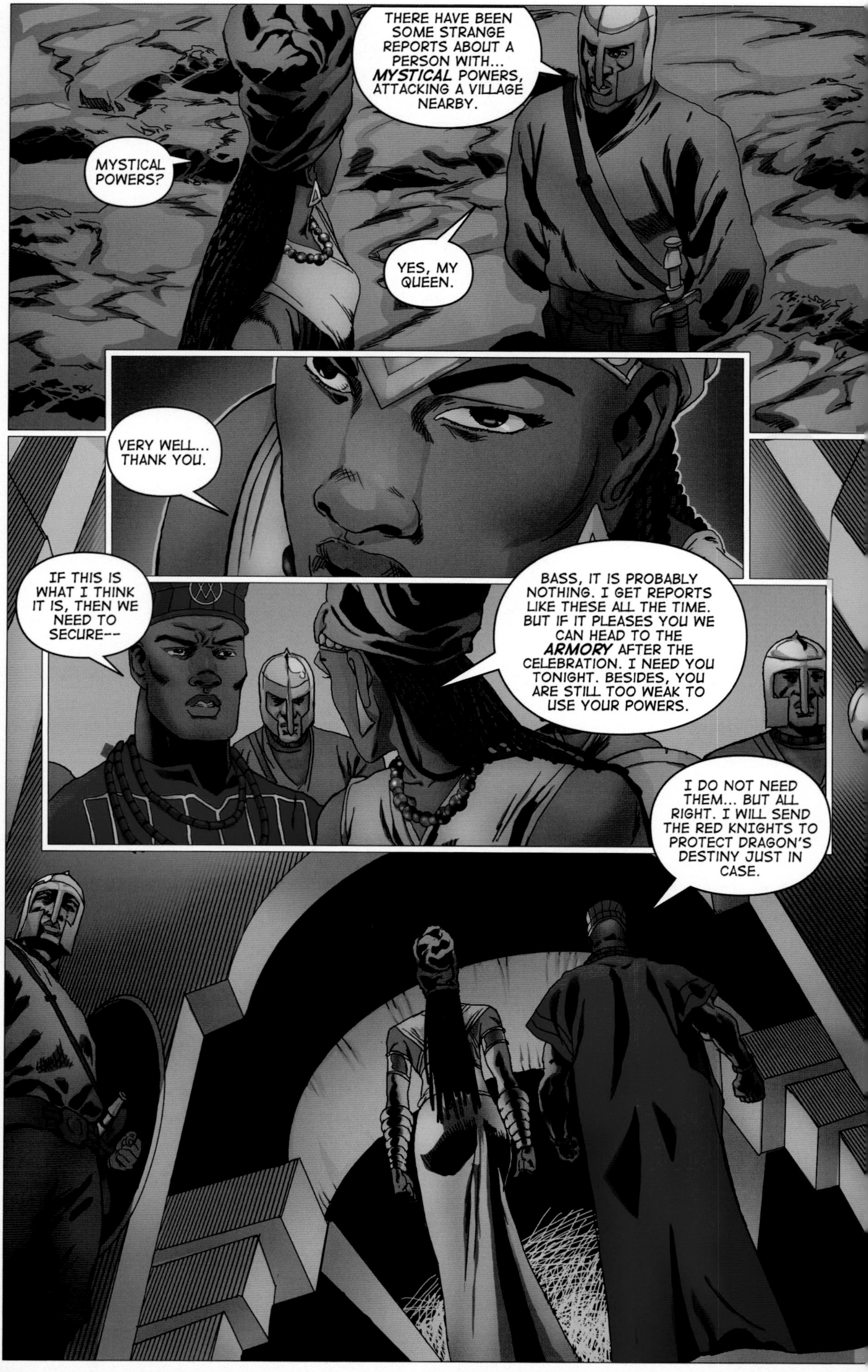
THERE HAVE BEEN SOME STRANGE REPORTS ABOUT A PERSON WITH... MYSTICAL POWERS, ATTACKING A VILLAGE NEARBY.
MYSTICAL POWERS?
YES, MY QUEEN.
VERY WELL... THANK YOU.
IF THIS IS WHAT I THINK IT IS, THEN WE NEED TO SECURE--
BASS, IT IS PROBABLY NOTHING. I GET REPORTS LIKE THESE ALL THE TIME. BUT IF IT PLEASES YOU WE CAN HEAD TO THE ARMORY AFTER THE CELEBRATION. I NEED YOU TONIGHT. BESIDES, YOU ARE STILL TOO WEAK TO USE YOUR POWERS.
I DO NOT NEED THEM... BUT ALL RIGHT. I WILL SEND THE RED KNIGHTS TO PROTECT DRAGON'S DESTINY JUST IN CASE.

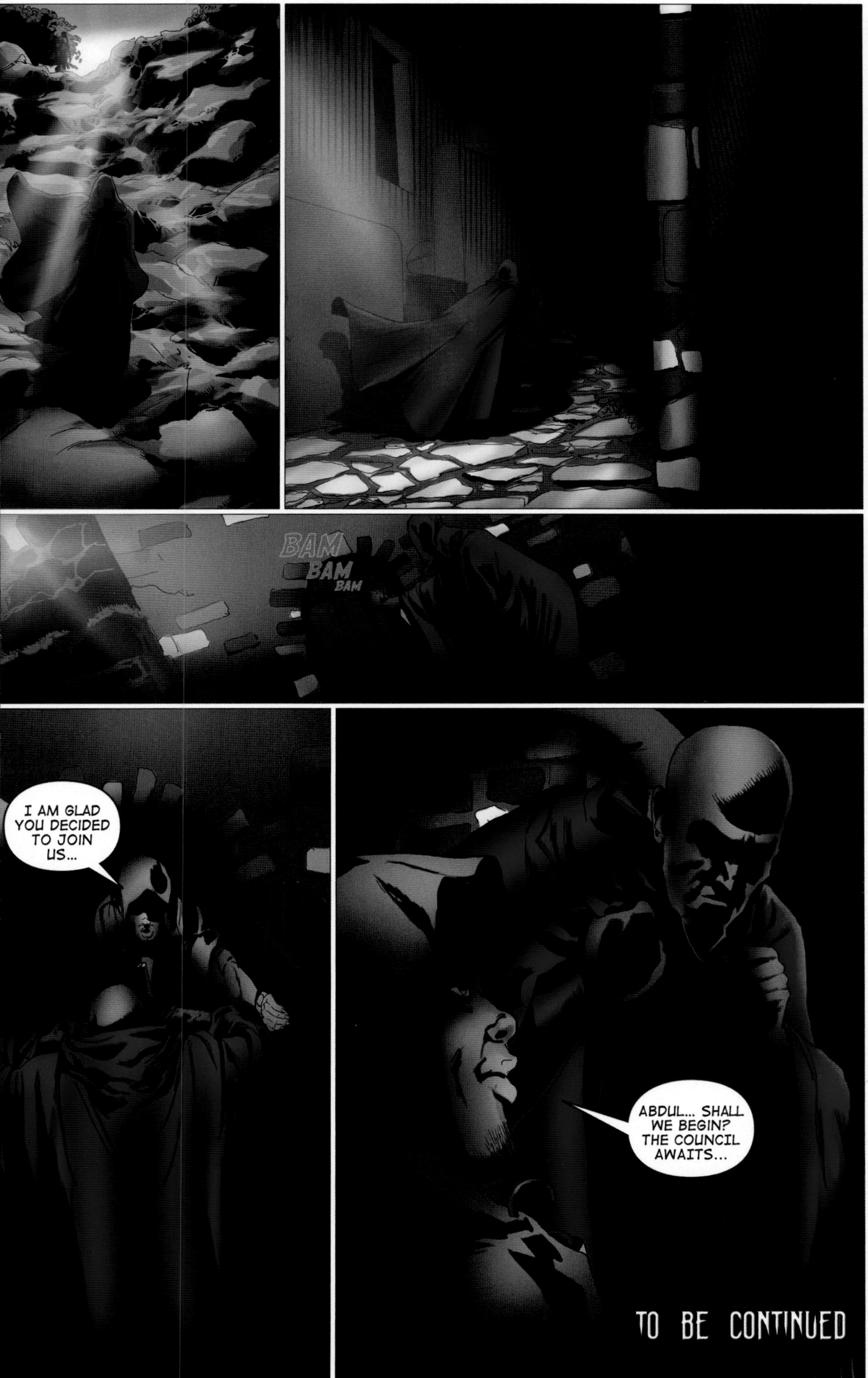
BAM
BAM
BAM
I AM GLAD YOU DECIDED TO JOIN US...
ABDUL... SHALL WE BEGIN? THE COUNCIL AWAITS...
TO BE CONTINUED

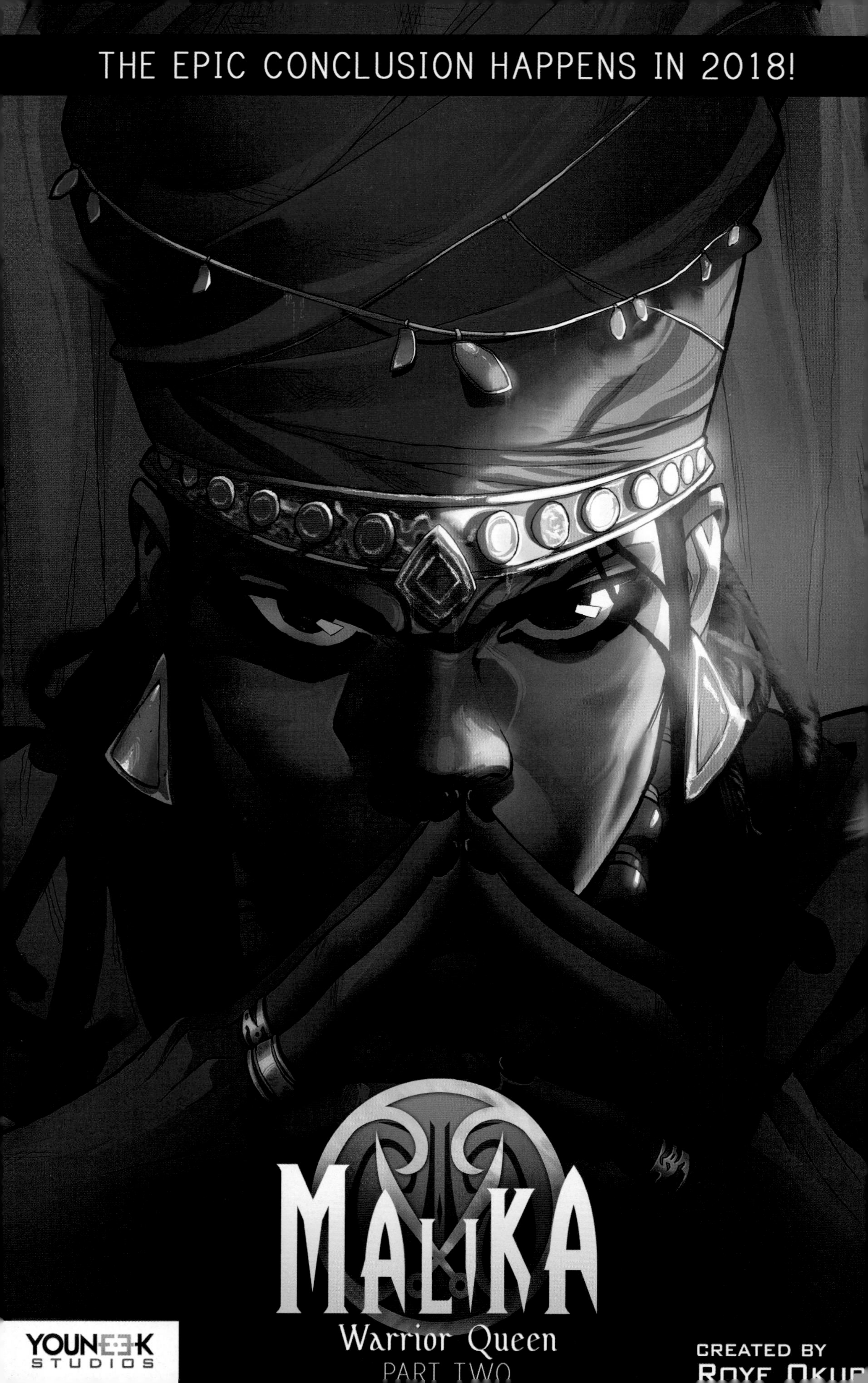
THE EPIC CONCLUSION HAPPENS IN 2018!
MALIKA
Warrior Queen
PART TWO
YOUNEEK STUDIOS
CREATED BY
ROYE OKUP

OPTIONAL READING ORDER

E.X.O.
THE LEGEND OF WALE WILLIAMS
PART ONE
E.X.O.
THE LEGEND OF WALE WILLIAMS
PART TWO
ROYE OKUPE
WINDMAKER
THE HISTORY OF ATALA
THE ART OF THE BOOK SERIES
MALIKA
Warrior Queen
ROYE OKUPE

THE YOUNEEK YOUNIVERSE

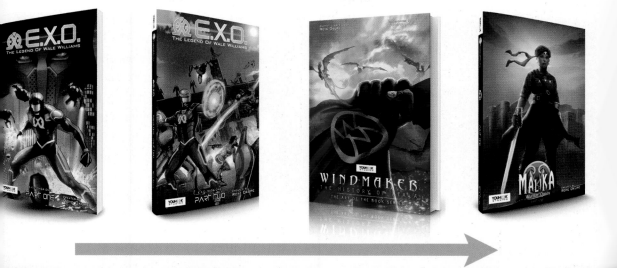

Coming off the hit graphic novel: E.X.O. The Legend of Wale Williams (Parts One & Two), which was featured on CNN, Forbes, The New York Times, The Washington Post and more, Malika is the fourth book in the continuity of a shared universe of graphic novels called the "YouNeek Youniverse." Dubbed "The MCU of graphic novels," the YouNeek YouNiverse is a combination of individual graphic novel series (E.X.O., Malika, WindMaker etc.) tied together with one continuous, overall plot that weaves through each individual story.

"We want to make it easy for anyone to get into comic book stories, which at the end of the day are just, well... 'Stories.' One of the inspirations behind the YouNiverse comes from something I see Marvel Studios doing very successfully with their movies. Marvel has masterfully crafted a system of connected movies (collectively called the Marvel Cinematic Universe or "MCU") that has attracted millions of casual, everyday fans that have never read a single comic book!" -

Roye Okupe, Co-Founder/CEO YouNeek Studios

Each title will have a different sub-genres and contain its own independent story, which will weave into an overall continuous story arc for the YouNeek YouNiverse. Another way to explain it would be to liken it to George R. R. Martin's "A Song of Fire an Ice" which is a series of novels, one of which is the critically acclaimed "Game of Thrones." In essence, the YouNeek YouNiverse is a series of superhero graphic novels, all with individual stories that serve collectively as an overall plot. So there will be no reboots, no events, no retcons and when a character dies, they are "more than likely" gone forever!

Go to YOUNEEKSTUDIOS.COM for more & to read for FREE!

E.X.O.® THE LEGEND OF WALE WILLIAMS
PART ONE (AVAILABLE NOW)

ORDER OUR BOOKS TODAY - YOUNEEKSTUDIOS.COM

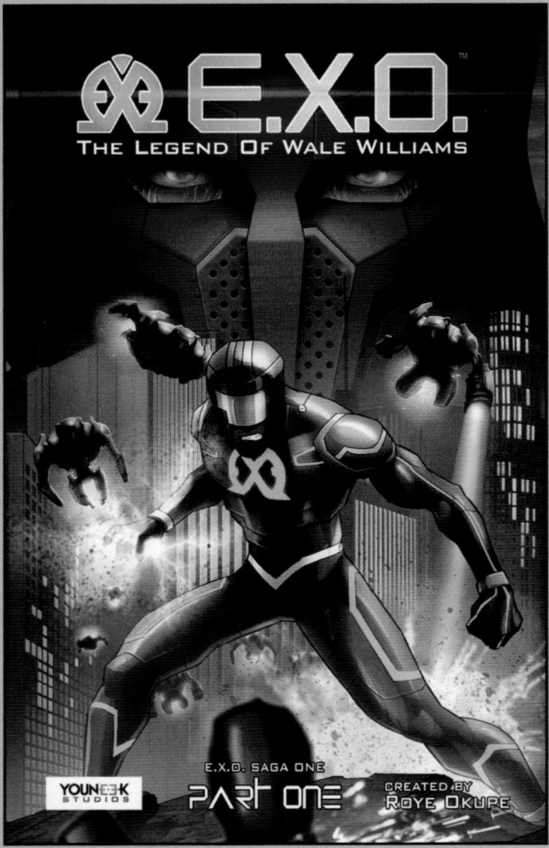
E.X.O.™
THE LEGEND OF WALE WILLIAMS
E.X.O. SAGA ONE
PART ONE
CREATED BY ROYE OKUPE
YOUNEEK STUDIOS

FEATURED ON CNN, FORBES, THE NEW YORK TIMES, THE WASHINGTON POST & MORE!

A science fiction superhero story about redemption, set in a futuristic, 2025 Africa! The 136 page graphic novel follows the journey of Wale Williams, an impetuous young adult who inherits a suit with super powers after his father goes missing. As he comes to understand the suit's powers, Wale realizes he must restore hope to his city by preventing catastrophic attacks from the sociopathic, Oniku, leader of an extremist group called The CREED.

136 pages - $14.99
First book in the YouNeek YouNiverse Continuity

"BOUT TIME." - JAMIE FOXX

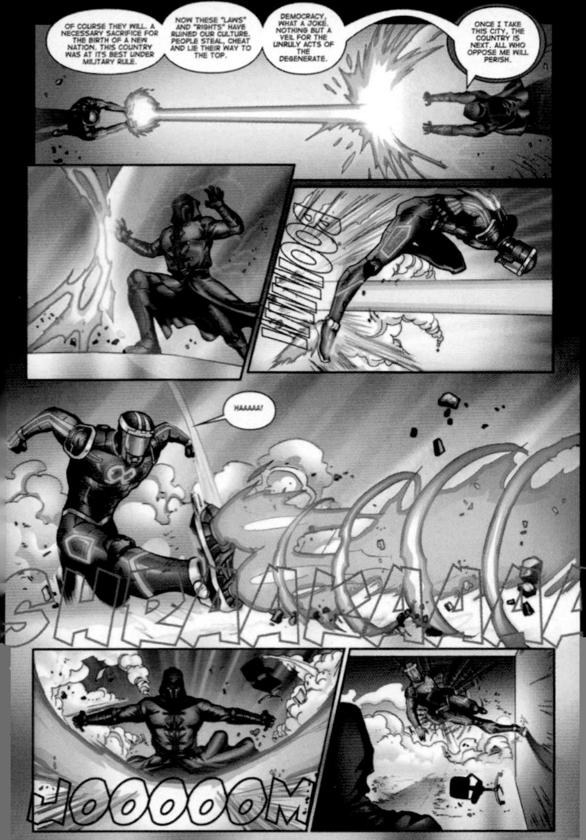
OF COURSE THEY WILL. A NECESSARY SACRIFICE FOR THE BIRTH OF A NEW NATION. THIS COUNTRY WAS AT ITS BEST UNDER MILITARY RULE.
NOW THESE "LAWS" AND "RIGHTS" HAVE RUINED OUR CULTURE. PEOPLE STEAL, CHEAT AND LIE THEIR WAY TO THE TOP.
DEMOCRACY, WHAT A JOKE. NOTHING BUT A VEIL FOR THE UNRULY ACTS OF THE DEGENERATE.
ONCE I TAKE THIS CITY, THE COUNTRY IS NEXT. ALL WHO OPPOSE ME WILL PERISH.
HAAAAA!

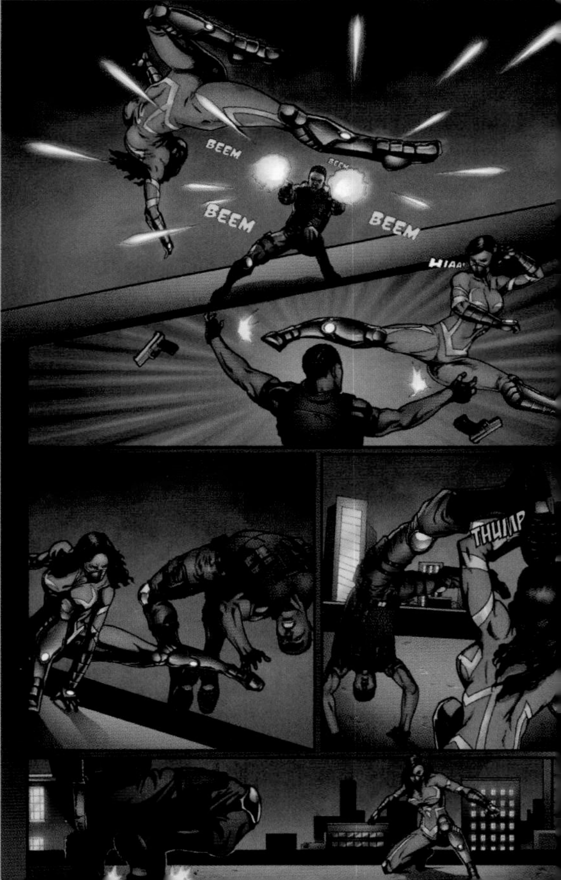
BEEM
BEEM
BEEM
THUMP

E.X.O. THE LEGEND OF WALE WILLIAMS PART TWO (AVAILABLE NOW)

ORDER OUR BOOKS TODAY - YOUNEEKSTUDIOS.COM

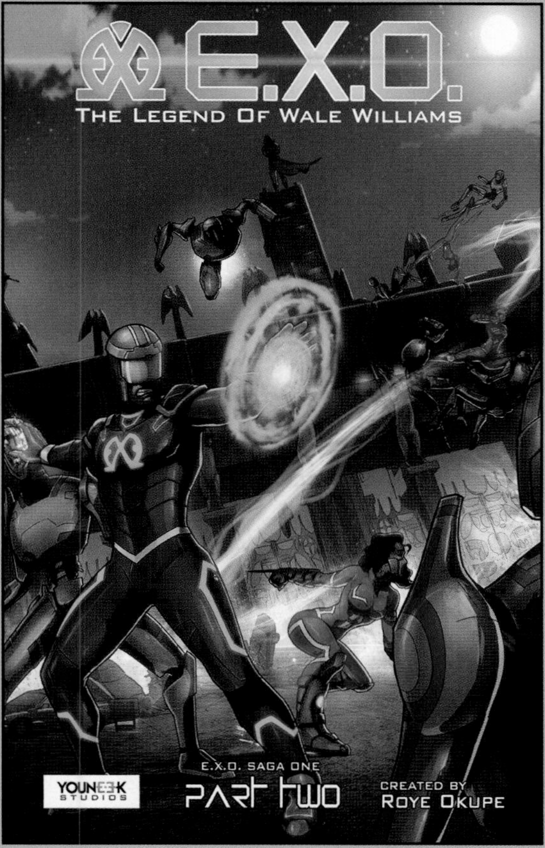
E.X.O.
THE LEGEND OF WALE WILLIAMS
YOUNEEK STUDIOS
E.X.O. SAGA ONE
PART TWO
CREATED BY
ROYE OKUPE

FEATURED ON CBR, NBC, BLEEDING COOL, ABC7 & MORE!

Part 2 continues to chronicle the journey of Wale Williams a.k.a EXO, who was last seen hanging on for dear life after his first encounter with the incredibly powerful and sinister Oniku, leader of the extremist group, The CREED. After his shocking revelation, Oniku now has all he needs to launch a crippling attack at the heart of Lagoon City, an attack that would be felt across the entire nation of Nigeria.

152 pages - $14.99
Second book in the YouNeek YouNiverse Continuity

"THIS IS A GOOD READ." - COMIXOLOGY

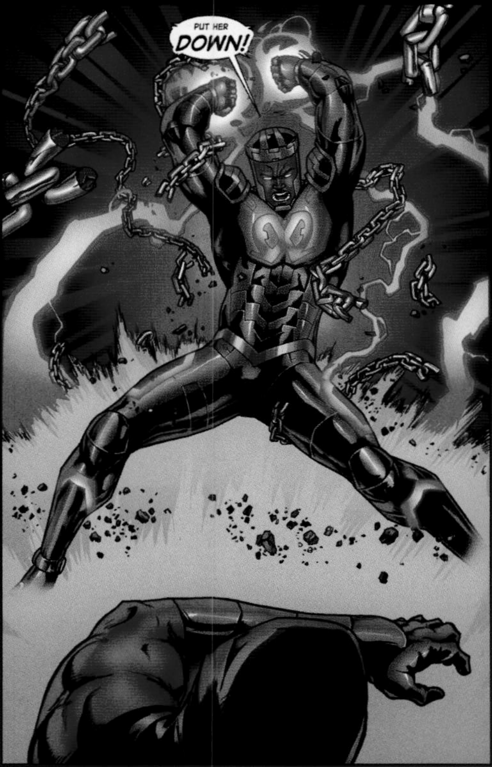
PUT HER DOWN!

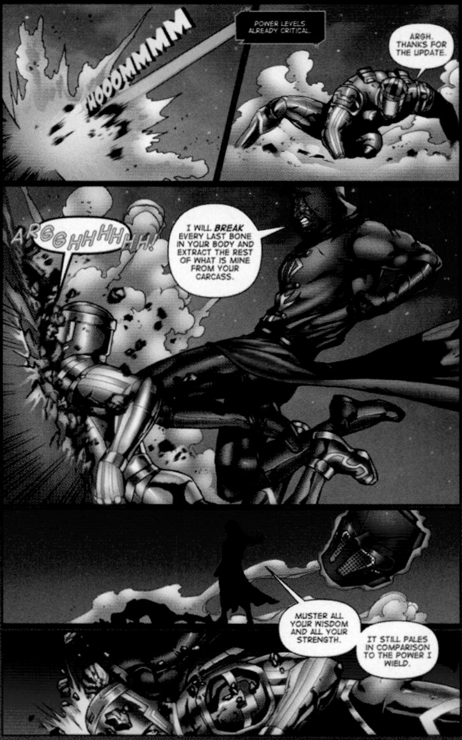
POWER LEVELS ALREADY CRITICAL.
ARGH. THANKS FOR THE UPDATE.
I WILL BREAK EVERY LAST BONE IN YOUR BODY AND EXTRACT THE REST OF WHAT IS MINE FROM YOUR CARCASS.
MUSTER ALL YOUR WISDOM AND ALL YOUR STRENGTH.
IT STILL PALES IN COMPARISON TO THE POWER I WIELD.

WINDMAKER™ – THE HISTORY OF ATALA
(AVAILABLE NOW)

ORDER OUR BOOKS TODAY - YOUNEEKSTUDIOS.COM

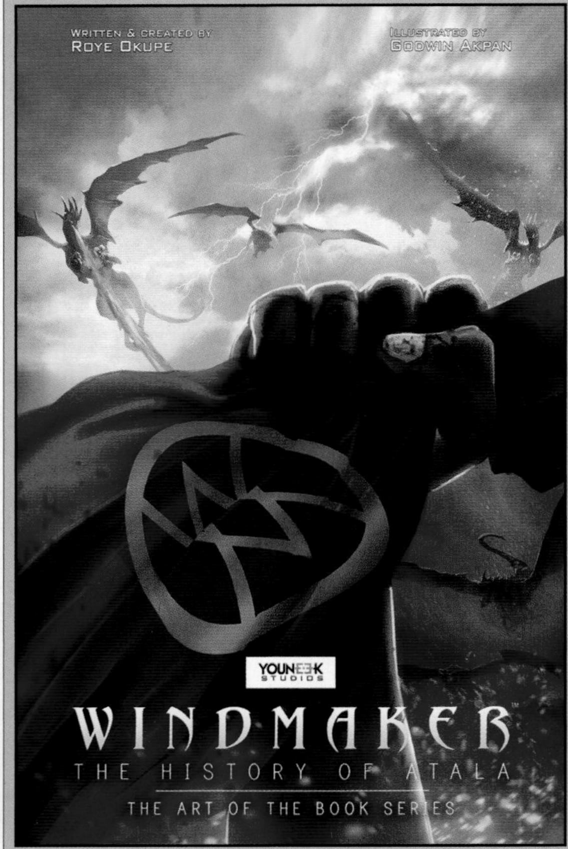
WRITTEN & CREATED BY
ROYE OKUPE
ILLUSTRATED BY
GODWIN AKPAN
YOUNEEK STUDIOS
WINDMAKER
THE HISTORY OF ATALA
THE ART OF THE BOOK SERIES

FEATURED ON KONBINI & THE WASHINGTON POST!

Inspired by African mythology, Windmaker: The History of Atala (Hardcover) pulls from the amazing depths of African history. With this art book, writer Roye Okupe sets the foundations for what is definitely a deep and meaningful universe of heroes. Illustrator Godwin Akpan's painting breathes life into the story in an amazing way. It's dragons, mythical relics, a feuding royal family & magical swords all mixed into in an awe inspiring African setting.

Hardcover Art Book - $24.99
Third book in the YouNeek YouNiverse Continuity

INSPIRED BY AFRICAN MYTHOLOGY

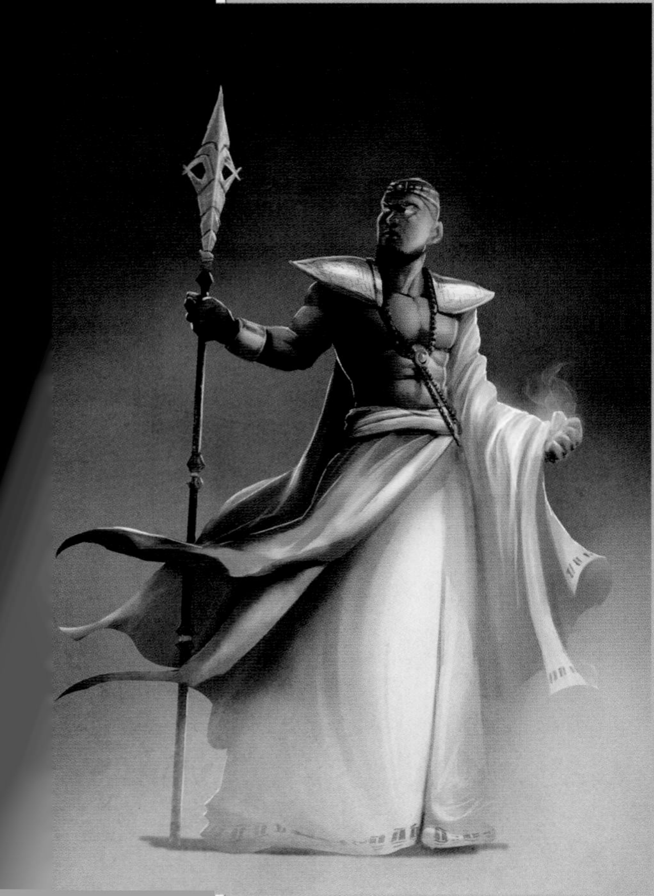

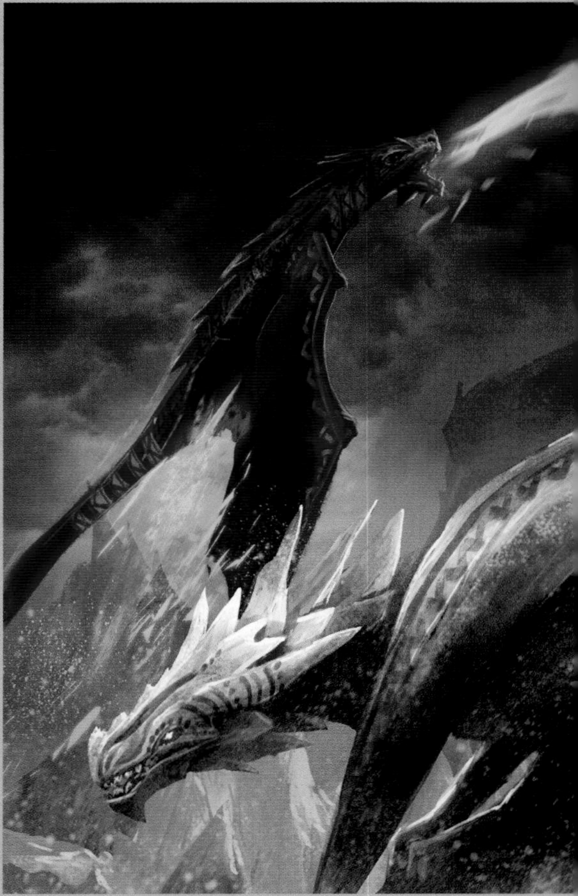

A SPECIAL THANK YOU TO OUR SPONSORS

Weird Realms
CLEVELAND'S NERD STORE
WEIRD REALMS IS PROUD TO HAVE BACKED THE CREATION OF MALIKA WARRIOR QUEEN.
WE ARE A COMIC AND GAME STORE IN CLEVELAND, OHIO DEDICATED TO PROVIDING AN INCLUSIVE SPACE WHERE ALL TYPES OF STORIES ARE TOLD. VISIT US IN CLEVELAND OR ON THE WEB AT WWW.WEIRDREALMS.COM!
THE INCAL
ROGER CORMAN'S CULT CLASSICS
STAR CRASH
BLACK
Hawkwind
DUNGEONS & DRAGONS
ILLUMINATI
HELLBLAZER
CONSPIRACY
HUMAN RACE
Valis
MALIKA

weirdrealms.com

facebook.com/weirdrealms • twitter: @weirdrealmscle • instagram: @weird.realms

216-694-8525 • 11508 Lorain Ave. Cleveland, Ohio 44111

LOEBIG iNK

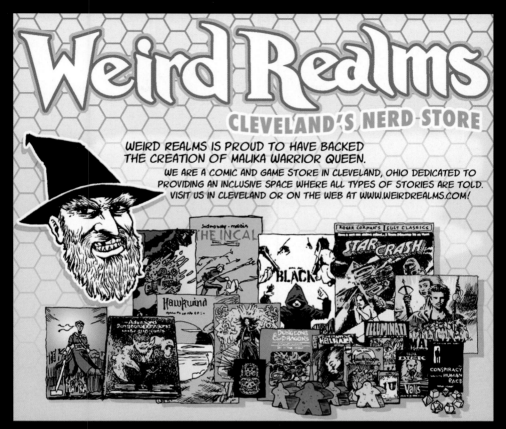

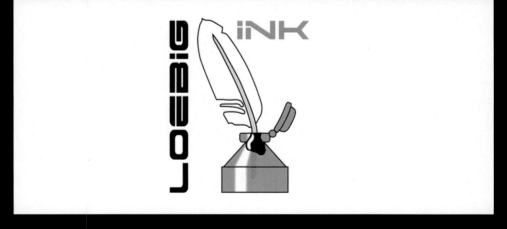

Loebig Ink, LLC is proud and privileged to support the creative, comic genius of Adewunmi (Roye) Okupe and Malika: Warrior Queen. From our first face to face meeting at Starbucks in downtown Silver Spring, MD, I knew that Roye and Malika were on a faith-inspired path to bring an amazing African Superhero story to life. Like Malika, Roye has answered a call to bring something special to a world that needs saving; a world that needs human superheroes.

A SPECIAL THANK YOU TO OUR KICKSTARTER BACKERS

Abimbola Adeniranye	Ramel Rocket-Man Hill	autumn brock
Omotola Thomas	MVmedia, LLC	Temi
Brian Loebig	C.R. Ward	A Naim
Beckett Warren	kalina vanderlei silva	Sherreka Burton
Adewale Odusanya	Tasha Turner Lennhoff	KidPositive
Ajibike Browne	Netobvious	R Cooke
Marta C. Youngblood	Roosevelt Pitt, Jr.	Iziah & Ry-Yon
Andre	Judd	Carrie Bell
Lamera	Jason Jackson	Lauren Bawden
Sid Sondergard	Jamal Narcisse	Andre washington
Adekunle Bello	Kate Bullock	Oyeronke Oyebode
Titilola Okupe	Vincent Baker	M. X. Jordan
Eric Outley	Simon Rushton	Ofeibea Loveless
S.Threadcraft	Jennifer Hicks	Obinna Onwuekwe
Chuks Oyem	Naseed Gifted	Eze Wosu
Brian Ka'im Wallace	Christina Devlin	Lesly Julien
David Massaro	James DiGioia	Greg Anderson-Elysee
Andrew Martin	Jacqueline washington	Gregory Lincoln
Greene County Creative	Pedastudio Team	Perry Clark
Chris Bishop	Therese Totten	Zeke Springer
Kimmi Mackenzie	Gary Simmons	William Green Jr
Femi Agunbiade	Chris Douglas	edwin walker
Marta Denise Collier	Jesse Alford	Jeff Lee
Ayomide Shittu	Emily Bibb	Adam Sadowski
Cas Thomas	Phoenix Dreams Publishing	tfaks
Kunle Malomo	William Satterwhite	Brandon Duke
Simon Polenz	Danny J Quick	William Anderson
Adedamola Adefemi	Brandon Easton	Erica Jones
Nina Everflow	Akinseye Brown	Clath Rin
mike kelley	Caitlin Shaw	Carrie M
Jaiye Moyela	Ben miller	Jeffaplus
Timl Omotayo	Drew Ford	Sharon Handy
Ayo Oseni	Ursula Murray Husted	Torsten Wollina
Regina Moretto	Rayan Turner	Alioscia Martinelli
Shamayahu (DintheAbary)	LaTasha Bundy	Emilio Rodriguez and James Rodri
Michelle van Gilder	Eddy Cozmo	Milton Hexadecimal
Malaika Mose	Hillary Shipps	Michael Toney
Dixie	L. R. Denzer	Krystelle Gélineau
Jerry D. Grayson	Kristopher Mosby	Eboni Dunbar
Stephanie Bryant	Kurt Rauer	Ian Yarington
Cedric	Carl Springer	Vincent Stoessel
Diana Wolf	Kristina Cunningham Bigler	Julian Purdy
Melissa J. Brooks	Jetamors	Antonio Pomares
Delhaye	Bethany Morse	Ashton
Nordee	Kayode Kendall	Glenn Fayard
Sean Andres	trojanzer	H. Roselyn Bloczynski
Ali	evan marmer	Brittany Jones
David Chaucer La Forest	TeJo	Cedric Neil Milton
Amanda I Walston	Michael Nedderman	Valancia

A SPECIAL THANK YOU TO OUR
KICKSTARTER BACKERS

Jacob Roberts-Mensah

Tess

Bernard Chan

Sean Jenkins

Brian Dysart

Krista Humphrey

Olayinka Lawal

Martin Reese

Sophie Lagace

Misha B

Unruly Designs

ClinkingDog

Chris Pramas

DivNull Productions

Luqman

Davery Bland

J.R. Murdock

Ron Brooks

Laura Duerr

Catherine Oyiliagu (Ezicat)

Zoe Lewycky

Olu Efunwoye

James

Andrew Lorenz

David E. McClain

Julie Restrepo

Willy Tekeu

Will Yeomans

Calvin Grace

T.K. Daniel

Victor Tenntungfui

Lars Westergren

Cathy Schwartz

Lala

Victor Williams

Maxwell Oginni

Jason Nolen

Byron Emerson

petiniaud

Mike Cooper

David

KyoshiroKami

JÃ½rgen Pollex

kamalloy

Tom Pouce

Michael S Edwards

Michael Benoist

Matrix

Steven Moye

Mike Grossman

Short Fuse Media Group, LLC.

Jay Nelson

Erin Subramanian

Kariane Lemay

Brander Roullett

Len Ahgeak

Rodney Thomas

Mohan Sarma

Michael Bowman

patty kirsch

Rikisha Sigler

Jake Palermo

Josh Medin

Andrew Wilson

Veronica Ramshaw

Devon

Charles Shropshire

Jerry Wright Jr

Derek Freeman

Joe Illidge

Salvatore Puma

Steven John Fuchs

Ellen Power

Richard Lowe

Benjamin Israel

Tevin Deante' Hill

Nightsky

James Lucas

Shean Mohammed

Jeffrey Underwood

Stephen Embleton

M.K. Palmer

Jerry SkÃ¶ld

Adrian Harper

John M. Portley

Christopher E O Williams

JoernStoppe

deezy

Paradox Girl

Jergall

Jake Ivey

Saturday AM

Micah BlackLight

Thomas Werner

Edem Dzodzomenyo

Victoria Stolfa

Whitney

Crystal M Rollins

Jim Ryan

Jim Otermat

maw

Contractor

Jim DelRosso

Brownie

David Wu

Quasi

Kenneth A. Brown

Ann Elliott

Darkspi

Francis Waltz

Karama Horne

Sharon Omotor

David

Murewa Ayodele

Raymond Thomas

Ronald T. Jones

Kadi Yao Tay

Marcela Peres

Sergey Anikushin

Chrisón Thompson

Jordan

Nikki

Jenny Underwood

Bill Ulrich

Ozhara

pagurus

adron

Reality Happens

Kaiju Den

Marcel Štefánik

LOCATION CONCEPT ART BY GODWIN AKPAN

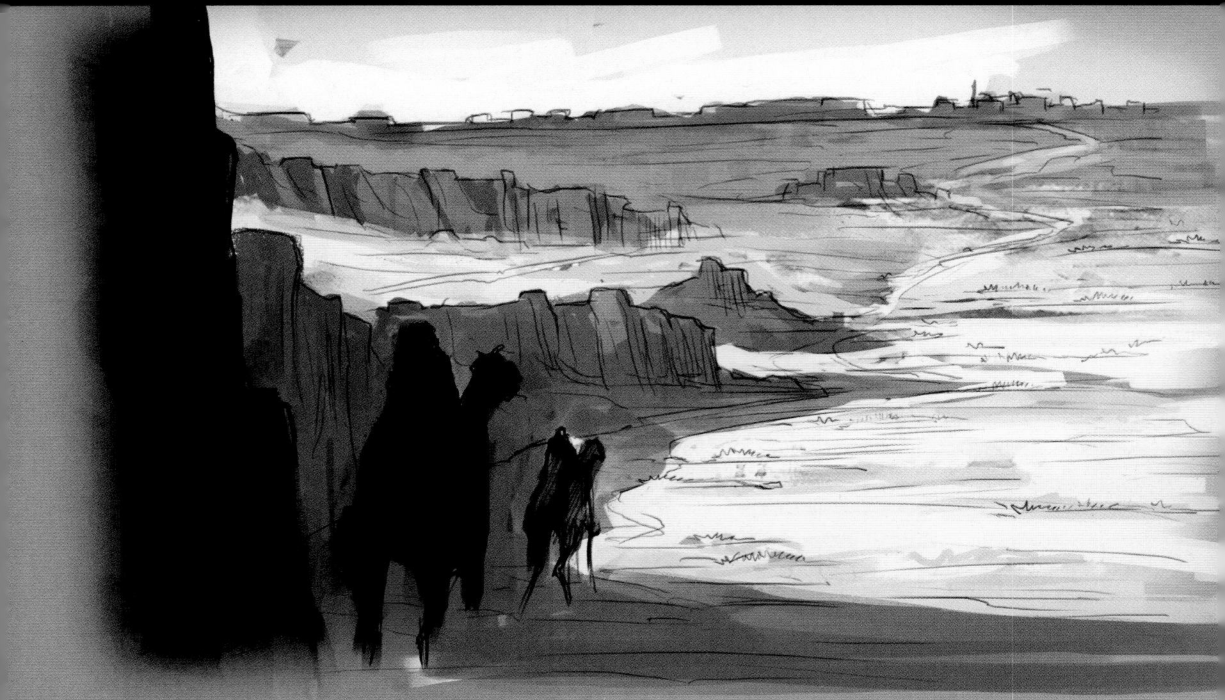

DESERT PLAINS LEADING TO CITY OF BAGA

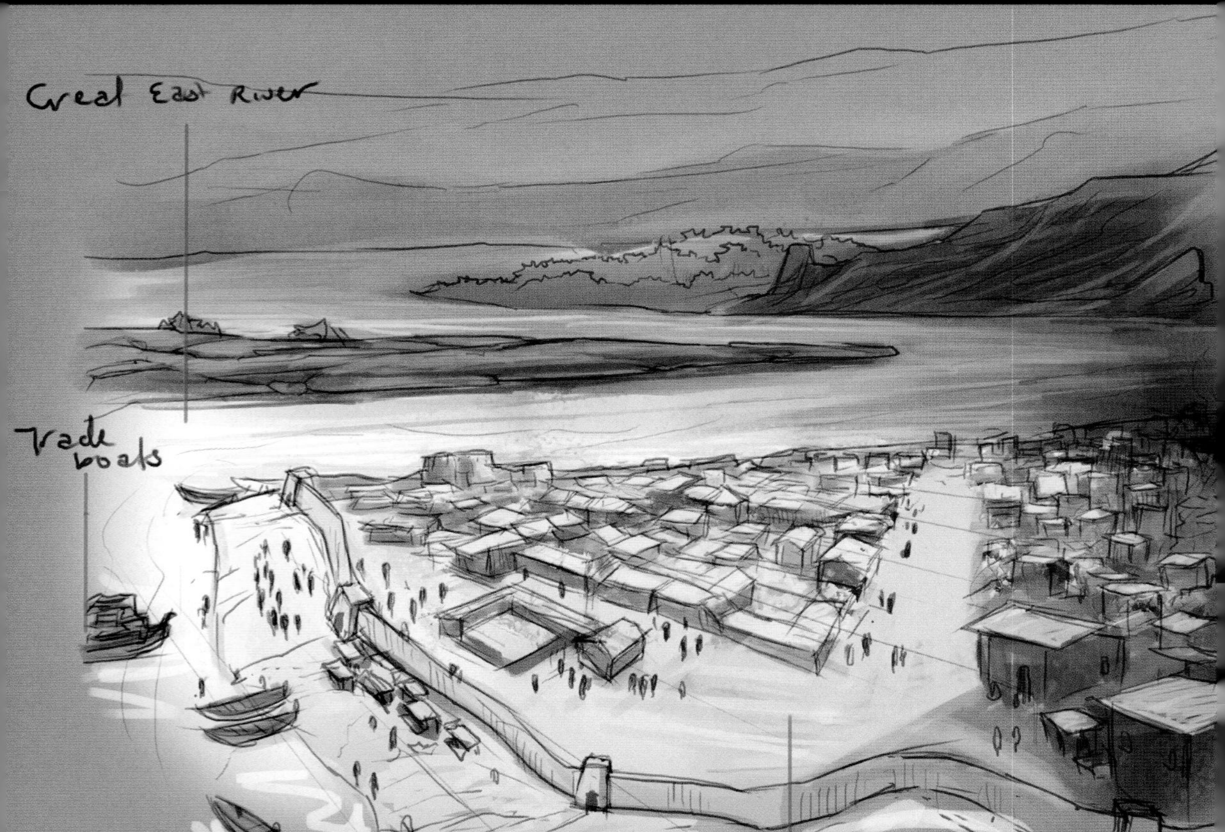
Great East River
Trade boats
Inside City

CITY OF CONFLUENCE

LOCATION CONCEPT ART BY GODWIN AKPAN

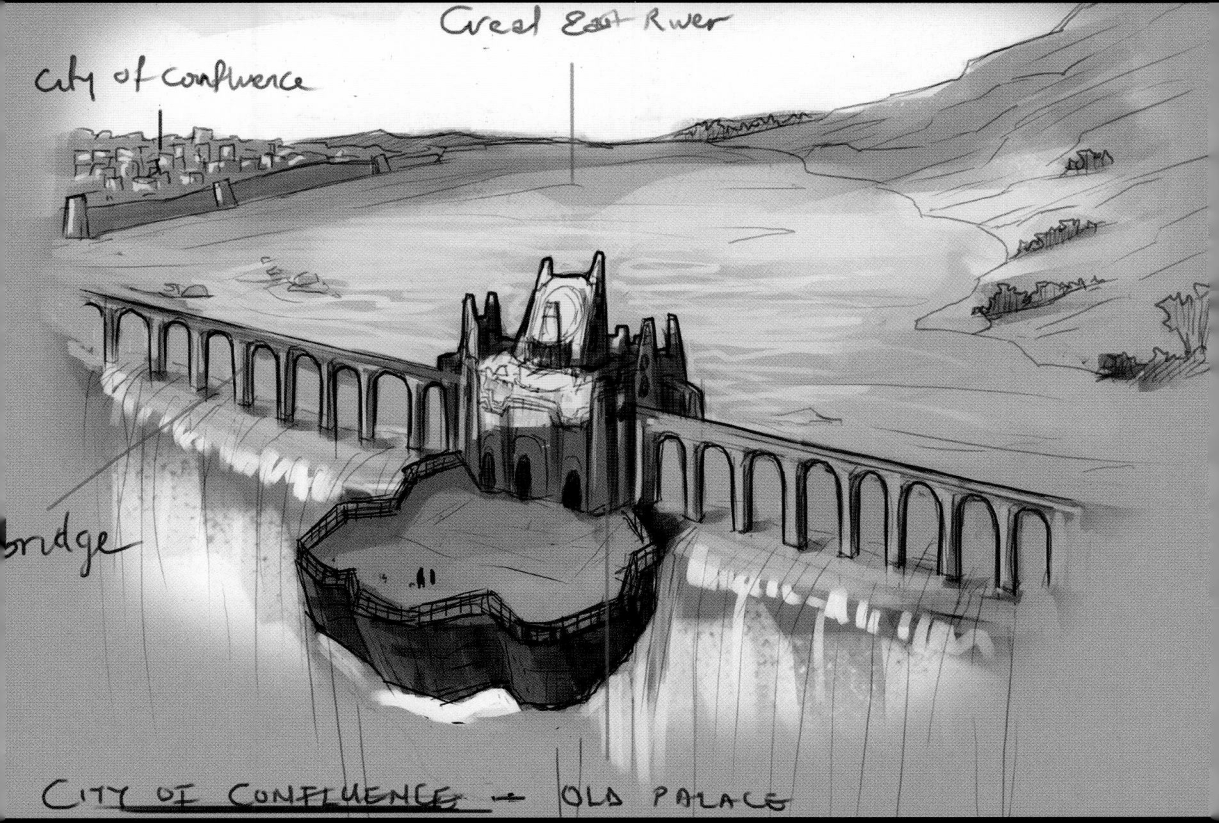
Great East River
city of confluence
bridge
CITY OF CONFLUENCE - OLD PALACE

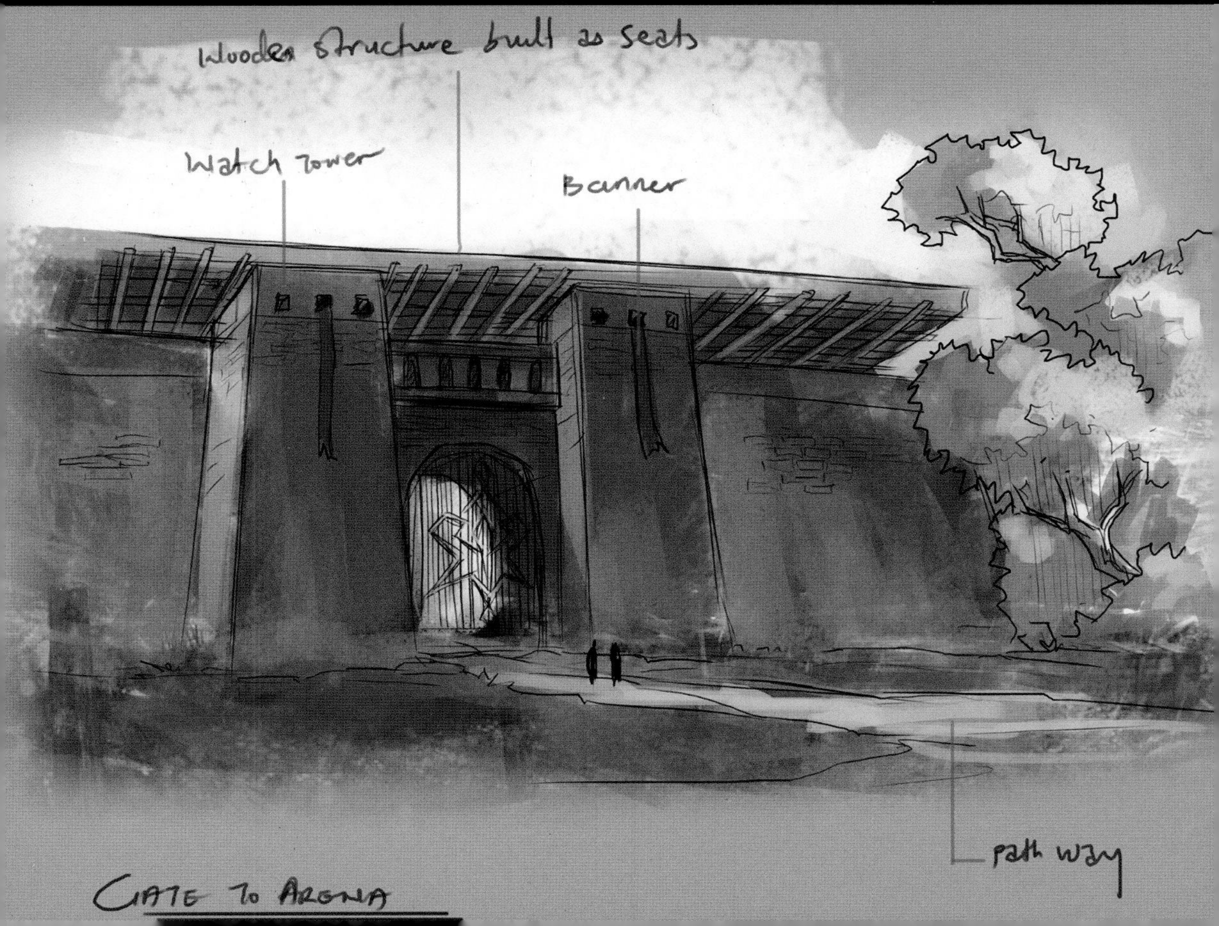
Wooden structure built as seats
Watch tower
Banner
path way
GATE TO ARENA

LOCATION CONCEPT ART BY GODWIN AKPAN

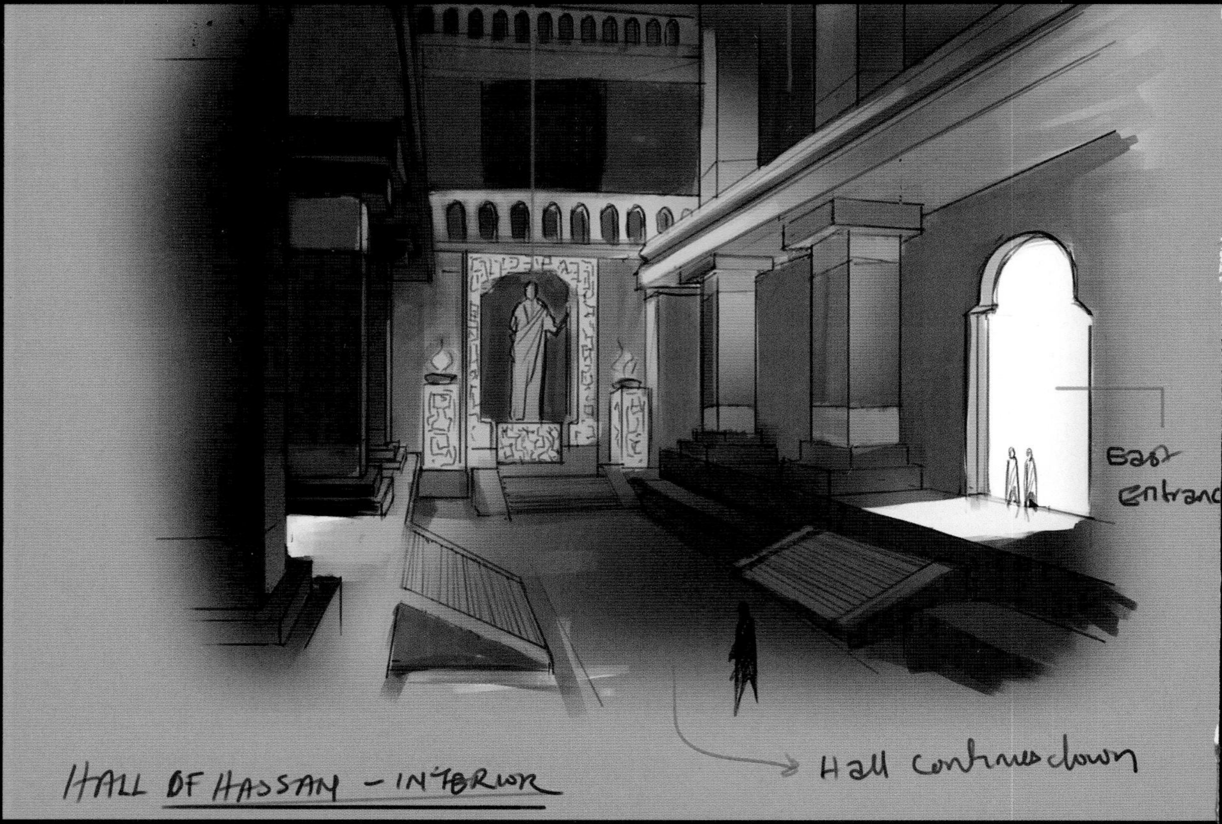
East
Entranc
Hall continues down
HALL OF HASSAN - INTERIOR

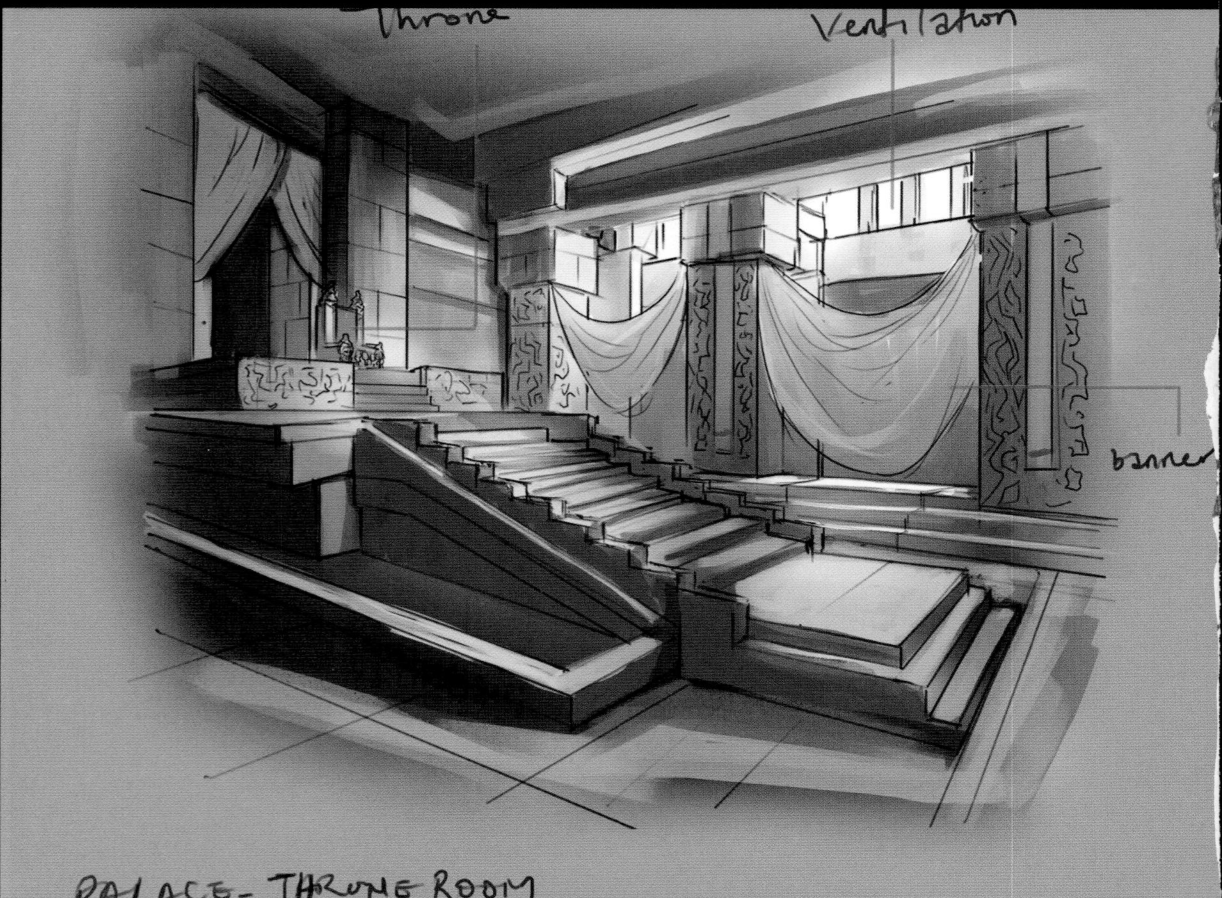
Throne
Ventilation
banner
PALACE- THRONE ROOM